Creativity 101
James C. Kaufman, PhD

Genius 101
Dean Keith Simonton, PhD

IQ Testing 101
Alan S. Kaufman, PhD

Leadership 101
Michael D. Mumford, PhD

Psycholinguistics 101
H. Wind Cowles, PhD

Intelligence 101
Jonathan Plucker, PhD

Anxiety 101
Moshe Zeidner, PhD
Gerald Matthews, PhD

James C. Kaufman, PhD, Series Editor
Director, Learning Research Institute
California State University at San Bernardino

James C. Kaufman is an Associate Professor at the California State University at San Bernardino, where he is also the director of the Learning Research Institute. He received his Ph.D. from Yale University in Cognitive Psychology, where his mentor was Robert J. Sternberg. Kaufman has authored more than 140 papers and written or edited 14 books, including the recent *International Handbook of Creativity* (with Sternberg, 2006), and *Essentials of Creativity Assessment* (with Jonathan Plucker and John Baer, 2008). Kaufman was recently named a coeditor of the official journal of Division 10 of the American Psychological Association, *Psychology of Aesthetics, Creativity, and the Arts,* and is the incoming editor of the *International Journal of Creativity and Problem Solving.* He is the associate editor of the *Journal of Creative Behavior* and *Psychological Assessment.* He received the 2003 Daniel E. Berlyne Award from the APA's Division 10 for outstanding research by a junior scholar and the 2008 E. Paul Torrance Award for creativity research from the National Association for Gifted Children. He has received awards for his professional contributions from CSUSB's psychology department and their college of social and behavioral sciences.

Creativity

101

James C. Kaufman, PhD

SPRINGER PUBLISHING COMPANY

Springer Publishing Company, LLC
11 West 42nd Street
New York, NY 10036
www.springerpub.com

Acquisitions Editor: Philip Laughlin
Production Editor: Julia Rosen
Cover Design: David Levy
Composition: Apex CoVantage, LLC

11 / 5 4

Library of Congress Cataloging-in-Publication Data

Kaufman, James C.
Creativity 101 / James C. Kaufman.
        p. cm. — (Psych 101 series)
    Includes bibliographical references and index.
    ISBN 978-0-8261-0625-4 (alk. paper)
    1. Creative ability.   I. Title.   II. Title: Creativity one hundred one.
III. Title: Creativity one hundred and one.   IV. Title: Creativity one oh one.
    BF408.K364   2009
    153.3'5—dc22   2008046851

Printed in the United States of America by Offset Paperback Mfrs.

Dr. Robert J. Sternberg has been the best mentor I could have
possibly hoped for—brilliant, supportive, and
a continual source of advice and inspiration.
I wouldn't be studying creativity if it weren't for him.
It is my honor to dedicate this book to him.

Contents

Contents

Acknowledgments

This book has been a long undertaking, and although I usually work quickly, this one has taken some time. I'd like to start by thanking Phil Laughlin of Springer, my editor and friend for six years and many books. It's been an absolute pleasure, even if it's meant tolerating the eternal optimism of a Pittsburgh Pirates fan. I look forward to many more books together.

Several of my students have been particularly helpful in researching, commenting, and critiquing this book. Ryan Holt has helped enormously with gathering research citations, and I have also had assistance from Sarah Burgess, Mariah Bussey, Candice Davis, Kristiana Powers, Bethany Pritchard, and Tessy T. Pumaccahua. Sheela Ramesh gave the manuscript a much-appreciated close read.

I have also greatly benefited from close and careful reads by a variety of top people in the field. Judith Schlesinger reviewed an earlier draft and (nicely) took me to task on some key creativity–mental illness points. Ruth Richards' early support and encouragement helped me gear up to finish the book.

In addition, I was moved by the extensive, thoughtful comments given by so many of my colleagues and coauthors. I had the good luck to meet John Baer early in my career, and his mentorship, friendship, and collaboration have been invaluable; John made sure that my descriptions of the domain-specific point of view were up-to-snuff. Ron Beghetto has shaped the way I view creativity as a developmental process, and my friendship with him and his family has been a source of great pleasure (and pancakes). Jonathan Plucker, an important voice for creativity across many organizations, has been a tremendous source of advice, support, pep talks, consultation, and friendship. Scott Barry Kaufman, my friend and brother-in-spirit, made sure that I was up to date on the intelligence and openness literature. Paul Silvia, an expert not only in creativity and aesthetics but also in how to write well (and often), gave me invaluable suggestions to make the manuscript smoother and easier to read. Finally, throughout my career I've been able to discuss and explore ideas about creativity with so many other great minds, including Adam Bristol, Christine Charyton, Jason Cole, Arthur and David Cropley, Claudia Gentile, Elena Grigorenko, Zorana Ivcevic, Aaron Kozbelt, Soonmook Lee, Paul Locher, Weihua Niu, Gunseli Oral, Jean Pretz, Roni Reiter-Palmon, Mark Runco, Janel Sexton, Jerome Singer, Dean Simonton, Jeff and Lisa Smith, the late E. Paul Torrance, Tom Ward, and Mary Waterstreet. Special thanks to grad school friends Adam and Jean for taking time to answer some specific questions for this book.

The late and much-missed John Horn took me under his wing when I was an undergraduate and taught me about life and crystallized–fluid intelligence. I am also grateful to Gwyn Boodoo, Bruce Bracken, Domenic Cicchetti, Ann Gallagher, James McLean, Jack Naglieri, Cecil Reynolds, and Sara Sparrow for their continued mentorship. Most essentially, I had the best possible advisor (in graduate school and beyond) in Bob Sternberg. He has been an incredible role model and a brilliant scholar, and I dedicate this book to him.

I give a big thank you to my friends at CSUSB who have been supportive of this and other projects, especially Mark Agars, Stacy Brooks, Allen Butt, Susan Daniels, Michelle Ebert Freire, Joanna Worthley, and all my students. My love to longtime friends Josh Butler, Wind and Esme Cowles, David and Aviva Hecht, and Nathan and Amy Stone.

Finally, the heart and soul of my life is family. I come from a family of psychologists, who have always been there for me. My sister, Jennie, and her family (Nicole Hendrix and Mitch, Brianna, and Leo Singer) have been a wonderful source of strength and friendship, as have my late brother's family (Milissa, Matt, Josiah, and Mikaela Kaufman and Kate Singleton). My parents, Alan and Nadeen, are often the first people to read my work and discuss my ideas; they have been loving pillars of support through my entire life (even as I sometimes argue that IQ tests are bad for not including creativity). The center of my life—my rock, my soul, my world—is always Allison. And my hope for the future is the sweetest person I know, Jacob.

Defining Creativity

few years ago, I was being interviewed by a journalist who asked me, "Engineers give us better machines. Doctors find cures. What does studying creativity do? Does it make better art? Is the goal ... to destroy the artist—and perhaps art itself—through a process of reductive demystification?" Aside from being an interesting break from the usual questions (such as, "Are all creative people crazy?"), this discussion made me think carefully about why studying creativity is important.

I think that the study of creativity *does* give us better art, and far from destroying the artist, I think it can improve an artist's life—or a scientist's life, or a businessperson's life. Creativity affects a lot of different people. Studying creativity and learning more about it also helps make the case that creativity is important. This statement—"creativity is important"—is not, however, a given assumption. On one hand, it is hard to imagine a teacher or a boss saying that they *didn't* want a creative student or employee. People who value creativity may point to its role in

1

inventions, in culture, in progress—in short, to most things that define our civilization. Yet, if creativity is so essential, why is it so absent from most educational or business assessments? If we want our students to be creative, why is creativity nowhere to be found on the SATs or GREs? With a few notable exceptions that I will discuss later, why do so few college admissions committees consider applicant creativity? If we want our employees to be creative, then why not toss in a measure of creativity in the personnel screening process to go with the ability, personality, interest, and integrity measures?

The answers to these questions are complicated. Many people have a gut reaction about studying and measuring creativity; one of my favorites is from Sherry Lansing, a one-time CEO of Paramount Pictures and a University of California Regent. "You can evaluate grammar, punctuation, and spelling, but not creativity," she told the *Chronicle of Higher Education* (E. Hoover, 2002). "How would *Ulysses* be graded on the SAT? How would Faulkner have been graded?"

The thought of grading Faulkner (or Mozart or Picasso) sounds absurd. The idea of "grading" Einstein or Bill Gates is a little absurd, too, yet we still have an awful lot of science and math questions on the SATs, GREs, AP tests, and so on that could theoretically provide a reasonable grade for them. Indeed, most of the things that scientists try to measure don't merit this type of reaction. Why? Some of the reasons lie in the nature of creativity itself. Many of the most common discussions of creativity are spiritual, psychoanalytic, or business-oriented. These approaches may yield useful information, but they're not particularly science-friendly.

Many of the earliest ideas about creativity were mystical and relied on divine inspiration (see a review of these ideas in Sternberg & Lubart, 1999). It's hard to claim that something is scientific or that it can be measured when the first people to talk about it were also talking about muses and demons. It's a little hard to take people's thoughts on the creative process seriously when they also may have believed that volcanic eruptions were caused by a trapped immortal sneezing fire (okay, I made that one up, but you get my gist).

Yet, creativity researchers often like using these mystical kinds of words in their article titles. I'm guilty of doing exactly this; I've used words such as *genius, lunatics,* and *madness* in my article titles, and I named one effect after Sylvia Plath (indeed, to the irate members of the Sylvia Plath Forum, I remain almost sorry). Why am I discussing my own use of these words, other than to illustrate my own hypocrisy? Because I know why I do it—it sounds cool. Creativity feels like a "grand" and "melodramatic" topic, and sometimes it's tempting to give in to the grandeur. But my guess is that agencies that fund grants are more impressed with titles such as, "Neural Interactions in Incremental and Episodic Memory" (a real NIMH grant title, in fact). And you know what? I would be, too. That grant sounds like the scientists know what they're doing.

However, the history of creativity research started with mysticism and continues on the mystical path to this day. A quick look on Amazon.com finds many bestsellers that focus on finding spiritual paths to creativity, gaining inspiration for discovering artistic confidence, reclaiming your creativity and dreams, unleashing creative forces within, and so on. These books may help some people, but they're not science by any stretch. There's nothing to back them up. Most fields within psychology don't have this problem; I don't see many books called *Tapping Your Inner Measurement Expert* or *Finding Peace and Love with Your Hippocampus.*

If you go beyond the creativity–mysticism work, what else is left? There's a lot on the role of creativity in Freudian theory and psychoanalysis. Again, there's nothing wrong with that—but we're not talking heavy-duty psychological science, either. I ended up studying more Freud in an undergraduate English class than I did in my entire graduate program in psychology. It's also a particularly negative way to look at creativity; much of the Freudian conceptions of creativity center around the idea that people are imaginative or create things as a way to sublimate their sexual desires. It's a little ironic that recent research indicates that creative people tend to have more sex than less creative people (Nettle & Clegg, 2006).

Another big area is creativity in the workplace. Much of the body of research and writing in this area is legitimate and insightful, and I will discuss it in detail. Some of the work in this area, however, is simply pop psychology. Being practical and applied is absolutely a good thing, but some of these approaches sacrifice any semblance of scientific validity and are light years away from empirical evidence. Most of the books on business creativity that you may find remaindered at Barnes & Noble or Borders are not necessarily foolproof. If learning to be a creative worker or leader was as easy as reading a book and realizing, "Hey, I just need to look at things differently sometimes," then everyone would be creative and live happily ever after—and every company would be an innovation engine.

Perhaps the biggest reason why creativity can feel like an unwanted Windows upgrade is that many people don't know exactly what creativity *is*. Ask a classroom full of students to tell you their definitions of creativity, and you'll get a lot of responses like "thinking outside the box." Yes, without question, but what, exactly, does that mean? One of the first goals of this book is to clarify the many different meanings of creativity.

It's not surprising that most people don't have a strong grasp of what it means to study creativity. If you look at the people who *do* study creativity, they are scattered across many different areas. Some are cognitive psychologists, others are in education. Some are in business; some are starting to pop up in neuroscience. It's hard to get a consistent agreement about a topic across psychology; it is even more difficult to get such a disparate group of thinkers to come together across fields.

Some people think of being creative the way they do about using public transportation—it's great that other people do it, but they don't want to do it themselves. Or others may think of it in the same way as being a vegetarian—a perfectly noble endeavor, but not something they could handle doing. Or, perhaps, it's simply something completely alien. "I'm not creative," they say. And these same people may then miraculously balance the family budget with innovative money management strategies, or keep a small child entertained for hours with made-up songs, or build a fence designed to keep a high-strung beagle in the yard.

Indeed, when you think of a creative person, who do you conjure up? Maybe you think of Van Gogh cutting off his ear and then painting a masterpiece. Or Alexander Fleming leaving a Petri dish out by mistake and discovering penicillin. More recently, you might think of Bill Gates and Steve Jobs revolutionizing the way people communicate, work, and think. But other images of creativity may come closer to home: your daughter building a structure with her Legos, or your uncle spontaneously making up a pun. Or maybe you on occasion may tinker with a new recipe, play guitar, create computer games, make funny faces, or tinker with new gadgets.

What do you think of when you think of a creative product or activity? Many people, for example, have received the spam e-mails from foreign countries in which someone writes of a "desire of going into a business relationship with you." His father died and left him a fortune, or she is the manager of a small bank trying to perform a large financial transaction. There are hundreds of millions of dollars up for grabs, and they need your help to provide an account for the money and put up a few thousand bucks in up-front costs. It's nothing, really, compared to the money you will be making. As you have (hopefully) guessed, it's a scam. The plans get postponed, more officials need to be bribed, and so on, until they have bled you dry. But here's the creative part: The other day I got an e-mail from the Antifraud Commission of Nigeria. They are busy prosecuting the nasty spammers and fraudsters and are suing them to compensate the victims. Indeed, I stand to gain nearly $500,000 as a witness and plaintiff, if I can just pass along the court expenses and initial legal fees. . . .

Here's another one: Are animals creative? Some would argue that the answer is yes, and in fact, there is even a framework for animal creativity (J. C. Kaufman & A. B. Kaufman, 2004). Let's take the satin bowerbird as an example. The males of the species do a nifty, complicated dance to attract the females. They puff out their feathers, they extend their wings, and they run around and make a funny buzzing sound (all in the name of love). Female satin bowerbirds prefer those males who provide the best show (Borgia, 1985). Sometimes, however, these dances can startle the females, making them less likely to mate (which somehow makes sense; try screaming "Boo!" during an intimate moment and see where that gets you). What recent research has shown is that male satin bowerbirds respond to startling their intended mates by reducing the intensity of their dances in the future (Patricelli, Coleman, & Borgia, 2006). So not only do these guys dance and put on a show, but they know enough to tone it down if they're not getting the right response. Teenage boys should be so lucky.

How about this one: John Cage was a composer who specialized in unorthodox compositions, finding music in a wide variety of sounds. One of his pieces was called 4'33". The piece consisted of 4 minutes and 33 seconds of silence or, as Cage called it, "unintentional sound." The pianist would walk out onto stage, open the piano, and simply sit for exactly four minutes and 33 seconds. Cage's idea behind this piece was that there is music all around us and we need to reject our preconceived notions about what music is (Cage, 1961; Hamm, 1980). Was Cage creative? Could silence be a creative piece of music? In 2002, composer Mike Batt's classical rock band, The Planets, released a CD with a song on it called "One Minute Silence," which is exactly what it sounds like. Cage's estate sued for plagiarism. Batt settled out of court for a six-figure amount (CNN.com, 2002).

Yet, consider this other lawsuit: Stu Silverstein compiled 122 uncollected poems of Dorothy Parker and published them as an edited volume. Penguin Books had earlier negotiated unsuccessfully to publish Silverstein's compilation as part of their collection of complete Dorothy Parker poems. Two years after Silverstein's book appeared, Penguin included the exact same 122 poems (no more, no less) in their collection in an uncollected poems section. Silverstein sued, noting that they included poems that he found embedded in letters and that Penguin used the same titles he gave untitled poems. Astoundingly, Penguin won—a judge ruled that a copyright can be claimed only for a creative contribution, and Silverstein's work as compiler and editor was not specifically creative but rather simply hard work. As a side note, the court had to legally define a poem and ended up with "poetry consists of poems, but not all poems are poetry" (S. Leith, 2007). Wow.

Here's another example: On November 3, 2003, the Patriots were losing 24–23 to the Broncos with 2 minutes and 49 seconds left to play, backed up to their own 1-yard line. Patriots coach Bill Belichick called for a deliberate safety, a play in which his quarterback kneeled down in his own end zone, conceding two points to the other team. This play put the Broncos up 26–23, and was an odd move to someone (like me) who doesn't know much about football. Instead of punting, the Patriots basically gave away two points. Why? What the move did was give the Patriots room to kick off. Instead of punting and getting the ball maybe 40 yards away from their own goal line, they were able to get the ball to the Broncos' 15-yard line (and further away from scoring). The Patriots were able to stop the Broncos and then scored a touchdown due to their new, improved field position (and a gutsy move by the coach), winning the game 30–26. The strategy easily could have backfired, but Belichick knew that he had a good field goal kicker who could likely tie the game up 26–26, even if the touchdown run didn't work ("Brady leads Patriots," 2006). In this strategy, the two points lost because of the safety were not particularly meaningful, and well worth the investment and risk. Is this creative football coaching? Would your opinion be different based on how much you know about football?

There are many, many other examples. In 2003, an odd phenomenon called "Flash Mobs" began, in which a large crowd of people would show up at a predetermined place and do a predetermined action (for example, gathering at a fancy hotel and then staring at a specific area). With hundreds of teenagers (or other people with too much time on their hands) participating in these flash mobs, it made the news as yet another example of odd behavior by the masses. Eventually, it faded into oblivion.

Is this creative or simply bizarre? What if I were to tell you that the originator of flash mobs was an eager devotee of social psychology experiments and was testing his own ideas about group behavior with a live participant pool? Would that it make it creative? In fact, that's what happened, and the originator is now a senior editor at *Harper's Magazine* (Wasik, 2006).

For every question we might tackle, another thousand pop up. What is creativity? Is it possible to find creativity in different pockets and nooks of our culture? Think about Deep Blue, the chess-playing computer that was able to defeat defending chess champion Gary Kasparov in the mid-1990s. Can a computer be creative? Consider the advertising campaign for an Ecuadorian foot powder, Pulvapies, which hyped its product on the eve of election night by advising voters to vote for whomever they wanted but to make sure to vote for Pulvapies for good health—and then managed to get their foot powder elected mayor of a small town (Mikkelson & Mikkelson, 2006). Does that count as creativity, or is it notable only because of the outcome? How about the toys and gadgets made by Archie McPhee, including a corndog-scented air freshener, an action figure of Marie Antoinette with an ejecting head, and Angry Scotsman chewing gum—do you have to find them amusing to consider them creative? Consider the Web site www.jowlers.com, which features many photographs of people in the process of shaking their head rapidly back and forth (thereby creating the effect of distorted facial features), or www.sleeveface.com, which offers people posing with LP sleeves covering their faces to create a new image. Certainly, jowler and sleeveface photographs are different and unlike other photographs; are they creative?

Think of the Paul Simon song, "Mother and Child Reunion"—does it strike you as more or less creative when you find out that he got the title from a chicken and egg dish at a Chinese restaurant? Maybe you can be a creative artistic consumer, interpreting movies or song lyrics in new ways. On the Web site Andy's Anachronisms (Taylor, 2003), a series of pop songs are interpreted as if they're about time travel. Most of these interpretations are not consistent with the typically assumed content of the song. "Once in a Lifetime," by the Talking Heads, is usually seen as a song about a mid-life crisis; Andy interprets lines such as, "And you may tell yourself—this is not my beautiful wife!" as referring to alternate universes created by time-traveling mistakes. However you think of creativity—*whether* you think of creativity—it is all likely different from how your neighbor thinks of it. There are many different ways in which someone can be creative, and there are almost as many different ways that people try to measure creativity.

This book is intended to be a brief and lively introduction to the field. It's not possible to summarize or describe all the work being done (or even to come close). In *Creativity 101*, I'll start by describing the history of how people began to study creativity and discuss different definitions. I'll explore the "Four P's" (person, process, product, and press), then I'll tackle four ongoing debates and research areas—the question of whether creativity is domain-general or domain-specific; how creativity corresponds to different constructs such as personality, motivation, and intelligence; the relationship between creativity and mental illness; and how creativity might (or might not) improve guidance and selection process. Finally, I'll discuss some thoughts for the future. Other creativity researchers might write (or have written) an entirely different book, and I would strongly urge an interested reader to seek out other volumes. I will present some recommendations in an appendix.

However, given that you're holding this book in your hands and not the others, go ahead and finish this one first (please).

A VERY BRIEF HISTORY OF CREATIVITY

The history of creativity research has two "eras" so far—before 1950 and after 1950. Before 1950, there was little serious research being conducted on creativity. Prominent thinkers have always *thought* about creativity. Plato argued that creativity (such as a poet's work) involved dictating whatever the Muse chanced to speak (see Rothenberg & Hausman, 1976). Freud wrote an essay on "Creative writers and day-dreaming," in which he wrote about the "strange being," the creative writer (1908/1959). Einstein frequently discussed imagination and creativity; he was once quoted as saying that "imagination is more important than knowledge" (Calaprice, 2000). Similarly, Vyogtsky and Jung wrote well-known essays on the topic. But none of these people *studied* creativity.

Most of the early researchers who may have discussed or studied creativity actually focused on something else. Francis Galton focused more on heredity and human ability, Charles Spearman and Alfred Binet wanted to measure intelligence, William James was interested in higher-level cognition, and Cesare Lombroso studied genius and madness (Becker, 1995). Others interested in questions of creativity were modern-day Renaissance types who are now long forgotten to even the ardent student of the field. W. S. Jevons taught logic and economy but dabbled in multiple fields (Mosselmans & White, 2001). George Bethune was a preacher, wrote popular hymns, studied fly-fishing, and was active in Democratic politics (Stedman, 1900/2001). As one psychologist wrote at the time: "It would seem futile to speak of a literature on the process of creative thinking" (Hutchinson, 1931, p. 392).

There were still isolated studies and papers. Chassell (1916) adapted or created 12 different measures of originality. Some of these tests tapped into problem solving, and others reflected high-level intellectual ability. However, some of these tests are remarkably similar to the same assessments used nearly 100 years later. In Chassell's Novel Situation tests, she asked college students six different questions, such as "If all water, because of some change in its chemical constitution, should contract instead of expand upon freezing, what would be the effect upon animal life, including man?" The responses were then graded for originality. Chassell's work predates by many decades the work of later pioneers—yet virtually no one cites or acknowledges her work.

Some of the other early work is less impressive. Witty and Lehman (1929) argue that creative geniuses, particularly creative writers, suffer from "nervous instability." They also provide no evidence or data to support their ideas (which, indeed, was a harbinger of research to come). Hutton and Bassett (1948), meanwhile, helpfully point out that lobotomized patients tend to be less creative.

Everything changed at the 1950 convention of the American Psychological Association. In his presidential address, Joy P. Guilford called for psychologists to increase their focus on creativity. He argued that creativity was an important topic and was not being studied or researched at the level it warranted. Before Guilford, less than 0.2% of all entries of *Psychological Abstracts* concentrated on creativity (Guilford, 1950). He helped move the field forward.

It is not true to say that Guilford single-handedly brought creativity from the realm of esoterica to prominence. On the other hand, it can often feel this way. What Guilford did was to both galvanize the field and make it acceptable to study creativity. Many of the ideas and studies that were published in the decade that followed his speech are still widely cited and respected. In contrast, there are only a handful of papers that are still commonly used from the decade before his seminal address. Indeed, a good starting place to talk about the science of creativity can be found in Guilford's own work.

GUILFORD'S APPROACH

Guilford (1950, 1967) placed creativity into a larger framework of intelligence in his Structure of Intellect model. He attempted to organize all of human cognition along three dimensions. The first dimension was called "operations" and simply meant the mental gymnastics needed for any kind of task. The second dimension, "content," referred to the general subject area. The third dimension, "product," represented the actual products that might result from different kinds of thinking in different kinds of subject matters. With five operations, four contents, and six products, Guilford's (1967) model had 120 different possible mental abilities. Indeed, he later expanded the model to include 180 different abilities, although the 120 abilities model is the one more often studied (Guilford, 1988). Perhaps true creativity could be figuring out a way to accurately measure a person's entire range of all 180 different abilities without having this person try to escape after the first 20 hours of testing.

One of Guilford's operations (or thought processes) was divergent thinking—analyzing your response to questions with no obvious, singular answer. If you're in the mood for playing along at home, take out a pen and some scrap paper and give yourself three minutes to answer this question: What would happen if we didn't need sleep?

It's either been three minutes or you didn't feel inspired. Your first impulse may be to wonder how your answers could be translated into creativity scores. The first step is to discuss how Guilford conceptualized the idea of divergent production. Although he had many different ideas about it (which makes sense, given that having many different ideas is a sign of divergent thinking), much of his work can be boiled down to four key components. The first one, fluency, is derived by counting all of your ideas. Did you come up with 5 possible results? 10? 15? I can't translate your number into a creativity score, but with the correct (and copyrighted) tables, you could figure it out.

Let's examine just what a fluency score does and does not represent. If I asked you another standard creativity question, which is to name uses for a brick, then maybe you'd mention that you could use it as a weapon, to build a house, as a paperweight, as a doorstop, as a kitchen tool, or as a parking brake. One singer–songwriter, Bill Berry, wrote a whole song called "The Brick," in which he rattles off the many possible things you can do with a brick (Schock, 1998). Your fluency score would simply be how many different things you named, regardless of their repetitiveness or practicality. If you say that you would use a brick to build an apartment, a condominium, a house, a shack, a wall, a fence—they all would count. If you say that you'd use a brick to fly to Spain, it would still count in your fluency score.

Flexibility looks at how many different categories you can name, or how many different types of ideas you have. Let's go back to not needing sleep. Maybe you said that people wouldn't need pajamas. That would count for both fluency and flexibility. But let's say that you also said that people wouldn't need pillows, bed sheets, mattresses, or blankets. All of these answers work just fine for fluency. Yet, they all represent the same category, not needing sleep-related objects. You would only get credit for one category for flexibility.

Originality is being able to produce the most unusual ideas. You might have said, for example, that if you don't need sleep, that people would have less physical intimacy (i.e., sex). It's a perfectly good response and usually gets a good laugh from people, but it's also one that many people might suggest.

I actually speak from expertise. Usually, the sleep example is the one I use in the talks that I give about creativity, which means that I've heard from probably 15,000 people. I know more about what might happen if people didn't need sleep than anyone has the right to know (and, indeed, I will be well prepared if such an occurrence transpires). People say that more work would be done (because there would be more time to work), that less work would be done (because people would be tired), that there would be more crime, less crime, happier people, sadder people, and so on. I've only encountered a few truly original responses. One of my favorite was when I discussed this concept in a theater class in Taiwan. One student said that "If we didn't need sleep, then clearly we are Martians, and therefore the differences that would exist would be the differences between ourselves and Martians."

One simple way of measuring originality is asking many people the same question and seeing how many times people give a response. If your response is rarely (or never) given, then it is more original. How, you may ask, can someone distinguish answers that are original from answers that are just plain weird? What if you were to suggest that not needing sleep would make everyone love the rock group Scissor Sisters? That's certainly original. What about "If people didn't need sleep, then binky rollo ponga zennadril?" At what point does an answer cross the line from being original to crazy? Broader definitions of creativity address this question by focusing on an idea's usefulness (as will be discussed in the next chapter). This distinction is also part of a larger question that will be discussed both in terms of how we can define creativity and in terms of the convoluted association between creativity and mental illness. For the purposes of originality, however, you're looking at uniqueness.

The final component of Guilford's model is elaboration. To review, *fluency* is the ability to produce a great number of ideas, *flexibility* is the ability to produce many different types of ideas, and *originality* is the ability to produce the most unusual ideas. *Elaboration* is the ability to develop these ideas. You say that people would get into more violent fights if there was no sleep? Okay, explain why and how. One way to conceptualize this ability is that if you draw a picture of a person, then "elaboration" would be the level of detail—is your person wearing a watch? Do they have earlobes? Shoelaces? Elbows?

One quick example to distinguish the four components was used in the *Essentials of Creativity Assessment* (J. C. Kaufman, Plucker, & Baer, 2008, pp. 18–19), and I will paraphrase it here. Let's say that your significant other wants to go out to eat and asks you to come up with different restaurants that might be a good choice. You might come up with a huge list of different restaurants (high fluency), you might come up with a wide range of food styles (high flexibility), you might think up a few restaurants that most people wouldn't have known (high originality), or you might focus on one type of food and rattle off every single place nearby (high elaboration).[1]

Some researchers have proposed modifications to these four categories. For example, one new coding method is to produce a "creativity quotient" by weighing both fluency and flexibility (Snyder, Mitchell, Bossomaier, & Pallier, 2004). Another scoring choice is to either code for originality based on national norms (from the standardized tests discussed later) or to score originality based on the responses of a particular sample (e.g., Runco & Dow, 2004). The second method might be useful if the sample you are looking at is not typical of national norms (for example, if you are looking at children with dyslexia, or adults who still like disco). Silvia, Winterstein et al. (2008) proposed subjective scoring of responses for originality so that all responses are evaluated by experts based on how creative they are (this method is often used with non-TTCT materials, as I will discuss later).

TURNING BRICKS INTO MEASURES

Guilford's four components of divergent thinking represent the foundation for the most popular measure of creativity, the Torrance Tests of Creative Thinking (TTCT; Torrance, 1974a, 1974b, 2008). Guilford (1967) also created similar measures himself (named, appropriately, the Structure of Intellect battery), and many others have designed similar tests (Getzels & Jackson, 1962; Wallach & Kogan, 1965). But the TTCT has continued to be the most popular, especially in deciding who gets into gifted programs (Hunsaker & Callahan, 1995).

---

1. Conversely, if you live in San Bernardino, you might simply acknowledge that Casa Maya is the best place to eat and agree to go there with no discussion.

The TTCT, developed by E. Paul Torrance, measures all four of these aspects of creativity with both Figural and Verbal forms (each has a form A and a form B that can be used alternately). The Figural forms have three subtests:

- Picture Construction, in which you use a basic shape and expand on it to create a picture;
- Picture Completion, in which you are asked to finish and title incomplete drawings; and
- Lines/Circles, in which you are asked to modify many different series of lines or circles (depending on the edition).

The Verbal form has seven subtests:

- Asking, in which you ask as many questions as you can about a given picture;
- Guessing Causes, in which you try to guess as many possible causes for a pictured action;
- Guessing Consequences, in which you try to guess as many possible consequences for a pictured action;
- Product Improvement, in which you are asked to make changes to improve a toy;
- Unusual Uses, in which you are asked to think of many different possible uses for an ordinary item;
- Unusual Questions, in which you ask as many questions as possible about an ordinary item; and
- Just Suppose, in which you are asked to "just suppose" that an improbable situation has happened (a made-up example might be, "What if elephants could talk?"), and then list the various ramifications.

Torrance (1974a, 1974b, 2008) provides extensive reliability and validity data in the technical-norms manual of the TTCT. Torrance and his colleagues typically gave the TTCT and compared the scores (usually with solid correlations) to other measures of creativity, or else they showed that gifted students scored higher on the TTCT than nongifted students. Torrance and Safter (1989) used one of the subtests ("Just Suppose") to conduct a long-range study looking at predictive validity. They found a solid relationship to creative achievement after more than 20 years. Plucker (1999) reanalyzed data from a different Torrance longitudinal study and found that divergent thinking was much more responsible for how people differed in creative achievement than were traditional IQ tests (the relationship between creativity and intelligence is an in-depth matter of its own and will be discussed in more detail in chapter four).

If Guilford kick-started the field of creativity and its scientific study, then Torrance served as its beloved international champion. The TTCT is also often used in other cultures, and validation studies have been conducted on translated versions of the TTCT in such countries as India (Tanwar, 1979), Hong Kong (Rudowicz, Lok, & Kitto, 1995), and Japan (Saeki, Fan, & Van Dusen, 2001). The basic structure and ideas behind the TTCT are present in tests developed in many additional countries (see, e.g., essays in J. C. Kaufman & Sternberg, 2006).

Even with Torrance gone, the Torrance Tests continue to be revised and modified. Flexibility was dropped from the most recent version of the tests because of its high correlation to fluency (Hébert, Cramond, Spiers-Neumeister, Millar, & Silvian, 2002). Replacing flexibility were two new categories in the Figural test, abstractness of titles and resistance to premature closure (Torrance, 2008).

Like anything that is at the top of any field for a long time, there are a multitude of criticisms of the TTCT. Some claim that the procedures for interpreting scores are not backed up by factor analysis (Heausler & Thompson, 1988); others point to how easy it is to change scores with different instructions (Lissitz & Willhoft, 1985); and still others have commented on the overly strong relationship between fluency and originality scores (e.g., Dixon, 1979).

Perhaps the most damning criticism is the question of whether a test of divergent thinking can measure all of creativity.

17

Clapham (2004), for example, gave the TTCT along with two measures of creative interests, and she found low or nonsignificant correlations. One reason might be that a measure of creative interests treats creativity as a broad and far-reaching thing, while divergent thinking (even when presented in different ways) is a narrower construct.

Creativity isn't necessarily just divergent thinking. The ability to engage in divergent thinking—to come up with many different responses, with outrageously innovative responses, and so on—is incredibly important. It's a cornerstone of creativity. But it's not all that creativity can be. I will spend the rest of the chapter and much of the next one discussing the different components of creativity, as we know it now. I will explore different definitions and conceptions of creativity, as well as many different ways of measuring creativity.

Some people act as if creativity began and ended with Guilford and Torrance. They're wrong. As is often the case, much of the problem lies in the distance between prophet and disciple. Torrance, along with his colleagues, argued for using several different methods to assess creativity (Cramond, Matthews-Morgan, Torrance, & Zuo, 1999), and he called for tests to be developed that extend beyond verbal and figural creativity (Torrance & Cramond, 2002). Teachers or administrators who rely *only* on the TTCT (or a similar instrument) are missing out on the complete "creativity" picture. Torrance himself would've likely been the first one to argue this point.

If creativity is more than just divergent thinking, then what exactly is it? Let's explore some other definitions of creativity.

MODERN DEFINITIONS

Guilford focused on creativity as a key part of human intelligence; others have focused their energies on trying to define creativity as its own construct. You might think that the question of defining creativity would be virtually its own discipline—yet creativity is often *not* defined. Plucker, Beghetto, and Dow (2004) selected 90 different articles that either appeared in the two top creativity journals or articles in a different peer-reviewed journal with the word "creativity" in the title. Of these papers, only 38% explicitly defined what creativity was. How could such a low percentage of papers actually define creativity? Maybe you could make a case for not defining the construct in a creativity journal—you could assume the intended audience already knows what creativity is (conversely, the intended audience may have 30 definitions of creativity and not know which one you are espousing). But, as Plucker et al. (2004) discussed, the noncreativity journals' rate of 33% defining creativity was actually *lower* than the overall average. Creativity is rarely defined, regardless of whether the intended audience is comprised of creativity experts or novices.

Most research and theory-based definitions of "creativity" boil down to two components. First, creativity must represent something different, new, or innovative (Amabile, 1983; Barron, 1955). This part raises a few questions (e.g., How new? Different in what ways?) that will be addressed later. However, unlike "originality," simply being novel isn't enough to qualify as being "creative." If I ask you to show me a proof for the transitive property in algebra, and you yell out "a herring!," this response is clearly *different*—but I wouldn't call it creative. I'd be more inclined to want to walk away from you backwards in a slow and nonthreatening manner than to consider you creative. Similarly, if you hire a contractor to work on your house and tell her that you especially value creativity, you will nonetheless be disappointed if she paves your driveway with rotten salami. It's different, and your driveway will be the most original on the block, but I wouldn't call it creative, and you likely wouldn't pay her.

So it isn't enough to just be different—creativity must also be appropriate to the task at hand. A creative response is useful and relevant. There are some circumstances (such as if you were doing a stand-up comedy routine) where yelling out "a herring" *might* be an appropriate response to an algebraic proof. But there are not many. A certain level of high quality is often linked with appropriateness—you not only fulfill task demands, but you do it well (Sternberg, 1999a; Sternberg, Kaufman, & Pretz, 2002).

I am reminded of a story from one of my students. She was talking about an event at her daughter's school, at which the children drew a picture of what they wanted to be when they grew up—doctors, lawyers, princesses, and cowboys. When it was one little boy's turn, he said, "When I grow up, I want to be a sandwich." Is this creative? Again, it's certainly different—most children do not aspire to be sandwiches—but it doesn't seem to meet the "appropriate" condition. Yet, this example calls into question where to draw the line. What about the child who wants to be a princess? That's at least possible (there are some unmarried princes lingering around somewhere), so it seems to be appropriate (if not terribly original). When does a child's aspiration cross the line from appropriate-and-therefore-potentially-creative to inappropriate? What if a child wants to sniff armpits for a living? I mean, it's *possible*, isn't it?

Another way of expressing the innovative–appropriate distinction is found in the Geneplore model (Finke, Ward, & Smith, 1992). This framework has two phases—generative and exploratory. Generation, the "novel" part, is generating many different ideas. Exploration refers to evaluating these possible options and choosing the best one (or ones). Guilford was also interested in the concept of exploration. In his Structure of Intellect model, a variation of the idea was called "evaluation" and was included as one of the operations. The exploratory or evaluative aspect of creativity is often overlooked; indeed, when you think of a creative person, do *you* think of someone pondering and selecting the best alternative? Yet, there is no doubting the importance of this component. "Creativity is allowing yourself to make mistakes," *Dilbert* cartoonist Scott Adams once said. "Art is knowing which ones to keep" (Adams, 1996).

Several researchers, perhaps most notably Runco (1991), have argued that the ability to evaluate and make creative ideas useful and helpful is often overlooked. There have been some studies of the importance of evaluative thinking (Okuda, Runco, & Berger, 1991; Runco & Chand, 1994), but this area is certainly one that merits more work.

WHAT DO YOU MEAN BY "CREATIVITY?"

Creativity research is much more than a basic definition and the concept of divergent thinking. When I talk about creativity, am I talking about a beautiful piece of art or an ingenious computer program? How about the sensation of the "a-ha" process when I suddenly understand what I need to do next? Maybe, instead, I'm talking about how a creative person behaves. Or maybe it's the synergy that happens when many different people share and exchange ideas together. Throwing all of these things together and labeling them as "creativity" is not much different than using the word "love" to mean your feelings for your mom, your best friend, your significant other, and spicy calamari. It may be technically correct, but it's not terribly useful.

It is important to distinguish between whether you are talking about a creative product, the creative process itself, a creative person, or a creative press (a fancy word that means environment; using it enables the nifty mnemonic of the four P's). These distinctions have been around for a while (Rhodes, 1962). They are not necessarily the only four possible ways of approaching creativity; as Runco (2007a) recounts, Simonton (1990) proposed "persuasion," with the logic that creative people impact the way others think, and Runco himself (2003) argued that "potential" should be one of the P's.

Not surprisingly, different creativity researchers have focused on each of these four facets, as we will see in the next chapter.

Modern Theories
of Creativity

lthough *The Four P's* sounds like it should be a doo-wop group, it is instead one way of approaching theories of creativity. I have placed many of the major theories of creativity into one of the four P's (product, process, person, and press/environment). Sometimes the fit is natural; sometimes I cram them in (the same way I pack my car trunk for a long road trip). My own interests tend to naturally gravitate toward the creative product and person, although there is much exciting work being done on all the P's.

THE CREATIVE PRODUCT

Of the four P's, the creative *product* is probably the most widely studied and measured. A creative product is a tangible item, product, response, or finished idea. It is the end result of a person's creative *process*, influenced by the *press* (aka environment).

One theory that presents a way of looking at creative products is Csikszentmihalyi's (1996, 1999) Systems Model. Creativity, according to this model, is an interaction between the domain, the field, and the person. A domain is a preexisting area of expertise. It could be as broad as mathematics or science; it could be as specific as game theory or particle physics. Creativity occurs when a domain is changed in some way.

The field is defined as the *gatekeepers*—teachers, editors, critics, and so on. The field can be thought of as the people who you need to impress if you want to be successful. The field interacts directly with the domain; the field shapes a domain (i.e., the editors of psychology journals help determine how the domain of psychology is advanced), and the domain shapes the field (i.e., it may be hard for someone trained as a psychologist to be hired by an education department, even if she can make tremendous contributions to the department, because some consider the domain of education to be restricted to people with specific training in education).

The third component is the *person*—the one who creates an idea or theory or piece of art. The success of such a creative product will likely depend on the interaction between the field (the gatekeepers) and the person. If a person creates a product that is uninteresting or offensive, the field will be unlikely to appreciate the product. A field can be a positive source of inspiration as well; a person may be mentored or advised by a more senior creator, or she may adapt and expand past work. Finally, the domain defines the space in which a person creates. A creative person designing a product within the domain of skyscraper building is not likely to use balsa wood and glue as a medium because skyscrapers *require* a certain level of strength and building finesse.

In Csikszentmihalyi's theory, the domain, field, and person work interactively. So, let's examine Bach's work. Let's say that while he was alive, the field did not believe his later work was creative in the domain of music. If this tidbit is true (and it apparently was), then according to Csikszentmihalyi, *Bach's work was not creative at that time.* It is only later, when our more modern critics, professors, and musicians recognized his talent, that his work could be called creative.

This theory should drive fear into the heart of the most successful creators. James Patterson? John Grisham? Sure your books sell now, but how about in 50 years? Steven Spielberg? Martin Scorsese? Let's see what film classes say in the next century. And, conversely, this theory may bring hope to people who fancy themselves as undiscovered geniuses. "Perhaps," a languishing poet might say, "my work will be found 200 years from now, and people then will realize I was misunderstood and unappreciated."

Yet, it is interesting to note that the work of Dean Simonton has discounted the myth of the unappreciated genius. He studied 496 operas and compared how they were initially received versus how often they are performed today. What he found was that, in general, operas that opened to good reviews and solid runs are the operas that are most commonly performed today (Simonton, 1998). Indeed, if you think of the most popular writers of the 19th century, you come up with writers such as Mark Twain and Charles Dickens—who were much more akin to the Jon Stewart and Stephen King of their time. Even more recently, the musicals of Harold Rome were considered the "high brow" theater of the 1950s, while Rodgers and Hammerstein were seen more as populist tripe. Yet, can you name a Harold Rome musical today? If you can, I'm impressed (and a little scared). If you can't, think of *Pins and Needles, Fanny,* and *I Can Get It For You Wholesale,* which introduced the world to Barbra Streisand.

Another area of research that discounts the neglected-genius idea is Simonton's work on career trajectories. Simonton has conducted extensive research on the relationship between age and achievement (see Simonton, 1997, for a review). He has found that most successful people begin producing in their 20s, peak in their 40s, and then gradually decline. Some fields peak particularly young; theoretical physicists and poets, for example, tend to make a major contribution by their mid-to-late 20s, or not at all (Simonton, 1994). A study by Kozbelt and Durmysheva (2007) looked at lifespan creativity in Japanese printmakers from the 18th century and found similar patterns and peaks.

An alternate theory has been proposed by Galenson (2005), who argued that different types of creators peak at different ages. He constructs two life cycles: early conceptual creators (finders), who burst onto the scene with a splash of greatness; compared to later-peaking experimental creators (seekers), who made contributions based on a vast body of work. Galenson argues that it is the type of approach that results in early or late peaks, not the domain. Simonton (2007) specifically addressed this question empirically and found that the question of domain (poetry vs. fiction) was equally important to predicting when a writer peaked; Kaufman and Gentile (2004) found that late-blooming novelists were more likely to be successful than poets.

One theory of creativity, the propulsion theory, focuses exclusively on creative products (Sternberg, 1999a; Sternberg, Kaufman, & Pretz, 2001, 2002, 2003). This theory describes eight different ways that someone can make a creative contribution and categorizes these contributions based on their relationship to the domain. The first four contributions all represent achievements that stay within the framework of an existing paradigm.

Perhaps the most basic type of contribution that someone can make is *replication*. Replication tries to keep things status quo—to reproduce past work. Think of a scientific study whose sole goal is to show that an earlier experiment can be reproduced, or maybe a romance novel that is mighty similar to earlier novels, with different main characters and a new setting. Or remember—if you dare—*Police Academy 6: City Under Siege.* Perhaps, instead, think of the people who spend Sunday afternoons in a museum, trying to copy a famous painting. Are they creative? Absolutely, and they help create that nice ambience that makes museums fun on the weekends. But these painters are not necessarily trying to advance the artistic domain.

The second type of contribution, *redefinition*, takes a new look at the domain. A redefinitive contribution doesn't necessarily try to push forward but rather tries to present a different perspective.

Think of the artistic work of Andy Warhol—taking everyday objects (such as Campbell's soup cans) and presenting them as art. Or the concept of "found poetry"—the ability to glean a poem from such nonliterary source materials as instructions on how to shampoo your hair or the quotations of Donald Rumsfeld. A good theater director may use redefinition—he or she may take a famous play and then put a new "spin" on it so that an audience may see something new. A good businessman may be able to see a new use for a product that hasn't sold well. A classic example is Art Fry of 3M, who found a new use for an adhesive that wasn't strong enough to sell as a glue—so he invented post-it notes.

A third contribution, and perhaps the type of contribution that achieves the most immediate success, is called *forward incrementation*. This type of contribution pushes forward the domain just a little. Maybe the creator makes a slight change in what already exists. These additions usually are not groundbreaking—it takes the domain in the same direction it was heading. Most successful Web sites are a result of someone nudging the domain a little bit further and applying an Internet sensibility. Amazon's success has been to present an online bookstore with infinite books. E-bay tackled auction houses. Numerous other Web sites have become travel agents, matchmakers, and so on. Think of really good genre writers. Many solid successes have introduced some twists. Jeffrey Deaver's hero Lincoln Rhyme is a quadriplegic, and Faye Kellerman's cop converts to Orthodox Judaism. My favorite is Harlan Coben's unlikely hero Myron Bolitar, a sports agent who teams up with his financial planner Win to solve crimes, sing musical theater songs, and generally kick butt.

The final contribution that stays within the existing definitions of a domain is *advance forward incrementation*. This contribution pushes the domain ahead two steps instead of one—and the creator often suffers for it. This type of creative product includes people who were a little before their time. Think of the musicals of Stephen Sondheim, such as *Sweeney Todd, Follies, Pacific Overtures,* or *Merrily We Roll Along*. The only one you've probably heard of is *Sweeney Todd*, although most are considered brilliant by true theater buffs. Sondheim's musicals represent an enormous leap forward from earlier theatrical shows. His intricate lyrics and complex music are still following in the path of previous creators (such as Cole Porter or Kurt Weill). One big push forward about his work can be found in his serious, dark subject matters. He writes about murderous barbers, a secret society that lives in department stores, Japanese imperialism, Georges Seurat paintings come to life, presidential assassins, and a partially deformed Italian woman's romantic obsession. One of Sondheim's shows tells us "Art isn't easy"; indeed, *Sondheim's* art isn't easy—and is an advanced forward incrementation (Gordon, 1992). Other examples of advanced forward incrementation include Andy Kaufman's provocative humor, Stravinsky's *Rite of Spring*, Faraday's work on magnetism, and Babbage's vision of a universal computer (see Sternberg, Kaufman, & Pretz, 2002, for a more complete description).

The final four types of creative contributions represent attempts to reject and replace the current paradigm. *Redirection* represents an attempt to redirect the domain to head in a new direction. The toy company Mattel, for example, helped redirect the domain of toy selling in the 1950s. Up until this time, toy manufacturers targeted wholesale suppliers and toy stores for their products. If companies decided to stock the toy, then it sold; if not, it didn't. Sometimes, manufacturers might try to target parents. But Mattel spent its last financial resources to purchase commercial time on the Mickey Mouse television show and reach the children directly. This decision changed the ways that toys were advertised (to many a parent's chagrin). Children all across America demanded Mattel's Burp Gun, and millions were sold (Panati, 1991; Stern & Schoenhaus, 1990).

If most of these contribution types represent "forward" thinking, *reconstruction/redirection* looks backwards. This contribution is an attempt to move the field back to where it once was (a reconstruction of the past) so that it may move forward from this point—in a different direction. An example of reconstruction/redirection is the Mahjong craze of the 1920s, which started when a businessman brought the traditional Chinese high-stakes, male-oriented mix of dice and dominos to America. The classic game was reconceptualized as a low-stakes, female-oriented leisure time activity and became a huge hit (Panati, 1991). Another example can be seen in a recent issue of *Mad Magazine*, in which they "rewrote" old Dave Berg observational humor ("The darker side of the lighter side," 2008). What if, they may have reasoned, Dave Berg were still alive and writing his old strip? They used his old artwork and rewrote the punchlines, incorporating modern issues and a slightly darker sense of humor ("The darker side of the lighter side," 2008).

Perhaps the most radical of all of the creative contributions is *reinitiation*. In reinitiation, the creator tries to move the field to a new (as-yet-unreached) starting point and then progress from there. Reinitiation is Marcel Duchamp entering a urinal into a 1917 art exhibit and calling it "Fountain." It is Lavoisier inventing a revolutionary new chemistry. It is Ian Finlay's poetry, which uses visual props such as wild flowers, stone, sundials, and glass combining with the words of the poetry to result in the overall creation of a certain emotion or feeling (Parker & Kermode, 1996). It is Eleanor Roosevelt serving as a radically different example of what a First Lady could be, bringing her own ideas and agenda to the role. She took a hands-on approach to a traditionally dignified status and used her position as a place to advance women's rights and civil rights (Boller, 1988).

Finally, the last contribution is *integration*, in which two diverse domains are merged to create a new idea. Consider, for example, Barry Goldwater's ability to integrate two very different facets of conservatism in his groundbreaking political tract *The Conscience of a Conservative* (1960). Goldwater bridged the gap between traditional conservatives and libertarian conservatives by appealing to aspects of both philosophies. He argued, for example, that the New Deal was a move toward totalitarianism and that the government should not be active in most aspects of life— yet, he also argued in favor of the government's need to sustain order and reinforce morality. He brought together the two different conservative factions by uniting them on the goal of fighting

Communism. Goldwater's ability to bring different types of conservative ideologies together helped establish conservatism as a strong force from the 1960s to the present day (Dalek, 1995).

Two of the most popular science fiction creations represent similar integrations of different fields. Gene Roddenberry's *Star Trek* and George Lucas's *Star Wars* both were able to integrate the fields of science fiction and westerns. *Star Trek* was a television show that was based on a similar concept as the western show *Wagon Train*—sturdy and resilient men and women prevailing over an assortment of different types of people. *Star Trek* used human and Vulcan characters and had them triumph over a variety of different alien species (Panati, 1991). In a similar vein, George Lucas used a famous western plot in a science fiction setting. The basic story of *Star Wars* closely mirrors the plot of the John Wayne classic *The Searchers*; again, however, the setting of the Old West is replaced by outer space. *Star Wars* also integrates the field of Japanese Samurai movies; the plot of *Star Wars: A New Hope* is reminiscent of *Kakushi Toride no San Akunin*. The character of Obi-Wan Kenobi can be seen to represent a Samurai warrior, while the two robots of R2-D2 and C-3PO resemble two crooks that were hired to help rescue a princess in the original Japanese movie.

The Propulsion theory proposes a model for categorizing different creative products. More difficult, however, is figuring out how to measure them. How do we determine if a poem is creative? Somehow, answering "ask people" seems too simplistic—but it usually works. The general concept has been around for quite a while (e.g., Cattell, Glascock, & Washburn, 1918; Getzels & Csikszentmihalyi, 1976), but Amabile (1982, 1996) has refined a method called the Consensual Assessment Technique (CAT), which incorporates opinions by qualified experts as a way to measure creativity.

A typical way of assessing creativity via the CAT might be to ask many people to write a poem or a story, or write a caption to a photograph, or else to draw a picture or make a collage. Other tasks (among others) that have been used include dramatic performance (Myford, 1989), music compositions (Brinkman,

1999; Hickey, 2001), and writing mathematical problems (Baer, 1994). Conceivably, the CAT could be used on any type of creative product.

Once you have many different samples, you ask experts to independently rate them (I will soon discuss who exactly can be an expert). The raters compare products to each other instead of an absolute ideal. A great deal of past research has shown that experts agree at a strikingly high rate (e.g., Amabile, 1983, 1996; Baer, 1993, 1998; Hennessey & Amabile, 1999; Runco, 1989b).

Raters tend to agree across cultures. Several studies have looked at judgments of creative work by both Chinese and American raters (e.g., Chen et al., 2002; Niu & Sternberg, 2001; Rostan, Pariser, & Gruber, 2002); generally, the cultures agreed with each other, although Niu and Sternberg found that Chinese judges generally gave higher scores. The finding of judges agreeing on creativity across culture has also been found with Japanese and Americans (Child & Iwao, 1968; Iwao, Child, & Garcia, 1969) and Greeks and Americans (Haritos-Fatouros & Child, 1977). Hennessey, Kim, Guomin, and Weiwei (2008) found solid reliability in judges in America, Saudi Arabia, South Korea, and China.

In a cross-cultural study of what variables affect a person's ratings, Paletz and Peng (2008) asked students from Japan, China, and the United States to rate products (either a meal or a textbook). Raters from all three countries valued novelty; however, Chinese raters placed less importance on appropriateness. In separately rating a product's desirability (as opposed to creativity), Chinese raters were more impacted by novelty.

In addition to studying creativity ratings across cultures, other studies have examined creativity ratings across one person's work. One study looked at captions written to a series of 12 different photographs (J. C. Kaufman, Lee, Baer, & Lee, 2007). Four experts rated these captions for creativity. Kaufman et al. found that not only did the experts agree on their ratings, but they also agreed across captions. In other words, if they thought that Joe Smith's caption for photograph #1 was creative, they also thought that his caption for photograph #10 was creative (without knowing it was the same person).

The reason why this finding is important is that if you're evaluating a lot of creative work, there's always the chance that some prompts may yield higher creativity than others. If I ask you to write a short story about "greed" or about "the sensation of biting into a chicken bone and hurting your front tooth that you had replaced a year ago," the odds are that people will write more creative stories about "greed." If your instinct, incidentally, was to pick the longer topic as being able to inspire more creativity, I think that you're wrong. The topic itself was creative (or at least different), but it would result in a long stream of very similar stories (how many different ways can you bite into a chicken bone?). Consider the (humorous) example of a bad creative writing prompt: "A husband and a wife are meeting in a restaurant to finalize the impending divorce. Write the scene from the point of view of the busboy snorting cocaine in the restroom" (Wiencek, 2008). Luckily, the J. C. Kaufman et al. (2007) study indicates that we may not need to study this issue using such radically different prompts; such differences are likely not terribly significant.

If creativity is assessed across several different products, what factors might impact how overall creativity is rated? In other words, let's say I'm making a judgment about an artist's career by walking around a museum gallery or listening to a greatest hits collection—what's the most important? S. B. Kaufman, Christopher, and Kaufman (2008) looked at expert ratings of a series of poems written by the same poet. They found that a number of factors predicted overall evaluation—the quality of a poet's typical work, for example, as well as the poet's best and worst work. Interestingly, they also found that the last poem read also was significantly related to overall assessment—in other words, the last song you hear on that greatest hits CD will have more than its due share of influence on your overall impression.

Another question to be explored is who are the best experts? In the J. C. Kaufman et al. (2007) study, it is less clear, because there are no established experts for writing captions to sentences.

I am unaware of any Benevolent Brotherhood of Caption Writers (and if you know of one, please don't tell me). It's different for the S. B. Kaufman et al. (2008) study on poetry, where the best choice of experts (published poets, as were used in the study) seems obvious.

What, for example, would I be qualified to rate? I can make a pretty good case for my being an expert of creativity. I can make a decent case for my expertise in noncognitive constructs in general, as well as cognitive psychology. Speaking a little more broadly, I'm perhaps an expert in psychology. I'm a musical theater buff, and I've seen shows such as *Bird of Paradise, Weird Romance,* and *Discovering Magenta,* which most theater fans have never heard of—does that make me an expert? I love dogs and spend many hours with them each day—am I an expert? The question becomes where to draw the line. I'm certainly an expert on my dogs Pandora and Kirby; by extension, I'm slowly becoming knowledgeable about Basset Hounds and Beagles and other dopey "B" dogs. But I'm only vaguely aware that Chihuahuas are little yippy things that don't like me.

Who's more of an expert on baseball: Bill James, a history and stat buff who can (almost) convincingly argue that Ichiro Suzuki is less valuable than the back-up third baseman on the Brewers and explain why the 1971 Padres had the best starting rotation of all time; or a second-string catcher currently playing for the Marlins who does not know anything about baseball that happened before 1998? Who should rate a child's drawings—her teacher, her mom, herself, her friends, a professional artist, a graduate student in art history, an art gallery owner, an editor of a children's art journal, someone who collects children's art, or a creativity specialist?

Certainly many different types of experts tend to agree on what's creative. Baer, Kaufman, and Gentile (2004) picked a total of over 300 poems, stories, and personal narratives selected from the National Assessment of Educational Progress. These creative writing pieces were produced by eighth graders in response to a wide variety of assignments and under varying conditions (i.e., in-class vs. take-home assignments). Thirteen different experts read all of the works; they represented three different possible categories of experts. One group consisted of psychologists who studied creativity, another group consisted of eighth-grade creative writing teachers, and the last group was writers and editors who specifically worked with school-age children. All three groups of experts showed inter-rater reliability (both within group and as a complete unit) at high levels—at an agreement of approximately .95 for stories and narratives and .87 for poems.

A further investigation used the same experts and a group of gifted "novices"—eight high school students attending New Jersey Governor's School of the Arts (a highly selective summer program) who were picked for their creative writing. The novices also showed solid inter-rater reliability (although lower than the experts), and their ratings significantly correlated with expert ratings. The correlation between the novices and the expert writers was (unsurprisingly) the highest (J. C. Kaufman, Gentile, & Baer, 2005).

The implications of gifted novices being nearly as reliable as experts are important in a practical way. Trying to get five professional artists to rate dozens of paintings requires a considerable level of resources. Artists and poets frequently get asked to evaluate work for competitions, and they are used to getting paid for it. It also takes them a long time. Gifted novices, however, are much easier to corral into participating in creativity research.

However, it is important to note that whereas gifted novices may be qualified experts, complete novices most assuredly are not. J. C. Kaufman, Baer, Cole, and Sexton (2008) had more than 200 poems rated by 10 expert poets and more than 100 complete novices (i.e., college students). Although both groups basically agreed with each other (expert agreement, not surprisingly, was higher than novice agreement), expert and novice judgments correlated only at $r = .22$. In a similar study using short stories as the creative product, the correlation between novices and experts increased, but novice rater agreement was still subpar (J. C. Kaufman & Baer, 2008). What does this mean? For creativity research, it means that college students are not qualified substitutes for experts in rating creative work. In a larger sense, however, it may point to the discrepancy between what experts may think of a creative work and what the general population may think. Film critics don't often pick the top grossing movie as the best movie of the year. The Oscars and the Grammys rarely are the same as the People's Choice and MTV Movie Awards. What the general population is looking for in a creative product is likely quite different than what someone working in that area would seek. As *Mad Magazine* argues, "There's a reason McDonald's doesn't put tarragon on their Big Macs" (Devlin, 2006, p. 48).

It is also worth noting that the correlation between novice and expert judgments may be even lower when comparing products that aren't from the arts. Nearly anyone can read a poem or listen to a piece of music and give an impression of how creative it is. It is more difficult to imagine any person off the streets being able to rate the creativity of a scientific theorem or mathematical proof (Simonton, 2004a).

There's still a lot of research that needs to be done on the CAT, but it's a technique that has advanced rapidly in the last 20 years and may well be the wave of the future. The level to which raters need to be "experts" may well influence its continued popularity.

I've talked about the creative product first in part because of my own interest in the topic and in part because of the many studies available on the creative product. There is also the sentiment that products last far longer than people; as Dean Simonton eloquently put it, when Albert Einstein "received the Nobel Prize for Physics in 1921, it was Einstein's ideas that were being honored, not his cognitive processes or character quirks" (2004a, p. 15).

THE CREATIVE PROCESS

A creative product is typically a tangible object, such as a short story, a painting, a design of a building, or a science experiment.

But studying the creative process is trying to hit a moving target—indeed, one that is zooming around the room like a deflating balloon. How do you study people being creative? Observe them? Hook them up with an EEG? Telling them to be creative on cue is a tricky subject in and of itself. "Okay, Sally, be creative. Go. Come on? What are you waiting for? Be creative!" Indeed, it is doubly difficult given that some research (to be discussed later) indicates that being aware of potential evaluation decreases creativity. One of the few studies of the creative process to avoid these pitfalls was Dunbar's (1995) investigation of scientific creativity. He spent a year observing biologists, using videotapes, audiotapes, and interviews, and concluded that creative scientists did not often experience sudden insight but rather used careful reasoning. This type of work, however, is quite difficult to do—both for the time commitment (it takes a long time to make someone feel comfortable in your presence, as documentary filmmakers know all too well) and the difficulty in finding willing participants. Would *you* let someone watch you while you tried to do something creative over a span of several months (or years)? The recent popularity of such shows as *American Idol* (and worse) indicates that for many people, the answer is "yes"—but then, are these the people we want to study to learn about creativity?

There have been other techniques used to study the creative process, some quite ingenious. Csikszentmihalyi introduced his concept of "Flow," or "optimal experience," which he calls the sensations and feelings that come when an individual is actively engaged in an intense, favorite pursuit—which could be anything from rock climbing to playing the piano. An individual must feel like his or her abilities are a match for the potential challenges of the situation to enter the Flow state—someone who never played the piano would not enter Flow when trying to master Beethoven, and a concert pianist would not enter Flow trying to play "Mary Had a Little Lamb" (Csikszentmihalyi, 1990; Csikszentmihalyi & Csikszentmihalyi, 1988). Csikszentmihalyi and colleagues' early studies on Flow asked participants to wear electronic paging devices. The study participants were then beeped at random times (during the day, not at three in the morning) and asked to fill out forms that asked what they were doing and how they were feeling (Graef, Csikszentmihalyi, & Giannino, 1983; Larson & Csikszentmihalyi, 1983; Prescott, Csikszentmihalyi, & Graef, 1981). With this technique, Csikszentmihalyi and colleagues were able to determine when people were being creative and in Flow (Csikszentmihalyi, Rathunde, & Whalen, 1993).

Much of Csikszentmihalyi's later work used a different technique, one that has been frequently used by others who study the creative process: interviews. People who have demonstrated a particular ability in creative fields are asked questions about how they are creative, what they do, how they think, and so on. One example of an investigation using this methodology is Susan Perry's (1999) study of creative writers. She interviewed more than 75 successful writers, ranging from popular favorites such as Sue Grafton and Jonathan Kellerman to critics' darlings such as T. Coraghessan Boyle and Robert Olen Butler. Perry used a structured interview in which she asked writers the same series of questions, such as "What were your thought processes before sitting down to work?"

As a book to read, Perry's work is terrific. As a pure research methodology, however, there are several dangers in this technique that make it less than ideal. For one, people don't always tell the truth. There is outright lying, of course, but there are other reasons as well. People may not take the question seriously; indeed, trying this technique on too many high school students may be a quick way to drive yourself crazy. Or people may be embarrassed by the question, or even offended ("How many times a day do you pick your nose?"). But people may also have beliefs that they may not fully realize and therefore couldn't express to an interviewer. These implicit attitudes can reflect automatic associations. So, for example, if Adam has a close friend who is a lawyer, then he may have positive feelings about lawyers—even if he is not quite sure why. His feelings may be purely unconscious, however; if someone asked him if he particularly liked lawyers, he might answer "no" (Greenwald & Banaji, 1995).

There are other dangers as well. Some creators may not want to talk about their art ("Talking about music," Bruce Springsteen once said, "is like talking about sex. Can you describe it? Are you supposed to?"). Further, people aren't always good at expressing their thoughts, particularly people who aren't skilled communicators. Perry's work avoids this problem (who better to articulate their thoughts then a group of writers?), but a last danger is true for all creators—some people do not understand their own creative processes. Just as many great baseball players are terrible managers (saying "Do as I do" doesn't always work), so may many great creative people be less skilled at articulating and explaining their own creative process. I'm reminded of the Leonard Cohen song "Hallelujah," about David playing a chord that made the Lord happy—yet still remaining baffled about the actual process of how he created the music. Just because we can do something does not mean we know how we are doing it.

Other researchers study the cognitive side of the creative process—how people think creatively. One of the early theories of creativity was by Wallas (1926), who proposed a model of the cognitive creative process. According to his five-stage model, you first use *preparation* to begin work on a problem. Next, there is *incubation,* in which you may work on other things while your mind thinks about the problem. In *intimation,* you realize you are about to have a breakthrough (this phase is sometimes dropped from the model), and then you actually have the insight in the *illumination* phase. Finally, with *verification,* you actually test, develop, and use your ideas.

More recently, the Geneplore model, as mentioned earlier, has two phases: generative and explorative. In the generative phase, someone constructs a preinventive structure or a mental representation of a possible creative solution (Finke, Ward, & Smith, 1992). For example, Elias Howe was working on his invention of the modern sewing machine. He couldn't quite get the needle correctly designed. Howe had an odd dream in which he was chased by savages who threw spears at him. The spears had a circle loop at the end—and Howe realized that adding the circle (or an "eye") to the end of the needle was the solution he needed (Hartman, 2000). The image of a spear with a circle at the end—the image that preceded Howe's insight—would be an example of one of these preinventive structures. They don't need to be as dramatic or sudden as Howe's story. Indeed, the generation of preinventive structures is only one part of the creative process according to the Geneplore model. The thinker must then explore these different preinventive structures within the constraints of the final goal. There may be several cycles before a creative work is produced.

The model focuses on the creative process, yet, most tests of the model have actually measured the creative product. In an experiment using the model, people were shown parts of objects (such as a circle or a cube). They were then asked to combine these parts together to produce a practical object or device. The creativity (and practicality) of the items is then assessed, much in the same manner as the Consensual Assessment Technique already discussed (e.g., Finke, 1990; Finke & Slayton, 1988). Interestingly, people produced more creative objects when they were told which parts had to be combined than when they could pick the parts themselves.

Other theories have also focused on cognitive-oriented components of the creative process. Michael Mumford and his colleagues have argued for an eight-part model, focusing on problem construction, information encoding, category selection, category combination and reorganization, idea generation, idea evaluation, implementation planning, and solution monitoring (Blair & Mumford, 2007; Mumford, Mobley, Uhlman, Reiter-Palmon, & Doares, 1991). Basadur, Runco, and Vega (2000) offer a simplified model centered around finding good problems, solving these problems, and then implementing these solutions.

Another theory about the creative process is the idea of Janusian and homospatial thinking (Rothenberg, 1991). Homospatial thinking is similar to the combination process just described—taking two different ideas and integrating them together to form a unique idea. Rothenberg (1988) used overlapping pictures in an experiment and found that people came up with more creative ideas than when the images were presented side by side. In a related experiment, Mobley, Doares, and Mumford (1992) asked people to combine categories to produce a new category. They found that when more diverse categories were presented, people created new categories that were more creative.

Janusian thinking, named after the two-faced Roman god Janus, is the process of conceptualizing two directly opposite ideas. Rothenberg's classic example is when Einstein initially thought of his famous theory of relativity when he had the idea that someone in the split-second act of falling has no gravitational field (at least during the immediate process of falling). This juxtaposition of two opposite ideas is Janusian thinking. Rothenberg (1996) argued that Nobel Prize winners were more likely to use this type of thinking. Janusian thinking doesn't have to result in genius ideas. You could use these insights to fix things around the house or tell stories to amuse your child.

Another approach to the creative process, related to Janusian thinking, focuses on the idea that creative people will be able to make associations between more remote concepts. An instant response to hearing the word "cow," for example, might be to think of grass (which cows eat), or milk (which cows produce), or bulls (with which cows discuss philosophy). Upon further thought, maybe you can connect cows with all sorts of things—cow's milk is used to make cheese, and goats are creatures that also produce milk, and both "holy cow" and "don't have a cow" are somewhat popular expressions. The idea behind the associative theory is that this connection can be measured by presenting three seemingly unrelated words and seeing if people can derive a fourth word that connects them (Mednick, 1962, 1968). This test is called the Remote Associates Test (RAT; Mednick, 1968) and has been updated by different authors (and sometimes called the Compound Remote Associates Task; see Bowden & Jung-Beeman, 2003). An example of a recent problem is Sleeping, Bean, and Trash. What word connects them (look away and think…look back)? It's "Bag." Sleeping bag, bean bag, and trash bag are all common phrases. The test is often used because it's fairly easy to administer and score; it is clearly related to creativity, although more heavily influenced by intelligence and verbal abilities than other measures. It is also the source of one of my solidly embarrassing graduate school moments; my professor was presenting on the RAT, and I was zoning out or doodling. I missed him say that he was going to present us with items that were unsolvable (I don't remember exactly why he gave us these items; I told you, I wasn't paying attention). One of the items caught my attention, and in the throes of puzzle-solving bliss, I shouted out the answer at the top of lungs: "Fish!" Alas, it wasn't. I still sometimes yell out, "Fish!," although at least now I *know* I'm being odd.

Many studies of the creative process use computer simulations in which they attempt to program a computer to "think" in a similar way as people. These computer models use many of the same principles behind artificial intelligence (Boden, 1999). Can we actually study artificial creativity? At first glance, computer models can be quite accomplished. BACON, one of the first such programs, used a series of rules and heuristics to rediscover Kepler's third law of planetary motion (Langley, Simon, Bradshaw, & Zytkow, 1987). Other programs have written a character-driven fictional story (Turner, 1994), and improvised musical jazz pieces (Johnson-Laird, 1988, 1991). Many of these programs differ from human creative functioning, however, in that the problems are given to the computer in structured form. In real life, however, much of creativity can be figuring out the problem in the first place (see Runco, 1994). Certainly, computer models of creativity seem to have much to offer, and it will be interesting to see what the future holds. Think of the Buggles' song "Video Killed the Radio Star" (now mostly remembered for being the ever-so-ironic first video on MTV), in which they sing about machines rewriting and taking credit for symphonies. Perhaps the machines will soon be writing their own symphonies in real life.

Why, you might think, do people still try so hard to study the creative process when this area may be the most difficult to pinpoint? Evaluating a creative product is not flawless, but as we've seen, it's possible. Studies of the creative process tend to rely more on theory or supposition and less on hard data. Yet, the creative process *feels* like it may be the most important aspect of creativity. A tremendous conversation between dueling academics in Thomas Stoppard's *Arcadia* (1993) captures the allure of the creative process itself quite well:

> It's all trivial...Comparing what we're looking for misses the point. It's wanting to know that makes us matter...If the answers are in the back of the book I can wait, but what a drag. Better to struggle on. (pp. 75–76)

Being able to capably evaluate the creativity of a Haiku or a collage, Stoppard's character would likely argue, is not the issue. It's the elusive process, the constant striving, that is the key. But these ideas, as appealing as they are, are less likely to come with good methods and data—they tend to revolve around theoretical ideas. And such processes can then lead us back to the spiritual and mystical approaches.

THE CREATIVE PERSON

If the difficulty in studying the creative process is in figuring out how exactly it can be done, the difficulty in studying the creative person lies more in figuring out which aspects of the creative person should be studied. There are a wide variety of different theories, often called "confluence" theories, which describe models of the many variables that may influence a person's creativity. Some of these models also touch on the creative environment.

Sternberg and Lubart (1996) propose an "Investment" theory of creativity, in which they argue that the key to being creative is to buy low and sell high in ideas. In this model, a creative person is like a successful Wall Street broker. Although some of the ideas in the model are focused on the creative process, they list six variables as being essential to creativity: intelligence, knowledge, personality, environment, motivation, and thinking styles. There are, indeed, patterns in these six variables that would describe a creative person. For example, people who are born into environments that value and nurture creativity tend to grow up to be more creative than people who grow up in environments that do not value (and may even punish) creativity. Other relationships between creativity and a wide variety of other variables will be discussed in greater depth later in the book.

Another economic-based theory is posed by Rubenson and Runco (1992, 1995), who look at creativity not in terms of buying and selling ideas, but in terms of costs and benefits. Creative potential, they argue, must take into account the costs of creativity, which can range from an activity taking up time to being psychically draining, compared to the possible benefits. The idea of creativity as human capital has also been proposed (Walberg & Stariha, 1992).

Amabile (1982, 1996) proposed the componential model of creativity. She argued that three variables were needed for creativity to occur: domain-relevant skills, creativity-relevant skills, and task motivation. *Domain-relevant skills* include knowledge, technical skills, and specialized talent. If you're going to be a creative mathematician, you'd better know your basic algebra and geometry. *Creativity-relevant skills* are personal factors that are associated with creativity. One example is tolerance for ambiguity—can you handle not knowing how a project might turn out or not knowing your plans for a weekend? Other creativity-relevant skills include self-discipline and being willing to take risks. Finally, Amabile singled out your *motivation* toward the task at hand. As will be discussed later, people who are driven more by enjoyment and passion tend to be more creative than people motivated by money, praise, or grades.

J. S. Renzulli (1978) has proposed two types of giftedness: schoolhouse (i.e., what would be measured by an ability or achievement test) and creative-production. Within creative-production, he argues for a three-ring conception of giftedness. These three overlapping rings are high intellectual ability, creativity, and task commitment. Examples of his components of creativity include Guilford's divergent thinking components (fluency, flexibility, and originality), openness to new experiences, curiosity, willingness to take risks, and sensitivity to aesthetic characteristics.

Even if you've selected the appropriate variables to study in a creative person the next, obvious question becomes: How do we select people who are creative? Before you select people, you need to decide the general type of creative person you want to study. There is a common division between "Big-C" and "little-c" creativity. Big-C creativity is the big time, genius-level creativity. Big-C is Mozart, Shakespeare, Louis Armstrong, Einstein, and Alexander Fleming. Big-C is the kind of creativity that lasts generations and will be remembered, used, or enjoyed a hundred years from now. One advantage of studying genius-level creators—particularly *dead* genius-level creators—is that it's easier to find information about them. The field of historiometrics, pioneered by Dean Simonton (1990, 1994, 2004a), looks at biographies and factual information about eminent people to gain insight into what makes a creative person (or a great leader).

In one classic study, Simonton (1977) divided the lives of 10 eminent composers (Bach, Beethoven, Mozart, Haydn, Brahms, Handel, Debussy, Schubert, Wagner, and Chopin) into 5-year periods and measured each composer's productivity based on both works and themes. Simonton then found several interesting results—perhaps of most interest, quality *is* related to quantity. The composers who wrote the most music also wrote the best music (with *best* being defined as most-cited and discussed across 15 different reference works). The most fertile time periods in terms of production were also marked by the best work. Simonton also found this same effect with psychologists (1985). Two-time Nobel Prize winner Linus Pauling may have sensed this phenomenon, once saying, "The best way to get a good idea is to get a lot of ideas."

Maybe, however, you're more interested in little-c, or "everyday" creativity. Little-c creativity is the way that everybody can be creative, even your great uncle who spends the entire day watching the Mets lose (e.g., Richards, Kinney, Benet, & Merzel, 1988). One example of theories that are more focused in little-c is layperson theories of creativity—in other words, what the average person on the street thinks about creativity. Most of these layperson theories are less concerned with analytical abilities (which are usually associated more with IQ tests) and focus instead on such characteristics as unconventionality, inquisitiveness, imagination, and freedom (Sternberg, 1985). Eastern conceptions, much more than Westerners, value the characteristic of "goodness," including "moral goodness," "contribution to the society," as well as the "connections between old and new knowledge" (Niu & Sternberg, 2002; Rudowicz & Hui, 1997; Rudowicz & Yue, 2000). According to standard Chinese traditions, a great person must not only satisfy his or her own needs as a human being but must also be devoted to other people and the interests of the society as a whole (Niu & Sternberg, 2006).

Little-c helps underscore the important and often essential role that creativity plays in everyday life (Richards, 2007). As I discussed earlier, nearly all of us can tap into our little-c creativity, sometimes on a daily basis. Little-c could be making up parody song lyrics to amuse someone, figuring out what might be substituted into a recipe if you don't have any eggs or milk, or doodling pictures of the people who are serving jury duty with you. Everyday creativity may not change the world, but it often makes the world more fun. Maybin and Swann (2007), for example, discuss how everyone can creatively enhance conversations or writing through wordplay and humor.

Some of the theories discussed in this book gravitate toward Big-C creativity, such as the propulsion model. With the possible exception of replication contributions, most of the categories are designed for the Big-C level. Your Uncle Steve probably isn't worried about how his creativity can impact his field (unless he is Steve Jobs, in which case I take back everything bad I ever said about my ancient 512K Mac).

Other theories are more focused on little-c. The Investment theory of creativity mentioned earlier in the chapter is an example (Sternberg & Lubart, 1995). The central key to this theory (buy low and sell high with ideas) is more relevant to someone's everyday creativity. People high in Big-C undoubtedly do exactly this same procedure, but such a model is more geared to the average person. It's hard to instantly picture a genius-level creator such as Mark Twain having to worry about which trends or ideas to follow—but these are exactly the concerns that people have everyday about their own creativity.

Beghetto and Kaufman (2007) argued that little-c is too broad of a construct. Everyone who isn't a Ray Charles or Buddy Holly is lumped as a little-c singer. Yet, where do you place a high school student falling in love with music? The everyday creativity that students experience as they learn a new concept or make a new metaphor is given short shrift in the world of little-c. A fourth-grade student doing a beginning scientific experiment (perhaps creating a volcano) is placed in the same category as a noted microbiologist. It's all considered little-c. Beghetto and Kaufman proposed a third category: mini-c. In mini-c, the initial spark of creativity doesn't have to be held up to the same standards that we use for typical everyday creativity. An idea or product doesn't need to be new and original, necessarily, just new and original to the student at the time. The quality or appropriateness would also not be held to the same standards as little-c creativity.

J. C. Kaufman and Beghetto (in press) further argue for a fourth category: Pro-c. They point out that there is not an appropriate category for individuals who are professional creators but have not reached highly eminent status. For example, the little-c category is useful for the everyday creativity of the home cook who can creatively combine ingredients to develop unique and tasty meals. The Big-C category is appropriate for chefs who have revolutionized the profession (e.g., James Beard, Marie-Antoine Carême, or Ruth Graves Wakefield). Yet, what about the professional chef who makes a living developing creative entrées (clearly surpassing the creativity of the innovative home cook) but has not yet attained (or may never attain) Big-C status?

J. C. Kaufman and Beghetto (in press) therefore propose the Four C Model as representing a developmental trajectory of creativity in a person's life. Early in life, a typical creator might be beginning to play with her creativity and exploring mini-c as she discovers new things. Most people will first experience mini-c early in life. Mini-c can be encouraged by teachers, parents, and mentors to nurture creativity. There are several discussions of the best way to foster a creativity-nurturing environment. Harrington, Block, and Block (1987), for example, show that rearing practices based on Carl Rogers' work (such as encouraging curiosity and exploration, letting children make decisions, and respecting children's opinions) later lead to increased creative potential. A person can continue to get mini-c inspirations and ideas across his or her lifetime as different domains and possible areas for creativity are explored.

After repeated attempts and encouragements, the creator might then reach the realm of little-c. Some people may happily remain at the little-c level for their entire lives; others may advance in some areas and remain at the little-c in other areas (e.g., an accomplished author who has advanced to the Pro-c level of writing, publishing many novels, may enjoy the little-c level of landscaping his garden or cooking gourmet meals). As part of this process of enjoying creativity in everyday life, the creator may stumble upon the area that he or she decides to pursue. With years of acquired expertise and advanced schooling, the creator may move onto the stage of Pro-c. Although she will still have mini-c insights, the creator has now achieved professional-level status and is capable of working on problems, projects, and ideas that affect the field as a whole. The creator may continue to create at the Pro-c level throughout her entire life, with specific peaks occurring at different ages based on the domain (e.g., Simonton, 1997). After many years have come and gone, the creator may achieve a lasting Big-C contribution to a field (e.g., the Nobel Prize), or the creator may have passed away, and history will make the final judgment as to whether she has entered the pantheon of Big-C or has been long-forgotten.

THE CREATIVE PLACE (ENVIRONMENT)

In the field of intelligence, the "nature–nurture" controversy is still a hot topic. Are people born with a certain amount of intelligence? Can we improve our intelligence? If we think that we're dumb, should we blame our parents for passing along "dumb" genes, or should we blame our parents for creating an environment where we were not properly encouraged? Note, incidentally, that *not* blaming parents is not an option.

This debate is not as heated in creativity. There are papers and presentations that discuss the genetics of creativity, but these tend to end with a question-and-answer session or a discussion section instead of fistfights. One noncontroversial statement alluded to before is that there are environments that can be more or less conducive to creativity. These environments range from the place and era of your early years to the place and social climate of your current workplace.

There has been an amazing array of work on the home environments and life situations that are most conducive to high-level creative work, much of it by Dean Simonton (some of which will be discussed throughout this book). Some studies show first-borns as being more likely to be accomplished (Roe, 1952; Simonton, 1987), but accomplished isn't necessarily the same as creative (although there is clearly some overlap). Indeed, Sulloway (1996) found that the first-born child was more likely to achieve power and privilege, but later-born children were more likely to be open to experience and revolutionary ideas. A first-born child might end up running the family business, whereas a later-born child might strike out in a new field and buck tradition. This trend extends across many domains—if you examine how prominent scientists reacted when Darwin proposed his classic (and controversial) theory of natural selection, 83% of the people who supported the theory were later-born children, and only 17% were first-born (Sulloway, 1996). Runco and Bahleda (1986), however, found that first-born children received higher scores on divergent thinking tests than middle and youngest children. Highest of all, however, were only children—yet, conversely, people with many siblings outperformed those with few siblings.

Schubert, Wagner, and Schubert (1977) found that significantly fewer first-born males volunteered for creativity training, while significantly more middle-born males volunteered (with no birth order effects found for women). This latter result can be interpreted in one of two ways, however; either firstborn males had less interest in creativity training, or they simply did not feel the need for creativity training, as they already considered themselves creative.

Although being a first-born or later-born child isn't totally about genetics, it's also not something that you have a whole lot of control over. Neither is losing a parent or experiencing a personal tragedy. Simonton (1994) reviews many studies that show that losing a parent before age 10 is much more common in eminent people than in average Joes. Other disasters that are more likely to befall the well-known include bouts of poverty, physical illness, and (to be discussed shortly) possibly mental illness.

Environment doesn't have to mean a home environment; different work environments can also be more or less conducive to creativity. Amabile and Gryskiewicz (1989) identify eight aspects of the work environment that stimulate creativity: adequate freedom, challenging work, appropriate resources, a supportive supervisor, diverse and communicative coworkers, recognition, a sense of cooperation, and an organization that supports creativity. Leader support is especially important to creativity among subordinates in the workplace (Amabile, Schatzel, Moneta, & Kramer, 2004). A good supervisor can inspire creativity through consulting with her workers, recognizing positive performance, and showing social and emotional support.

Amabile and Gryskiewicz (1989) also discuss four aspects that restrain creativity: time pressure, too much evaluation, an emphasis on keeping the status quo, and too much organizational politics. External events, such as downsizing, also can negatively impact creativity in the workplace (Amabile & Conti, 1999). During larger times of economic depression, industries that require innovation (such as those in technology) may suffer more globally (Amabile & Conti, 1997a, 1997b).

One specific example of a work-related influence on creativity is how much conflict occurs with group performance. Kurtzberg and Amabile (2000) propose that a moderate amount of conflict about the task itself will lead to more creative outcomes. However, other types of conflict, such as those that relate to personal relationships or to the actual process of working together, will lower creative performance (and, generally, not be a lot of fun).

Similarly, the idea of "psychological safety" has been proposed as a mutual feeling in a group that risk-taking is okay (Edmondson, 1999). One way that psychological safety can be increased is by a leader meeting with team members and talking honestly and openly with them (Roussin, 2008); another is to enable employees to speak up and voice dissatisfaction (Detert & Burris, 2007). Ford and Sullivan (2004) argue that experiencing psychological safety can aid both innovative contributions and personal satisfaction.

An environment can refer to contexts beyond personal and work; it can also be seen as the context in which someone is assessed for creativity. Sometimes the environment can interact with personal traits. One study of undergraduates found that having a wider breadth of attention was correlated with writing poems that were judged to be more creative and that distracting noise disrupted creative performance more in those students with a wide breadth of attention (Kasof, 1997). Hillier, Alexander, and Beversdorf (2006) studied the impact of an auditory stressor (a small amount of white noise) on cognitive flexibility. What they found was that basic cognitive functioning (measured with verbal and figural tasks) was not affected—but scores on a remote associations test (which measures creativity to a degree) were affected. A level of white noise that did not impact intellectual performance made people slower and worse at a creativity-related task.

Another consistent finding is that instructions to be creative typically increase a person's performance on divergent thinking or creativity tasks (Harrington, 1975; Shaeffer, 1969). Katz and Poag (1979) found that telling college students to be creative led to an increase in fluency scores in males, but not in females. One possible explanation they suggested was that given that the task was verbal, males may need the boost more given their typical inclination toward figural and spatial tasks.

Many subsequent investigations have explored the specifics of how instructions can impact creativity. One study found that instructing people to be creative, practical, or analytical raises performance in these areas; if the instructions match someone's preferred thinking style, a particular increase was noted. So someone who is told to be creative and who naturally has a creative thinking style will show the largest amount of increased creativity (O'Hara & Sternberg, 2001). The impact of simply telling people to be creative has been found across cultures (America and China) and domains (verbal, artistic, and mathematical; Chen, Kasof, Himsel, Dmitrieva, Dong, & Xue, 2005). Runco, Illies, and Reiter-Palmon (2005) found that telling someone to be creative in a specific way (i.e., "think of things that will be thought of by no one else") resulted in higher divergent thinking scores than simply telling them to be more creative in a general way. Runco, Illies, and Eisenman (2005) found an interaction between the instructions (emphasizing originality, appropriateness, both or neither) and the type of DT task (realistic or unrealistic). Realistic tasks with appropriateness-focused instruction drew more appropriate ideas, and unrealistic tasks with originality-focused instructions produced more original ideas.

Similarly, people's creativity can be manipulated via social norms. Adarves-Yorno, Postmes, and Haslam (2007) asked participants to create a leaflet in two tasks: one that subtly emphasized

words (discussing reasons to go to college) and another with images (discussing fashion). Their identity was either salient (having
them wear nametags) or not (using numbers on the nametags).
In the identity-salient condition, people were more likely to "con-
form" in their creativity (using more words in the college leaflet
and more images in the fashion leaflet). The findings were further
strengthened in a second study by the authors in which group
membership was made more important.

What can be gathered from these discussions of creative products, people, processes, and environments? Plucker et al. (2004)
offer a nice definition of creativity: "Creativity is the interaction
among aptitude, process, and environment by which an individual or group produces a perceptible product that is both novel
and useful as defined within a social context" (p. 90). In other
words, creativity is the how (ability and process) and the where
and when (environment) made by the who (individual or group)
making the what (a specific product both new and useful). When
I discuss the role of motivation and creativity later on, I'll add in
the "why."

One reason for the complexity of their definition is that they
conceive of creativity as being an intricate, highly contextualized
concept that cannot be simply defined in a few quick words.
Indeed, is creativity the same thing if the product is a poem or
a mathematical proof or a business plan? Are the people who
are creative in music similar to the people who are creative in
engineering? Would the same environment stimulate a person's
creativity in both art and computer science domains? In the next
chapter, I will offer a new theory to help answer some of these
questions.

Is Creativity One Thing or Many Things?

During the last four months of 1987, the world lost a number of renowned creative people. One such loss was Bob Fosse, director and choreographer extraordinaire noted for his openly sexualized dances in which even the slightest movement—a turn of a knee, a tilt of a head, a roll of a hip—had meaning (Grubb, 1991). Other people who passed away during this period include James Baldwin, a teenage preacher who became a civil rights activist and author, whose landmark *Go Tell It on the Mountain* remains a classic 50 years later (Parker & Kermode, 1996); Joseph Campbell, perhaps the world's foremost expert on mythology; famed violinist Jascha Heifetz (who happened to be my fourth cousin); Henry Ford II, who took over as CEO of the Ford Motor Company and helmed its expansion; and Nobel Prize–winning Walter

Brattain, who built the first transistor. Of course, the list could go on: Jacqueline du Pre, Alf Landon, Woody Herman, Dan Rowan, Jean Anouilh, Harold Washington, and many others.

The Fosse "style" has been assumed into modern theatrical dance so much that it is becoming a cliché. Fosse worked his way up through vaudeville, into choreographing musicals, and then taking on director roles, as well. He became one of the few show people to be as much of a star if not more so than the actors on stage. Indeed, many casual theater-goers are aware of the name "Bob Fosse" and may know a little bit about him; only someone who is a student of musicals would be able to just as quickly name Fred Ebb and John Kander as the authors of *Chicago* and *Cabaret*, two of Fosse's biggest hits. *Pippin* was a smash on Broadway; can anyone but an ardent fan identify John Rubinstein as the original titular character?

Yet, what if Fosse had decided, early in his life, to pursue creative writing like James Baldwin? Would we still be reading his stories (perhaps about his unhappy home life or successive series of girlfriends)? Or what if Fosse became fascinated by mythology, instead? Or what if he decided to pursue cars, transistors, or politics? Might there be a "Fosse Motor Company?" Meanwhile, let's ponder the reverse—might Walter Brattain be remembered as a Broadway hoofer if that was how his muse appeared? Could Henry Ford II have left the family business and devoted his life to playing the violin?

The answer to these questions lies in the nature of creativity. If creativity is truly and completely "general," or if it is one thing, then the answer would be yes. A Fosse would be a "Fosse" no matter what domain he chose. A Jascha Heifetz or a James Baldwin or a Joseph Campbell would show his creativity in any variety of domains. If, on the other hand, creativity were "domain specific," then such a transition would not be as easy. Someone with an aptitude for poetry might not necessarily be able to use this creativity to compose music or solve mathematical problems.

There is an intense debate over a similar question in the intelligence field. Some researchers argue passionately for a general factor of intelligence, g, in which there is one factor that is largely responsible for academic performance (among many other things). Other researchers argue just as passionately against g, offering instead theories of multiple intelligences or theories that paint a broader and more complex picture of intellectual abilities. A quick search on the main psychology article database for "g or general" and "IQ and intelligence" turned up 13,483 hits; a good place to start for a spirited discussion on this is Sternberg and Grigorenko (2002). The debates can sometimes have a nasty edge to them—g advocates can point to an astounding array of data in their favor that they accuse the anti-g crowd of ignoring; the anti-g contingent can point to an unpleasant connection between the g theory and racist ideas and implications.

Is there a c, analogous to intelligence's g, that transcends domains and enhances the creativity of a person across many different areas? This question has fueled numerous debates in the literature (Baer, 1998b; J. C. Kaufman & Baer, 2005a, 2005b; Plucker, 1998; Sternberg, Grigorenko, & Singer, 2004), although the two alternate sides are converging in the middle.

THE PROBLEM WITH GENIUSES

If we start at the highest level of creativity, where there is no doubt that the products in question deserve such recognition, then only a few have reached eminence in more than one domain. At first blush this comparative lack of double- or triple-talented stars seems like a strong argument for domain-specificity. Think of the true Renaissance men or women: Leonardo Da Vinci, Benjamin Franklin, Paul Robeson, Johann Wolfgang von Goethe, Bertrand Russell, and Marie Curie (Physics and Chemistry) and Linus Pauling (Chemistry and Peace), who both won Nobel Prizes in two different categories. There just aren't that many.

Miss Piggy may sing (in *Muppets Take Manhattan*) about wanting to be a neurosurgeon, movie star, scuba diver, singer, airplane pilot, model, and veterinarian (in addition to having Kermit's children), but she's not real. There simply are not many cases of impressive creative work across many domains. Indeed, it's not surprising that most creativity researchers who focus on the highest levels of creative eminence, the true geniuses and legends, tend to take a domain-specific approach (e.g., Csikszentmihalyi, 1990; J. C. Kaufman, 2001a; Simonton, 1994; Sternberg, Kaufman, & Pretz, 2001, 2002; Weisberg, 1999).

One conclusion that might be drawn is that creativity is indeed domain-specific except in extraordinary cases. A problem with this, however, is that geniuses aren't necessarily the best people to study. Several creativity researchers, perhaps most notably Ruth Richards (e.g., Richards, 1990; Richards, Kinney, Benet, & Merzel, 1988), have argued that there is a danger in equating creativity only with higher-order accomplishments. For one thing, this type of thinking leads to people devaluing their own creative contributions. If you're an aspiring composer and consider only Mozart, Beethoven, and Bach as being truly "creative," you're setting yourself up for failure (or, if not, you're a narcissist).

Remember that there is an important distinction between studying genius-level creativity compared to studying everyday creativity. If we're talking about genius-level creativity, there are additional considerations to worry about. In order to attain greatness (or even "goodness") in any given field, it requires a tremendous amount of knowledge and practice. On average, this process requires approximately 10 years from beginning to enter a field to making any kind of substantial contribution (Bloom, 1985; Hayes, 1989). These 10 years are spent learning the mechanics of the field, discovering all of the practical issues that can't be taught in a book, and obsessively plying one's trade. These 10 years do not represent a basic apprenticeship, in which one might be taught how to shine shoes. Rather, these are years of active experimentation and new ideas (Gardner, 1993). Despite the earlier discussions about the importance of the domain, the 10-year rule holds up fairly well across these domains.

There are, of course, some differences. In domains where creative excellence may entail very similar work—especially performance areas such as chess, sports, or playing music—10 years may be just right. Fields more dependent on ever-changing standards of creativity and less focused on technically perfect performance may take much longer than 10 years (Simonton, 2000). The 10-year rule is also pretty consistent, regardless of when someone first enters a field. Mozart, for example, began composing at age 5, in 1761—and his first major composition, "Exsultate, Jubilate," debuted in 1773. Steven Spielberg shot his first home movies (such as *Escape to Nowhere* and *Battle Squad*) around 1961, when he was 15 years old. His first significant movie, *Duel*, was released in 1971, when he was 25. *Jaws* was released 4 years later.

To rise from being merely creative to being a superduperstar has its own set of requirements. Subotnik (2000, 2004a, 2004b) sees expertise as a continuum, in which once you reach a certain level of expertise there still lies the peak of elite talent (which sounds better than superduperstar). It is here, in what Subotnik calls *elite talent*, that the truly great stuff gets done. So, going back to Spielberg, once he achieved renown and success with *Duel* and *Jaws*, he kept progressing. He made *Close Encounters of the Third Kind* and *E. T.* As he grew older, his masterpieces dealt with serious subject matter and aimed to inform as well as entertain; think of *Amistad, Saving Private Ryan,* or *Schindler's List.*

Subotnik and Jarvin (2005) interviewed over 80 top music students at different stages of their career. To go from being competent to expert required a stronger emphasis on technical proficiency. Going from expert to elite talent brought in new components, such as creativity, charisma, and practical intelligence. Some scholars have argued that having too much knowledge may actually hinder creativity because it can lead to inflexibility (Frensch & Sternberg, 1989; Schooler & Melcher, 1995). However, Bilalić, McLeod, and Gobet (2008) questioned whether expertise truly comes with such negative side effects. They found that although some expert chess players were inflexible, they were more likely to be flexible if they had a greater level of expertise. Such findings indicate that the rigid expert stereotype may be an urban myth.

Knowledge of a topic or category (if not expertise) may decrease originality. Ward (1994) asked students to imagine animal life on other planets, and found that nearly everyone used Earth-based animal characteristics (such as eyes and legs) as a basis for their alien creature. These results held even when students were asked to describe alien animals that were extremely different from Earth beings (Ward & Sifonis, 1997), and similar patterns emerged for a variety of different concepts (such as food or tools; Ward, Patterson, Sifonis, Dodds, & Saunders, 2002). Ward and his colleagues (Ward, 1995; Ward, Dodds, Saunders, & Sifonis, 2000) argue for a path-of-least-resistance model, in which people tend to rely on standard examples of a given domain to generate new ideas in that same domain. It is possible to break out of this least-resistance trap, particularly if you are given instructions that encourage you to think more abstractly about the task (Ward, Patterson, & Sifonis, 2004).

Gardner (1993) proposed that a creator may take a second 10 years to create his or her second great piece of art. Could there be a similar 10-year rule that advances the creator from mere goodness to greatness? S. B. Kaufman and J. C. Kaufman (2007) present evidence for such a rule. They studied 215 contemporary fiction writers. Writers took an average of 10.6 years between their first publication and their best publication. Just as there is evidence that creators take 10 years from the time they put the pen to the paper, there may also be evidence that another 10 years pass before a truly elite work is produced.

These findings make it much harder to discuss the question of being creative across many different domains (Plucker & Beghetto, 2004). Most people simply won't be allotted enough years to live in order to pursue elite greatness—let alone mere talent—across many fields. As much as one might love to see how Martin Scorsese might approach architecture, or how Bill Gates might tackle interpretative dance, it's not going to happen anytime soon. And even if someone did magically have 140 or 150 years instead of the usual paltry 60 to 90 years, there are many aspects of creativity that are tied to age. Most scientists make their most important contribution before or around age 40. Artists are usually even younger. As I mentioned earlier, some individuals in fields such as theoretical physics and poetry can peak as early as their twenties (Simonton, 1994).

There are many reasons for these patterns of decline; one possible reason can be found in the intelligence literature. The theory of fluid and crystallized intelligence, also called "Gf-Gc," presents two different types of intelligence (Horn & Cattell, 1966). I will discuss this topic later, but in brief: Fluid intelligence, or Gf, measures your ability to adapt and be flexible in new situations. Crystallized intelligence, or Gc, looks at acquired knowledge. Gf and Gc are roughly equivalent to the Performance and Verbal scales (respectively) on the Wechsler tests.

Many different studies have used the standardization samples of IQ tests to compare people's intelligence across different age groups. Recent work by A. S. Kaufman (2000, 2001; this Kaufman is not me, but is my father, for readers keeping score at home) used data from all three editions of the Wechsler Adult Intelligence Scales to compare people across different age cohorts. A. S. Kaufman controlled for educational level, thereby accounting for the big difference in graduation rates in age (regardless of whether it was the "Greatest Generation," it was never known as the "Best Educated Generation").

What A. S. Kaufman found was a little scary. First, the good news: Verbal scores (Gc) maintained pretty well. They peaked around ages 45–54, and didn't really get terribly low until about age 80. This bit of information should be quite encouraging—you'll likely remember reading about this study for a mighty long time. The bad news: Performance scores (Gf) peak around 20–24 and start dropping at a rate of about 5 IQ points a decade. Scores are notably lower by age 40. If you're in your late twenties or older, then your ability to problem solve and deal with new stimuli is dropping *as you read these words*. This is not necessarily the best news for someone contemplating a creative career change.

59

It is possible that the drops in fluid intelligence may be counterbalanced by other factors (such as experience) that enable people to stay at least somewhat successful with advancing age. Ng and Feldman (2008) conducted a large meta-analysis that studied job performance and age; one of their 10 dimensions of job performance was creativity. They found no relationship between age and creativity when measured either as a self-report or when measured by supervisor ratings.

Roskos-Ewoldsen, Black, and McCown (2008) looked at creativity as measured by both the Torrance Tests and a creative invention task. They found no differences on the Torrance Tests, but they did find that younger adults (aged 18–22) outperformed older adults (aged 61–86) on the creative invention task. However, these differences disappeared when they accounted for differences in working memory. It may be that the differences in fluid intelligence, as discussed by A. S. Kaufman (2001), and poorer working memory may be responsible for declines in creative performance across most domains with advanced age.

ARNOLD SCHWARZENEGGER, RENAISSANCE MAN?

One problem with making any larger conclusions about the lack of renaissance people is that using such a high standard asks a different question. The reasons why someone may not be incredibly accomplished in more than one area may be much more related to practical issues (such as lifespan) than to the fundamental structure of creativity.

There are certainly many people who have achieved the Pro-c level of creative achievement in two domains. William Carlos Williams and Anton Chekhov, for example, are two famed writers who were also medical doctors (Piirto, 1998); the deeper question remains, however, of whether they were *creative* medical doctors. Accomplishment is not always the same thing as creativity.

Their success in their chosen fields may be argued as an indicator of creativity but not as proof.

It is certainly easy to identify others who are successful in multiple fields, and it can be fun identifying people with seemingly discrepant interests. Byron "Whizzer" White is but one of many athletes to become notable in another field (although he's the only notable athlete to become a Supreme Court justice). John Glenn, like many others, became a successful politician after a top-notch career in another area (in his case, being an astronaut). Vladimir Nabokov was a well-known entomologist whose collection of caterpillar genitalia is still exhibited in the Harvard Museum of National History—and is likely better-known for writing such novels as *Lolita* (Powell, 2001). Omar Sharif is a recognized film actor and bridge player. Many scientists who have contributed great things are claimed by many fields—Herbert Simon, for example, impacted Psychology, Economics, Computer Science, and other disciplines (see essays in Augier & March, 2004).

Among people still active, Brian May is the founding guitarist of the classic 1970s band Queen—and he has a Ph.D. in Astrophysics and has written about the history of the universe (May, Moore, & Lintott, 2008). Danica McKellar, who grew up on television as *The Wonder Years'* Winnie, went on to get a Ph.D. in mathematics, helped discover an original theorem, and is working at inspiring young girls to go into math (McKellar, 2007). Mike Reid was a Pro Bowl defensive lineman who then became a Grammy-winning singer–songwriter. Many genre writers have expertise in another area, whether it's forensics anthropology (Kathy Reichs), psychology (Jonathan Kellerman, Stephen White), law (Linda Fairstein, John Grisham, Scott Turow), medicine (Robin Cook, Michael Crichton, Tess Gerritsen), secret service (John le Carré), politics (Ken Follett), graphic design (Alex Kava), or field ecology (Nevada Barr).

But another problem—and issue to be considered—is what exactly constitutes a creative domain? Do we give multiple credit, let's say, to H. G. Wells, who was a highly successful journalist and creative writer, or do we lump it all as "writing"? How about someone like Angela Lansbury, who has grandly triumphed in movies, on television, and on the stage—or is it all "acting"? Or Mel Brooks, who has succeeded as a comic actor, writer, director, songwriter, and so on—yet all his work has a fairly unmistakable "Mel Brooks" feeling to it?

Conversely, where do we classify Alan Greenspan? He reached a certain level of accomplishment (perhaps little-c) as a saxophone player before realizing that he didn't have what it took to be truly successful as a musician; he then fell back on economics, where he has been quite successful. Many successful actors are almost-been athletes, and many moderately successful child actors grow up to find acclaim elsewhere (Mayim Bialik, of television's *Blossom*, is finishing her Ph.D. at UCLA in Neuroscience). If you've spent time watching the various VH1 tribute-to-the-'80s shows, you know how many of the glam-rock or new wave musicians are doing something else today. Tommy Heath, for example, the lead singer of Tommy Tutone (who sang the song about Jenny, at 867-5309), is now a computer programmer.

A further question is, what is considered a creative accomplishment? Many people get opportunities in a second or third domain solely because of their success in a first domain. Does anyone remember the 1985 Chicago Bears' hit song "Superbowl Shuffle?" It's not as if these guys went on to great operatic careers (or, in most cases, even continued on in great football careers). How do we consider the latest trend of actors wanting to be singers or directors, singers wanting to be actors, sports stars wanting to be actors or singers, and so on? Shaquille O'Neal didn't get his acting and singing breaks because of his inherent charm or smooth vocalizations—he was just famous. The level and degree of his success in these secondary domains is questionable. Many of the Monty Python crew have gone on to be successful in related (such as writing musicals) and unrelated (such as writing books on medieval history) areas. Yet, who knows how much of this subsequent acclaim is simply because no reasonable person could say "no" to anything they wanted? If John Cleese called me up and asked if he could borrow my toothbrush, I'd give it to him in a second (and then sell it on eBay).

An opportunity is an opportunity, though, and you can't blame someone for how he or she first got a chance. The key is what someone can do with that opportunity—I am reminded of how Evita sings that she was lucky and in the right place but that she nonetheless deserves credit for being able to fill the open gaps as well as she did. Rising to the occasion and taking advantage of an opportunity to be creative and reach people is its own talent. I feel perfectly comfortable "crediting" Paul Newman with being a creative actor and businessman. I am happy to consider Robert Redford as being creative in acting and in founding festivals and institutes that promote independent film (Sundance). Oprah Winfrey is a successful, Oscar-nominated dramatic actress, and her talk show has provided her with an opportunity to be creative in several different domains that I'm not fully sure how to distinguish (Is she a political activist? Humanitarian?). In fact, one of the few living people I could think of who had succeeded in *more* than two *absolutely distinct* domains that involve creativity was Arnold Schwarzenegger. He was a body-builder and weightlifter (and I would argue that his level of success in that sport—like any sport—would require considerable creativity). He was a movie star. And now he's the governor of California. Athletics, acting, and politics: three pretty unrelated areas, all of which require creativity. Arnold Schwarzenegger, Renaissance Man?

However, what do all of these examples actually prove? The concept of domain specificity does not say that people are only allowed to be creative in one domain; it instead suggests that the underlying components of creativity are different from one domain to another. In other words, were the elements that enabled Danica McKellar to be successful in acting and math the same? Or is she creative in both acting and math in much the same way that someone might be able to run a mile in 4 minutes and learn French (both great abilities, but quite unrelated)? In some ways, all of these examples simply show that it is possible to be creative in more than one area—and of course it is. It may be rare, but it's possible. If creativity was truly domain-general at the eminent level, then you might expect these examples times a thousand—people who could write novels like John Updike and cook like Wolfgang Puck and plan psychology experiments like Albert Bandura. Yet, multiple-domain successes are the exception, not the rule.

A more difficult question is how to consider someone like Albert Einstein or Albert Schweitzer. Einstein, of course, was a legendary physicist, and Schweitzer was a renowned doctor and humanitarian. Both are often also considered to be philosophers. When I discuss the question of renaissance men and women in class (or in conversations), the two Alberts often are mentioned. I feel a little skeptical, to be honest. I am in no way disputing their unfathomable creativity in their primary domain but rather wondering if their philosophizing would have been brilliant enough to stand on its own. In other words, if Albert Einstein were a shoemaker, would his concepts and ideas about peace or knowledge ever be quoted or discussed? What if he was simply a professor of philosophy—could he get published in the first place? I'm not a philosopher, and I don't know. Maybe Einstein's insights (or Schweitzer's) were so brilliant that they would be remembered today regardless of their origins. But my strong guess is that their philosophical works are given more regard than is merited *based on the philosophy alone*. This is not to say, again, that Einstein wasn't creative—he was. But I feel less compelled to include him as an example of someone who was super-creative in more than one domain.

So there may be many reasons for why we don't have many people who excel in multiple creative domains that extend beyond the issue of whether creativity is domain-specific or general. Indeed, we return to the problem with geniuses. What happens when we focus, instead, on everyday creativity? How would an "average" person's creativity differ across domains?

The answer turns out to have a lot to do with how creativity is measured.

EVERYDAY CREATIVE PRODUCTS VS. THE EVERYDAY CREATIVE PERSON

The question of domain-specificity vs. domain-generality has been around for a while. Frank Barron and his colleagues at the Institute of Personality Assessment and Research (IPAR) were among the first to study creative people in specific careers; they studied architects, scientists, mathematicians, entrepreneurs, and writers, among others (e.g., Barron, 1965, 1969, 1995; see also Richards, 2006). Much of Barron's work focused on the similar personality traits found in many creative people (as will be discussed later); he was less focused on how people in one career differed from those in another.

Typically, the answer to whether creativity is domain-specific or general depends on the methods used to ask the question (Plucker, 2004). If a study focused on the creative product, then creativity often appears domain-specific. John Baer has conducted much of the recent research that argues for domain-specificity. In several different studies (e.g., Baer, 1991, 1994), he tested students ranging from second graders to college students. He had these students produce creative work through writing poetry, writing short stories, telling stories out loud, creating mathematical equations, creating mathematical word problems, and making a collage. Baer consistently found low and usually nonsignificant correlations between creative ability in these different areas. In other words, a student who wrote a creative poem was *not* more likely to also tell a creative story or write a creative mathematical equation (a creative algebraic equation might use numbers in a playful or unusual way). Several other studies have found similar results (e.g., Han, 2003; Runco, 1989b). If you remove variations due to IQ, the small correlations get even smaller.

In contrast, standardized assessments typically focus on the creative *person*, and scores often are all grouped together as representing one central construct. Many of these studies rely on people describing or answering questions about their own creativity (e.g., Hocevar, 1976; Plucker, 1999). There is a question as to how much insight someone might have into herself or himself—can you accurately describe how creative you are (or how charming, or how funny)? Some people can, some people can't. The actual extent to which people can accurately self-assess their own creativity will be discussed later.

In addition, people are influenced by what they may implicitly think about creativity. There are certain characteristics or behaviors that you might associate with being creative in general—perhaps taking risks, or liking to try new things. But there are also certain things that you may associate with being creative in a certain area. Your image of a creative scientist may be of Albert Einstein thinking deep thoughts or of a mad Dr. Frankenstein cackling in his lab. But it is certainly different from your image of a creative poet.

One study asked nonartists, amateur artists, and professional artists to name characteristics they associated with artistic, scientific, and everyday creativity. All groups came to some consensus—but a different consensus for each type of creativity. In addition, each group was different (Runco & Bahleda, 1986). Another study found that even among successful creators in a single domain (art), people working in different media had both different conceptions and personal definitions of creativity—definitions that they shared with other artists in the same media but *not* with artists working in different media, such as painters versus graphic designers (Glück, Ernst, & Unger, 2002). Wickes and Ward (2006) studied gifted children's implicit conceptions of creativity and found that they described risk-taking and inquisitiveness as key components of their own creativity, yet they considered artistic talent and motivation as being important for other people's creativity.

Finally, some studies have found that different cultures have different implicit views about creativity, as discussed earlier (e.g., Niu & Sternberg, 2002; Runco & Johnson, 2002; however, see Lim & Plucker, 2001, for evidence that Koreans and Americans share implicit views of creativity). Which group does agree on conceptions of creativity? The creativity researchers themselves, who tended to converge on key traits and developmental factors (Runco, Nemiro, & Walberg, 1998).

THE AMUSEMENT PARK THEORY

John Baer and I have developed the Amusement Park Theoretical (APT) model of creativity to integrate generalist and domain-specific views of creativity. We are not the first to try to synthesize these ideas. Others, for example, have proposed a "hybrid" view in which creativity is primarily general but appears domain-specific in "real world" performance (Plucker & Beghetto, 2004). According to this theory, the level of specificity changes according to social context and matures as a person advances from childhood into adulthood.

The APT model uses the metaphor of an amusement park to explore the nature of creativity (Baer & Kaufman, 2005; J. C. Kaufman & Baer, 2005a, 2005b, 2006). We start with the initial requirements. What do you need to go to an amusement park? First off, you need the time off to go. Amusement parks usually take up an entire day; trying to cram everything into 1 or 2 hours would just be silly. If you don't have a day to take off, you probably won't be going to an amusement park. But having the time is just the beginning. You need money to get in. You need a way of getting to the amusement park. You need the basic desire to go—if, like me, you are terrified of roller coasters, then you likely won't be going to a Six Flags (or one of those anonymous hard-core roller coaster palaces on the sides of the freeway), even if given 2 weeks off work and a few thousand bucks.

APT: INITIAL REQUIREMENTS

Initial requirements are things that are necessary, but not by themselves sufficient, for any type of creative production. They include such things as intelligence, motivation, and suitable environments. Each of these factors is a prerequisite to creative achievement in any domain, and if someone lacks the requisite level of any of these initial requirements, then creative performance is at best unlikely. There are some exceptions, of course, as in the rare autistic children who create celebrated paintings (e.g., Buck, Kardeman, & Goldstein, 1985). Higher levels of these initial requirements, in combination with other more domain-specific factors, predict higher levels of creative performance in general. It must be noted that although all of these initial requirements are necessary for creativity in any domain, the specific degrees of intelligence, motivation, and suitable environments needed to succeed in different areas of creative endeavors vary (just as the height requirements found at different rides may vary depending on the nature of the ride).

As an example of this, intelligence is an important contributor to creative performance in all domains, but it is much more highly correlated with creativity in certain domains than others. Picturing a less-intelligent creative dancer or woodworker, for example, may be easier to do than picturing a less-intelligent creative physicist. But *some* degree of intelligence is needed for creativity activity; there's a reason why rocks don't compose sonatas (other than the fact that they don't have opposable thumbs).

Similarly, when I talk about motivation, I'm not being specific about what things motivate people or what techniques they may use to motivate themselves. I'm simply referring to the motivation to get up off the couch and do something. If someone is not motivated to do something—*anything*—for any reason, then that person isn't going to be creative. Someone who lies on the couch all day and doesn't have the motivation to do anything will not be creative. A writer who never translates his or her ideas into words at the keyboard is not going to be a creative writer (or any type of writer).

Finally, environments are important in both the past and present tenses. A person who grows up in a culture or in a family in which creative thoughts or actions are not encouraged (or are even punished) will have a harder time being creative. A person living or working in an environment that is supportive of original thought is more likely to be creative than a person in an environment that discourages such thought. Being creative is a different thing to a woman living in Saudi Arabia or Pakistan as compared to a woman living in England or Portugal. And no matter what the country, a child growing up in an abusive household may have a more difficult time expressing novel ideas than may a child growing up in a nurturing family.

As with motivation, I mean environment here in a general way. There are also certainly specific environmental influences to be found at other levels of the model, such as a family that invites study or inquiry in one area (e.g., music) but not in another (e.g., engineering), or an environment that contains the tools and materials necessary to one kind of creativity but not another—if you grow up with an abundance of sports equipment but no musical instruments, then your environment is more conducive to athletic creativity than to musical creativity.

APT: GENERAL THEMATIC AREAS

Once you have decided to go to an amusement park, you must decide what kind of park you wish to visit. Maybe you are in the mood to go to a water park and splash around. Or perhaps you are feeling more daring (or you don't like the way you look in a swimsuit), and you want to enjoy extreme roller coasters or those rides that plunge you into free fall. Maybe you want to see animals or fish, or you want to visit a theme park centered on a cartoon character.

Just as all of these different places fall into a larger category called "amusement parks," so can many different types of creativity fall into larger categories that are called general thematic areas. How many general thematic areas are there? 1? 10? 100? The question of articulating all of the important different thematic areas is, perhaps, an ancient one. In Greek mythology, there are nine muses—goddesses who helped inspire those mortals who would attempt to be creative in the arts or sciences. There were initially three muses—Melete (muse of Practice), Mneme (muse of Memory), and Aeode (muse of Song). But these three muses were soon expanded to nine (although the muse of Memory lives on when we try to remember the order of the planets and use a Mnemonic).

Consider the expanded list of muses and what they represented (D'Aulaire & D'Aulaire, 1992):

- Calliope: Epic poetry
- Euterpe: Lyric poetry/music
- Erato: Love poetry
- Polymnia: Sacred poetry
- Clio: History
- Melpomene: Tragedy
- Thalia: Comedy/pastoral poetry
- Terpsichore: Choral song/dance
- Urania: Astronomy/astrology

These nine muses could easily be reread as nine general thematic areas. Clearly, our values and conceptions of creativity have changed from the times of Greek mythology—one senses a certain focus on poetry that is, unfortunately, not as present in modern day. But even all those years ago, the choice of muses showed certain awareness about creativity. If you were creative and looking to be inspired, you might need different stimuli depending on your area of creativity. An alternate interpretation, of course, is that these nine goddesses simply preferred these particular nine areas, and no mortals were brave enough to suggest that they become more creatively diversified. If there's one thing that mythology has taught us, it's that you don't try to argue with an angry goddess (also, if a god with winged heels gives you a shield and sword, he probably wants something from you).

In more modern days, the debate continues. Feist (2004) uses the phrase "domains of mind" and has proposed seven: psychology, physics, biology, linguistics, math, art, and music. Gardner (1999), famously, has proposed eight intelligences; although they are usually interpreted as aspects of intellectual ability, they serve just as well as areas of creative achievement (e.g., Gardner, 1993). His eight areas are interpersonal (i.e., dealing with other people), intrapersonal (dealing with yourself, so to speak), spatial, naturalistic, language, logical-mathematical, bodily-kinesthetic (which could be dancing or playing baseball, for example), and musical. Holland's (1997) model of vocational interests could also apply to creative interests; his six categories are realistic, investigative, artistic, social, enterprising, and conventional.

J. C. Kaufman and Baer (2004) tried to figure out how many general thematic areas there were by asking people to rate themselves on their own creativity across many domains. First, they asked 241 college students to rate their creativity in nine areas—science, interpersonal relationships, writing, art, interpersonal communication, solving personal problems, mathematics, crafts, and bodily/physical movement. They next did a factor analysis of their responses (for people who don't know, a factor analysis is a spiffy way of interpreting many different variables and condensing them into fewer variables. I could go into more detail, but I prefer the Sidney Harris cartoon that uses the explanation of "and then a miracle happens").

They found three factors from these nine domains: Creativity in Empathy/Communication (creativity in the areas of interpersonal relationships, communication, solving personal problems, and writing); "Hands On" Creativity (art, crafts, and bodily/physical creativity); and Math/Science Creativity. Interestingly, these are pretty close to three factors found in the area of student motivation—writing, art, and problem solving (Ruscio, Whitney, & Amabile, 1998). Rawlings and Locarnini (2007) replicated the factor structure and found that professional artists scored higher on the "Hands On" factor, and professional scientists scored higher on the Math/Science factor.

A study of Turkish undergraduates found a slightly different factor structure, with an Arts factor (art, writing, crafts), an Empathy/Communication factor (interpersonal relationships, communication, solving personal problems), and a Math/Science factor. Bodily/kinesthetic was not associated with any factor (Oral, Kaufman, & Agars, 2007).

Carson, Peterson, and Higgins (2005), in creating the Creativity Achievement Questionnaire, selected 10 domains, which loaded onto two factors: the Arts (Drama, Writing, Humor, Music, Visual Arts, and Dance) and Science (Invention, Science, and Culinary). The tenth domain, Architecture, did not load on a factor.

Another, similar line of research has been by Zorana Ivcevic and her colleagues, who have studied self-reported creative behaviors instead of self-ratings on overall creative areas. Ivcevic and Mayer (in press) tested college students with open-ended questionnaires and group discussions, which then resulted in a comprehensive assessment of creativity across specific behaviors. Factor analysis of these behaviors resulted in three second-order dimensions: The first factor was dubbed the creative lifestyle and included crafts, self-expressed creativity, interpersonal creativity, sophisticated media use, visual arts, and writing. This factor is comparable to both the "Hands On" factor and the Empathy/Communication factor from J. C. Kaufman and Baer (2004). The second factor was dubbed performance arts, and encompassed music, theater, and dance. Although it is not directly comparable to J. C. Kaufman and Baer's three factors, it is most similar to the "Hands On" factor from J. C. Kaufman and Baer (2004). The third factor, intellectual creativity, represented creativity in technology, science, and academic pursuits. This factor is akin to J. C. Kaufman and Baer's (2004) Math/Science factor. In a separate investigation, Ivcevic and Mayer (2007; see also Ivcevic, in press) used a creative activities checklist in combination with a personality inventory to derive five "types": Conventional, Everyday Creative Individuals, Artists, Scholars, and Renaissance Individuals.

The next study to build off of the work by Kaufman and Baer and Ivcevic and Mayer expanded the number of domains. This new study asked over 3,500 people to rate their own creativity across 56 different domains (J. C. Kaufman, 2006; J. C. Kaufman, Cole, & Baer, in press). Still using the miracle of factor analysis, we found seven general thematic area factors:

- Artistic-Verbal
- Artistic-Visual
- Entrepreneur
- Interpersonal
- Math/Science
- Performance
- Problem-Solving

These seven factors were found as hierarchical second-order factors—in other words, there is some type of "c" analogous to "g," but such a single construct is only part of the broader picture. It is interesting to note that some general thematic areas were strongly related to the "c" factor (i.e., overall creativity). Performance and Artistic/Visual were strongly related, whereas Math/Science was the least related to creativity. One theory is that mathematics and science may not fall into people's conceptions of creativity (J. C. Kaufman & Baer, 2004; J. C. Kaufman, Cole, & Baer, in press). The average person may not consider such areas as math or science as representing their mental images of what it means to be creative. This idea is consistent with Paulos's (1988) idea of innumeracy, the inability to accurately use numbers and chance. "Romantic misconceptions about the nature of mathematics," Paulos wrote, "lead to an intellectual environment hospitable to and even en-couraging of poor mathematical education and psychological distaste for the subject and lie at the base of much innumeracy" (1988, p. 120). Perhaps we should not be surprised to find that a society that does not value mathematical ability also does not as-sociate creativity with mathematics. It would be interesting to see if this same pattern was found in Asian populations; although Western perceptions of creativity typically revolve around the arts (e.g., Sternberg, 1985), studies of Eastern perceptions do not show this same connection (Rudowicz & Yue, 2000). Similarly, the idea of humor being related to creativity (especially interper-sonal creativity) is found in Western cultures (Sternberg, 1985) but not in the East (Rudowicz & Hui, 1997).

It should be emphasized that these seven factors still only reflect people's perceptions of themselves, and there are many reasons why such perceptions might be inaccurate. After all, nearly all people believe they are above-average drivers. A quick jaunt on any major city freeway will clearly establish that not only is this discrepancy statistically impossible, but the opposite (and equally statistically impossible) option is true—*no one* is an above-average driver.

It is also important to note that factor analysis is not the only approach to winnow down the number of general thematic areas. Silvia, Kaufman, and Pretz (in press) apply latent class analysis to large samples of both creative accomplishments and creative self-ratings (if factor analysis intimidates you, then la-tent class analysis will follow you home and beat you up). In essence, latent class analysis determines whether you can divide up a group of people into subgroups. In analyzing people's re-ports of creative accomplishments, there was one big subgroup of people who did not list any notable creative achievements. There were smaller subgroups that indicated creative proficiency in visual and performing arts. In a second sample that gave self-ratings, subgroups did not emerge; differences in creativity across domain tended to produce factors (which can correlate with each other) and not latent classes (which cannot).

Regardless of what the general thematic areas actually are, what do they mean for the APT model? Let's assume that you have enough brains and motivation and are in a suitable environment—the general thematic areas are the next step. Each of them requires different skills and traits. For example, there might be a certain profile of abilities and preferences that you might associate with someone interested in the musical/performance general thematic area. Some might be abilities (such as a sense of pitch), and some might be more personality-related (probably more extraverted, since it's hard to perform with stage fright). Someone more inclined to be creative in the mathematical/scientific general thematic area might have a completely different profile.

G. Park, Lubinski, and Benbow (2007) conducted an interesting study that examined intellectual patterns of ability and eventual creativity in different domains. Using math and verbal SAT scores given to people at age 13, they then tracked these same people's accomplishments 25 years later. Unsurprisingly, early prowess was associated with eventual success. However, a person's specific strengths (in this case, math vs. verbal) predicted patents (math) and literary publications (verbal). Although the authors offered this study as evidence of an IQ–creativity link (which it certainly provides), I also see evidence of the separation of different creativity domains. It would be fascinating to see how a more diverse battery of tests might predict even more specific creative works (such as our seven general thematic areas). Similarly, Wai, Lubinski, and Benbow (2005) found in the same population that math and verbal SAT scores predicted success by occupation—math SAT scores predicted success in science-related fields, and verbal SAT scores predicted success in humanities-related fields.

Maybe certain types of intellectual ability would be especially important to some general thematic areas and not others. Some areas might require specific patterns of thinking styles or levels of emotional intelligence, others less so. Certain types of personality might be vitally important for some areas. Sociability might be essential for others. We're still working on finding out these patterns. But our theory doesn't end here.

DOMAINS

We've now spent considerable time discussing how many general thematic areas they are, but this question is only one piece of the puzzle. Indeed, once you have decided on a type of amusement park to visit, there are still many more decisions left. Even within one genre, there are many different parks to choose from. If you want roller coasters, do you choose Six Flags or Disneyland? If you've decided on an animal theme, do you pick the San Diego Zoo, Sea World, or the Wild Animal Park?

Similarly, within each of the general thematic areas are several more narrowly defined creativity domains. For example, the Painting/crafts general thematic area might include drawing, painting, woodworking, pottery, sewing, scrapbooking, making collages, and many other things. And each of these domains may have a unique profile of related strengths and weaknesses.

Let's compare, for example, a creative poet and a creative journalist. Both would fall in the general thematic area of artistic-verbal (or, following Feist or Gardner, linguistics or language). Indeed, there will likely be many similarities between the two writers. Both will have strong verbal abilities and a love (or at least tolerance) of the written word.

Despite their similarities, creative writers and journalists have different goals. Consider, for example, Thomas Boswell's (1989) explanation of the differences:

> That's one difference between a reality writer and a fiction writer. The beat journalist's ultimate goal isn't a dramatic or poetic effect, much as any writer lusts after such moments of luck…"That's right" is what we're after, more than "That's beautiful." (p. xii)

Journalists and creative writers work often under radically different conditions and with varying expectations—a top-notch journalist may have to crank out a piece in 10 minutes to make a deadline, whereas an equally respected novelist may be allowed 10 years to perfect a book. Creative writers such as novelists, poets, and, to a lesser extent, playwrights may be introverted or avoid social encounters; their success or failure depends on a product that may be created with little outside input. Journalists, in contrast, must thrive on such interactions because much of their work typically involves gathering information and opinions from other people.

Indeed, journalists and poets show many individual differences. For example, journalists and other nonfiction writers outlive poets by approximately 6 years, although this is only at the most eminent level (J. C. Kaufman, 2003). Many other differences are less readily apparent—journalists, for example, have been found to have different thinking styles than poets (J. C. Kaufman, 2002). Within Sternberg's (1997) Mental Self Government model, there are three types of thinking styles: Executive, Judicial, and Legislative. Executive thinkers prefer to follow directions, to carry out orders, and to work under a great deal of structure. Legislative thinkers prefer to create things and to be self-directed. Judicial thinkers prefer to compare, contrast, and analyze different types of ideas. Some domain comparisons would give you pretty obvious differences—a scientist would probably be more likely to think in a Judicial way than a dancer. But even with the journalist–poet distinction, there are differences. Journalists tend to be more Executive and less Legislative in their thinking than poets.

If motivation is important as a general construct at the initial requirements, the *type* of motivation is more important at the level of domain. Perhaps the poet does his or her most creative writing when motivated by a desire to create a beautiful poem, whereas the journalist may put forward his or her best and most creative work under a deadline (or perhaps when angling for a front-page story). One's motivation to write may be quite strong for one kind of writing but at the same time weak for another.

Knowledge plays a large role at the domain level. Let's explore domains that fall under the math-science area. Chemistry, physics, biology, and geology may all fall under the same area and may all involve a certain type of analytic and precise thought. However, the knowledge bases for these four natural science subjects are strikingly different, with only modest overlap, as are the knowledge bases that are foundational for work in the social sciences, such as the differences between psychology and political science.

Some personality traits may also be particularly useful in some domains. For example, being conscientious may be vitally important for scientists. However, it may be of little importance (or possibly even harmful) for those in other fields (such as, perhaps, artists). Similarly, some traits may prove to be related to creative performance in one domain in only a minor way, but at the same time be overwhelmingly important in another (i.e., although openness to experience is of some importance for mathematicians, it is *essential* for artists; see Feist, 1999). Environment and opportunity are also components here. As an example, some creative acts require a particular *kind* of nurturing background. A child who wants to play the violin (or take up horseback riding) may be out of luck if his or her family cannot afford lessons. If that child's sibling has an interest in poetry—which requires less of a financial investment to get started—then poverty may be less of an obstacle for him or her. And if one is working for Exxon, the working environment may be more conducive to creativity in the domain of geology than in the domain of pure math.

MICRODOMAINS

Imagine that you have gone to a zoo, such as the world famous Wild Animal Park. All the activities at the Wild Animal Park involve animals, but they still vary greatly. Maybe you want to spend time feeding leaves to long-necked giraffes. Maybe you want to look at the lions stretching and majestically sunning themselves. Or else you might not feel like walking around, so you take the WGASA monorail and see the animal preserve from the comfort of a slow-moving train.

Similarly, there are many commonalities among all the tasks that are part of a domain. Yet, there are still big differences in what one needs to know, and what one needs to know how to do, in order to be creative when undertaking different tasks in that domain. It's rather like the transition from undergraduate to graduate education. As an example, everyone in a graduate program in psychology may be preparing for a career as a psychologist, but future clinical psychologists, social psychologists, and cognitive psychologists likely take few of the same courses. Similarly, studying fruit flies intensively for 5 years may help one develop creative theories in one of biology's microdomains but be of little use in another, and practicing on a 12-string guitar may help one perform creatively in some microdomains of the music world but not others.

The nature of what creativity is can vary by microdomains under the same domain. Howard Gardner and his colleagues argue for the twin concepts of *axis* and *focus,* two ways of looking at creativity in its many forms (Connell, Sheridan, & Gardner, 2003; Keinänen & Gardner, 2004; Keinänen, Sheridan, & Gardner, 2006). *Axis* consists of vertical and horizontal orientations, which focus on the constraints in the task. Vertical orientations have restrictive constraints; think about being creative in programming computer code or singing an opera aria. There are specific ways of how something is done, and the creativity comes in the slight variations. Horizontal orientations have few constraints; think of a slapstick comedian or an abstract painter. When I cook, I cook in a particularly horizontal way. Granted, I'm using the word "cooking" quite loosely (it mostly consists of making instant mashed potatoes, much to my wife's dismay). But I toss in everything— meat powder seasoning, sliced almonds, cinnamon, grated cheese, hot sauce, and so on (often in the same dish). In contrast, really good sushi is made in a vertical way. There are specific rules for how sushi is made and presented, and the creativity in cooking comes from how the chef can work within those rules.

Focus has modular tasks and broad situations. Modular tasks are specialized (think mechanical engineering), while broad situations are more general (think advertising). Three of my favorite courses to teach, for example, are Critical Thinking, Psychology and the Movies, and Intelligence and Creativity. Critical thinking is a broad situation—the course can kind of cover whatever I want it to, so I end up minimizing topics such as Venn diagrams and maximizing topics such as what you should do if you have a heart attack in the middle of a crowded street. Psychology and the Movies is a more modular class. The topics can range quite a bit, but they all have something to do with movies, and they all begin with me screening a movie. The topics might change from "how people with mental illness are portrayed" to "examples of creativity in film," but the class is going to deal with movies in some way. Intelligence and Creativity is even more modular. The class covers (not surprisingly) intelligence and creativity. What I talk about is limited to (also not surprisingly) intelligence and creativity.

Keinänen et al. (2006) use the examples of dance and law, and I'll paraphrase their law example. A small-town lawyer is an example of a vertical axis and a broad focus. Most of the law that goes on in a small town is typically pretty traditional—most small-town lawyers will not rewrite the law books, making it in the vertical axis. Yet, the focus is broad; a lawyer who only specializes in hostile corporate takeovers, for example, would not survive long in this situation. A good small-town lawyer will be able to do many different things. Trust and Estate law is also vertical (again, there are many specific restraints in place for how things can be done), yet with a modular focus (i.e., specialized). Mergers and Acquisition law, meanwhile, shares a modular focus with Trust and Estate law—but has a horizontal axis. There are much fewer constraints on what a Mergers and Acquisition lawyer can do, and something new and different is more likely to be rewarded. Also in the horizontal axis but with a broad focus is cyberspace law—something that is almost completely new (hence, horizontal) but spread across many different areas, from copyright infringement to slander (hence, broad).

STRANGE BEDFELLOWS

No theory can explain everything, and there are still a lot of weird connections that go on. On one hand, the nested hierarchy of microdomains grouped within domains grouped within general thematic areas feels nice and tidy. On the other hand, there are all sorts of things that are left unexplained. Just as there are important similarities among the differently themed roller coasters located in different theme parks, there may occasionally be connections among domains and microdomains in different general thematic areas that will surprise us. In studies with elementary and middle school children, for example, Baer (1993) found relatively small and generally statistically nonsignificant correlations among the creativity ratings given to different kinds of creative products (including poems, collages, mathematical word problems, equations, and stories), but there was a surprisingly consistent (but as yet unexplained) correlation between creativity in writing poetry and creativity in producing interesting mathematical word problems. These two tasks would seem to be comparatively unrelated—they come from different general thematic areas—yet there has to be some kind of link somewhere.

In addition, there will also always be strange bedfellows that make sense only upon closer examination. Someone may decide to pick their amusement parks based only on how good the popcorn is at the food court. Someone else may only go to cheap amusement parks (Big Dave's Generic Roadside Attraction). In a similar way, microdomains or domains may be selected for reasons that are less obvious. Bill may be a multitalented renaissance man, but he may be motivated to do things that will impress Jane—and *only* do things that will impress Jane. So Bill may learn how to be a creative chef and cook her delicious meals, and he may become a creative poet and write sonnets to her beauty, and he may become a creative animal trainer and teach a flock of seagulls to spell out her name in the sky, and he may become a creative Web programmer and build a great Web site at www.JanewillyoupleasegowithmethanksBill.com. Yet, if you only looked at the microdomains that Bill pursued, the resulting data would look like gobbledygook (unless, of course, Jane had a whole host of similarly single-minded suitors).

ADVANTAGES OF THIS TYPE OF MODEL

I am not arguing that the APT Model is the only or best such model that integrates domain-specific and domain-general perspectives—indeed, the hybrid model discussed earlier does a great job as well (Plucker & Beghetto, 2004). There may be future or in-press models that integrate these viewpoints. The question of creative domains needs to be addressed, however, in any major conceptualization or assessment. Older assessments, such as the divergent thinking tests, tend to assume that creativity is domain general. There is a preponderance of evidence for some amount of domain specificity in creativity. Few researchers, even those who may lean toward the general side of the spectrum, would agree with the domain-general leanings of divergent thinking tests. I believe that these tests' reliance on this singular concept is one reason that other creativity assessments have gained favor over the past decade.

OTHER WAYS TO APPROACH CREATIVITY

Ah, you may say, these ideas are all well and good, but what is most interesting is the relationship between creativity and individual factors, such as motivation, intelligence, and personality. If you just said that, then you are in for a treat, as this topic is *exactly* what I'll be talking about next. If not, then just read every fourth word for a secret message.

Where Does Creativity Fit In? Personality, Motivation, and Intelligence

ontrary to the impression I may have given in the first chunk of the book, there are other constructs that are studied besides creativity. How do these other constructs stack up to creativity? Where does creativity fit into the broader spectrum of cognitive and noncognitive traits and abilities? I chose three specific constructs to discuss: personality, intelligence, and motivation. As with most of the topics in this book, I could have chosen many other areas to explore in more detail, but I selected these three because I believe there has been more work on the relationships between these constructs and creativity, that the research done is quite interesting, and because their initials spell out "Pim," which was Anne Frank's nickname for her father Otto. So, in this chapter we'll explore whether there is a particular personality that is more associated with creativity. We'll talk about how certain types of motivation may help people be more creative. And we'll analyze the relationship between intelligence and creativity (are they simply the same thing?).

CREATIVITY AND PERSONALITY (AKA OPENNESS TO EXPERIENCE)

There are many different personality theories, but the one that is most commonly used in current research (and one that is backed up by a ton of data) is the Five Factor theory of personality (Goldberg, 1992; Hofstee, de Raad, & Goldberg, 1992). The Five Factor theory reduces all of the different possible personality variables into five broad factors: neuroticism, extraversion, openness to experience (sometimes just called openness), conscientiousness, and agreeableness. These factors are sometimes called the "Big Five," kind of like the Five Families in *The Godfather* but with more data and fewer button men. Neuroticism measures an individual's emotional stability (or lack thereof). Extraversion is how outgoing and sociable someone is, whereas openness to experience conveys someone's intellectual and experiential curiosity. Conscientiousness taps into one's discipline, rule-orientation, and integrity, and agreeableness is friendliness and being good-natured (Kyllonen, Walters, & Kaufman, 2005; McCrae & Costa, 1997).

There are other measures that are popular based on different theories (such as Eysenck's Personality Questionnaire, which looks at extraversion, neuroticism, and psychoticism; the 16 PF; the MMPI; and the Myers Briggs), but I'm going to stick to the Big Five for the sake of simplicity (and better data).

The personality factor most associated with creativity is openness to experience. Indeed, one way that researchers study creativity is by giving creative personality tests. The questions on these tests tend to be openness to experience–type questions, and they usually ask you to rate how much you agree with statements such as:

1. I have a good imagination.
2. I enjoy playing with my ideas.
3. Going to an art museum sounds like a fun time.
4. Gosh, I like thinking deep thoughts.
5. I bet it would be fun to make up a story and see where it takes me.
6. My waffles are better than store-bought.

I made up the last one (although if you said it was true, contact me care of the publisher). The first five are pretty typical of what creative personality tests are like. Basically, they ask if you think you're creative or deep in a few different ways, and they see how much you seem to be open to new experiences. As I mentioned earlier, openness to experience is one of the "Big Five" of the personality factors, and it's the factor most associated with creativity. The factor is split into openness to fantasy (a good imagination), aesthetics (artistic), feelings (experiencing and valuing feelings), actions (trying new things, many interests), ideas (curious, smart, likes challenges), and values (unconventional, liberal). More recently, DeYoung, Quilty, and Peterson (2007) argue that each of the Big Five can be split into two distinct factors. Openness to experience, they argue, can be broken into intellect and openness. They use conceptions of openness based on a multitude of tests, including the main test that assesses the Five Factor Theory. Most of the specific subcomponents of openness to experience (all except for ideas) are more related to the openness component than the intellect component.

Some of the subcomponents seem less obviously related to creativity. Some who are high on openness to experience in the actions category will like eating new foods or learning a new language, for example. It makes sense that this same person will be creative, but the connection is less direct. That subcomponent seems more related to sensation-seeking and risk-taking. Values and feelings also make sense but are less obvious (there are many creative people who are straitlaced, calm, and conservative). The other subcomponents sound like creativity because they *are* creativity.

It is unsurprising, therefore, that there is a near-universal finding that openness to experience is related to a wide variety of creativity measures, ranging from self-reports of creative acts (Griffin & McDermott, 1998), verbal creativity (King, McKee-Walker, & Broyles, 1996), studies of creative professions (Domino, 1974), analysis of participants' daydreams (Zhiyan & Singer, 1996), creativity ratings on stories (Wolfradt & Pretz, 2001) and autobiographical essays (Dollinger & Clancy, 1993), creative activities and behaviors throughout life (Soldz & Vaillant, 1999), self-estimates of creativity and scores on the Barron-Welsh Art Scale (Furnham, 1999), and psychometric tests (McCrae, 1987). Silvia, J. C. Kaufman et al. (in press) found that students who showed expertise in visual and performing arts were more open to experience than students without such creative accomplishments. The related quality of being tolerant—measured at age 27—was predictive of creative accomplishments at the age of 72 (Feist & Barron, 2003). It is also interesting to note Dollinger's (2007) study of creativity and conservatism. Even when controlling verbal ability, students who self-rated themselves as more conservative reported fewer creative accomplishments and produced photo essays rated as less creative than those produced by their more liberal classmates.

Being open to new experiences may also help creative people be more productive. King et al. (1996) found that people who were creative and high on openness to experience were more likely to report creative accomplishments. Those people who were creative and low on openness to experience, however, showed comparatively few creative accomplishments.

This general finding of the power of openness to experience seems to extend across domains. Feist's (1998) extensive meta-analysis of personality and creativity found across many studies that creative scientists were more open to experience than less-creative scientists, and artists were more open to experience than nonartists.

McCrae (1987) looked at the subcomponents and their relationship to several divergent thinking measures (mostly looking at some aspect of fluency). All subcomponents were significantly correlated; the smallest correlation was found for actions. These relationships stayed significant (although weakened) even when McCrae controlled for vocabulary scores and years of education. In Dollinger and Clancy's (1993) study of personality and autobiographical essays, the aesthetics facet was significantly linked to creativity for both men and women, and the ideas facet was also associated with creativity in women.

Perrine and Brodersen (2005) examined openness to experience, interests, and artistic vs. scientific creativity (all via survey measures). Five of the six subcomponents were related to artistic creativity—all but values—with the strongest relationship being found in aesthetics. Ideas and values—but not the other subcomponents—were related to scientific creativity. When interests were added as a variable, the results stayed consistent, with artistic interests helping to predict artistic creativity and investigative interests helping to predict scientific creativity.

A similar way of looking at the openness to experience factor is Zuckerman's (1994) work on sensation-seeking. Just as openness to experience is made up of one part creativity and one part risk-taking, so is sensation-seeking a comparable mix. His dimensions are boredom susceptibility (intolerance for being bored), disinhibition (taking social risks, such as excessive alcohol intake or one night stands), experience seeking (needing new experiences, which can include art or museums), and thrill and adventure seeking (taking physical risks, such as bungee-jumping).

BEYOND OPENNESS TO EXPERIENCE

The research on openness to experience, despite a few loose ends, is pretty clear. The other factors are more complex. The research on conscientious and creativity, for example, shows a strong domain effect. Creativity in the arts has shown a negative relationship to conscientiousness—creative artists tend to not be conscientious. This finding has been consistent across creativity ratings on stories (Wolfradt & Pretz, 2001) and in biographical data (Walker, Koestner, & Hum, 1995), and an arts-based creativity measure (Furnham, Zhang, & Chamorro-Premuzic, 2006). J. C. Kaufman (2002) found that creative writers were less conscientious than journalists. Feist's (1998) meta-analysis found that artists were less conscientious than nonartists. There may be a possible interaction between openness to experience and conscientiousness; among people who are high in openness to experience, conscientiousness may reduce creativity as scored in a test of fluency (Ross, 1999).

Feist (1998) also found that although scientists were much more conscientious than nonscientists, creative scientists were not necessarily more conscientious than less-creative scientists. In fact, although only four studies found a link between low conscientiousness and high creativity in scientists, the effect was strong.

Chamorro-Premuzic (2006) did an interesting study looking at how creative thinking and conscientiousness differed in predicting student success. He found that creativity was associated with how well students performed on their dissertation, whereas conscientiousness was more associated with performance on exams. Creative students tended to prefer oral exams, group projects, and working on their dissertation; more conscientious students preferred multiple choice and essay exams. Moutafi, Furnham, and Patiel (2004) suggest that less intelligent people may overcompensate by being very conscientious in order to be successful. Perhaps a similar relationship exists with creativity; creative students enjoy activities that allow them to be creative and set their own timetable, whereas less creative students may emphasize tasks that they can accomplish via sheer willpower (such as studying for exams).

What does this all mean? In the arts, creative people are much less conscientious. In the sciences, there is an overwhelming tendency in general for conscientiousness; your average scientist is likely more conscientious than your average artist (and they pay us to figure out this stuff). But when you're looking within a domain, just at scientists, the factor doesn't particularly help and may hurt. Interestingly, King et al. (1996) found that conscientiousness helped less creative people produce more creative accomplishments. Putting this and Feist's meta-analysis together, perhaps genuinely creative scientists don't need to be as conscientious as people who are making advances with more sweat and late nights than moments of inspiration.

It is also important to look beyond just the arts and sciences. George and Zhou (2001) studied openness to experience and conscientiousness in organizations, and they found that a supervisor's feedback and the structure of the task were essential in relating the two personality factors to creative behavior on the job. In situations where people received positive feedback from supervisors and had an open-ended task, those who were high on openness to experience produced more creative results. When a person's work is closely monitored, then people who are high on conscientiousness will produce less creative results. In addition, people who are highly conscientious may be more likely to nitpick, be generally unhelpful, and create a negative work environment; these factors then interact to produce a strikingly low level of creativity. Conscientiousness is typically associated with positive work outcomes (i.e., people showing up for work on time and getting projects completed by deadline), so this type of negative finding is fairly unusual. It is interesting to note that a different study in the workplace, Gelade's (1997) investigation of advertising and design workers, also found a negative relationship between creativity and conscientiousness (and a positive relationship with neuroticism, extraversion, and openness to experience).

Of the remaining three personality factors, one of them—neuroticism—opens up a can of worms that I'll discuss in a later chapter. This factor is tied to a wide variety of mental disorders. Mental illness and creativity deserves its own chapter (or its own book), if only to sort out the actual data from the many strongly held opinions and personal feelings.[1]

The fourth factor, extraversion, is a bit more muddled. There may be a mild link between creativity and extraversion, or there may not. This connection was found with creativity measured through fantasy stories rated for creativity (Martindale & Dailey, 1996), in an analysis of biographical data (Furnham & Bachtiar, 2008; King et al., 1996), and with divergent thinking tests (Furnham & Bachtiar, 2008; Richardson, 1985; Schuldberg, 2005; Srinivasan, 1984). G. Leith (1972) found that extraverted people produced both a greater number of responses and more original responses. In Silvia et al.'s (2008) study, students with performing arts experience were more extraverted than students with visual arts experience or no creativity-relevant experience.

Yet, Roy (1996), in a study of fine artists (in comparison to other professions), found that the artists were more introverted than nonartists; Mohan and Tiwana (1987) found similar results with a group of creative writers. Several other studies found no significant relationship at all (most notably Matthews, 1986; McCrae, 1987). Feist's (1998) meta-analysis shows that scientists were much more introverted than nonscientists—but creative

---

1. It is also important to remember that what may be data for you are personal feelings for others. When my work with poets and mental illness had a wave of media attention, I was at first surprised at the many blogs that seemed to take great delight in calling me a jerk and criticizing my work (and the photo on my professional Web site). But aside from the usual stream of folks who just enjoy insulting people, I found several people who intelligently and eloquently articulated the personal nature of my research. I might study "poets" as part of my research; for many of these people, poetry is their life.

scientists were more extraverted than less-creative scientists. There was a small effect for artists being more extraverted than nonartists.

The fifth factor, agreeableness, has perhaps the mildest relationship to creativity. Feist's (1998) analysis found that creative scientists were less agreeable than less-creative scientists, and artists were less agreeable than nonartists (also found by Burch, Pavelis, Hemsley, & Corr, 2005). King et al. (1996) found that agreeableness negatively correlated with creative accomplishments (although the relationship was modest at $r = -.23$). However, there is not the same extensive body of work associating this factor with creativity as it exists in some way with the other four factors.

A final note is that personality tests (like creativity tests) have often been accused of being susceptible to faking. To combat this, Hirsch and Peterson (2008) devised a "fake-proof" version of the Five Factor Model, in which respondents were forced to choose between two good options. In other words, instead of being asked whether you agree with statements such as "I try to help people," you would be asked to choose which is more like you, "I try to help people" or "I like thinking deep thoughts." This new version, excitingly, predicted creativity and academic achievement better than traditional measures of the Five Factor Model. I eagerly await future studies with this new version.

SELF-ASSESSED CREATIVITY: IS IT WORTH ANYTHING?

Personality is nearly always measured by asking people questions about themselves. Can we learn about creativity by the same method? Think about simply asking people to rate themselves for creativity. It sounds easy and maybe a little too good to be true. Would the scores be worth anything? Would everyone just say, "Yes, I'm incredibly creative, oh naïve researcher"? If not, maybe we could abandon all of these complicated divergent thinking tests and consensual assessments.

A typical question might ask, "Rate your creativity on a scale from 1 to 10." Another format is to show a picture of a typical IQ bell curve and ask, "Using a scale with 100 being average, rate your own creativity." Although these types of questions are often used as part of larger questionnaires, surprisingly few studies have specifically examined self-estimated creativity.

Unsurprisingly, self-report measures tend to correlate highly with each other (e.g., Fleenor & Taylor, 1994; Goldsmith & Matherly, 1988; J. C. Kaufman & Baer, 2004). There are some studies that show that self-assessed creativity relates to some measures of creativity. Furnham and his colleagues (Furnham, 1999; Furnham & Chamorro-Premuzic, 2004; Furnham et al., 2006) asked students to assess their own creativity and administered the Barron Welsh Art Scale and a Five Factor personality test. They found that self-assessed creativity was significantly related to creativity as measured by the Barron Welsh Art Scale. They also found that self-assessed creativity was correlated with conscientiousness (although the correlation with openness to experience missed significance). M. Park, Lee, and Hahn (2002) found self-reported creativity to significantly correlate with all scores on the Torrance Tests of Creative Thinking (TTCT) except for fluency, and Phillips (1973) found that self-assessments differed between high scorers on the TTCT and low scorers (with high scorers rating themselves as more creative). Furnham, Batey, Anand, and Manfield (2008) found self-assessed creativity to have significant but low correlations with divergent thinking tasks and self-reported creative activities—although Eisenman and Grove (1972) found no relationship between self-reported creativity and creative activities.

There is other research, however, that indicates that self-assessed creativity does not necessarily correspond to measures less reliant on paper and pencil (or computer keyboard). Lee, Day, Meara, and Maxwell (2002) used three measures of creativity (verbal, pictorial, and self-report) and found little relationship among the three measures. Priest (2006) found that students' self-assessment of the creativity of their musical compositions did not predict expert ratings of these same compositions. J. C. Kaufman, Evans, and Baer (in press) tested fourth graders in four domains of creativity (math, science, art, and writing) with a self-assessment and a rated creative product. The two scores were not related in *any* of the four domains.

It does make sense at a gut level that people might not always be in touch with their own abilities or qualities. Shows such as *American Idol* reveal just how many people think they are talented or creative or special—and are not. At a broader level, people often are simply unaware of how bad or incompetent or untalented they actually are (Dunning, Johnson, Ehrlinger, & Kruger, 2003). If you spend some time on YouTube or LiveJournal and see or read people's creative output, you already know that for every truly interesting or different video or post, there is plenty of other unfunny, painful, and navel-gazing material right alongside the good stuff.

There is a theoretical basis for self-reported creativity being a meaningful concept at higher levels of creativity and less important at lower levels. Part of the reason is the idea of meta-cognition, the ability to monitor one's own learning, perform self-evaluation, and then make plans accordingly (Everson & Tobias, 1998; Flavell, 1979). Someone who was high in metacognitive abilities would know his or her limitations, be able to seek help, and estimate success with reasonably high accuracy. There are some theoretical links between metacognition and creativity (e.g., Naglieri & Kaufman, 2001). Several theorists have argued that metacognition is connected to creative problem solving and that someone who is high in metacognitive ability should be a more creative problem solver (Davidson & Sternberg, 1998; Feldhusen & Goh, 1995; Jausovec, 1994).

Yet, what goes up usually goes down—and whereas high metacognition will lead to better creative performance, low metacognition may lead to lower creative performance. Indeed, Kruger and Dunning (1999) argue that people who do poorly in intellectual (and social) realms may suffer from a "double whammy"—they are not only underperformers, but they also have lower metacognitive abilities and therefore are unable to recognize their poor performance.

People who may be poor at determining their own creativity may nonetheless be able to identify their most creative work. Runco and colleagues (Runco & Dow, 2004; Runco & Smith, 1992) found that people who tended to produce more original responses also were better at rating their most original responses to a divergent thinking task. Silvia (2008c) asked people to pick their best responses to a similar divergent thinking task, and then examined whether they were more likely to choose responses that outside raters considered creative. Silvia found that people were able to discern their more creative responses—and that people who were more open to experience were more likely to choose accurately. At the Big-C end of the spectrum, Kozbelt's (2007) analysis of Beethoven's self-critiques found that the great composer was a reasonably accurate rater himself.

A final point to ponder is the relationship between self-efficacy ("I think I can, I think I can") and creativity. Higher self-efficacy is associated with higher creativity (Bandura, 1997; Prabhu, Sutton, & Sauser, 2008). Tierney and Farmer (2002) proposed the concept of creative self-efficacy as representing a person's beliefs about how creative he or she can be. These beliefs are often rooted in a situational or narrow context (e.g., Jaussi, Randel, & Dionne, 2007). A broader view of creative self-efficacy examines creative personal identity, which is also reflective of how much someone values creativity (e.g., Randel & Jaussi, 2003). In other words, believing that you are creative may be important as a factor by itself, regardless of whether you actually are creative. The importance of self-beliefs can be further seen as we dig into the motivation literature.

CREATIVITY AND MOTIVATION

Just as I did with personality, I'm going to cram an entire century's worth of copious research into a manageable discussion by focusing on one key issue: intrinsic vs. extrinsic motivation and its relationship to creativity. Someone who is intrinsically motivated is performing an activity because he or she enjoys it or gets personal meaning out of it. It's as simple as that. You do something because you like to do it or because you feel like what you are doing has great worth. In contrast, extrinsic motivation is doing something for an external reason, such as grades, money, or praise. Neither one is inherently better or worse. There are some areas where it's hard to be intrinsically motivated, such as cleaning toilets. There are some aspects of cleaning toilets that might inspire intrinsic motivation—a pride in one's accomplishments, a strong work ethic, and so on. But the experience itself is unlikely to be rewarding.

There's a reason why you have to pay people to do that. Some activities are easy to categorize—I play with my dog Kirby because I love doing it. Nobody's paying me anything (or if they are, Kirby's funneling away the money to a Swiss bank account and not telling me). When I was in graduate school, I would occasionally volunteer to do MRI studies where I had my brain scanned while I performed some random task. I chose to do these studies because of the $40 they were paying me, which translated into about eight eggplant-sausage calzones at Town Pizza. But other things are somewhere in the middle. I enjoy teaching a lot, but would I do it without any financial compensation? Probably not. Certainly, I would rarely grade papers or midterms—particularly multiple choice tests that involve repetitive circling of answers—if I weren't getting paid for teaching the class.

Here's where it gets tricky, too—why am I writing this book? It's certainly not for the money. Any academic-oriented book that isn't self-help or an introductory psychology textbook doesn't make enough money to pay more than minimum wage per hour worked. Yet, extrinsic motivation can be praise ("Dr. Kaufman," said in an alluring voice, "I really enjoyed your book about creativity...") or external evaluations and reviews. Perhaps if writing this book were a purely intrinsically motivated task done for the sheer joy of writing it, it wouldn't matter if anyone ever read it. I could write it and then delete the files off my computer (but my publisher probably wouldn't be pleased).

Conversely, maybe it is the communication of my ideas that I find meaningful. I may not love the writing process enough to do so without sharing my work, but the discourse process might be the meaningful component for me—writing this book and having colleagues (and students) read it, respond to it, and perhaps get their own ideas about creativity. This aspect of writing would still represent intrinsic motivation.

Related to motivation, unsurprisingly, are goals. There are learning goals (also called mastery goals), in which you do something because of the learning you achieve while doing it. You might take a night course in Spanish or Introduction to Tiramisu because you want the knowledge from the course. You don't really care whether you get an A or an A-. Another type of goal is the performance goal—you are focused on how well you perform a task and are less concerned with how much you learn while doing so (Nicholls, 1979). If you need to pass an exam to get out of taking Remedial Math, you care much more about doing well on the exam than about learning from it. Your goals shift with the task. Let's take cooking, for example. Sometimes you might want to learn new things and try cooking a new dish. You care less about the success of the actual product than the new techniques or combinations that you can apply to future meals (for example, salmon and honey don't usually mix). Other times, you might cook to impress someone, and it's more important for the meal to turn out perfectly than for you to learn something.

Learning goals are associated with intrinsic motivation. If your goal from a task is to learn how to do something, then you are more likely to be doing it out of enjoyment or for the meaning of the activity. Performance goals are associated with extrinsic motivation. If your goal is to get a perfect final product, you are more likely to be doing this task for a reward or external value. These connections aren't too shocking.

Ability factors into which goals and motivations work best. If you have learning goals, it doesn't matter how much ability you have; your goal is, after all, to get better. It's equally possible to improve when you're starting from a place of poor ability (Elliott & Dweck, 1988). If you have performance goals and high ability, then you're usually going to do pretty well, also. If you want to write a great poem or give a great speech or juggle 10 chain saws, *and* you are high in poem-writing, speech-giving, or chainsaw-juggling ability, then the world will be a happy place. The problems come up, however, when you have performance goals and run into a snag. If you feel like you aren't good enough, you are much more likely to give up. This situation produces a learned-helpless type response (Elliot & Church, 1997; Middleton & Midgley, 1997).

Another potential problem is called the "hidden cost of rewards" (Lepper & Greene, 1975, 1978; Lepper, Greene, & Nisbett, 1973). If you offer people a reward to do something that they already find interesting, then you may *decrease* intrinsic motivation. If you enjoy drawing pictures and I start giving you money for drawing pictures, then you may choose to draw fewer pictures for your own enjoyment. According to this theory, offering extensive praise, rewards, or performance incentives may backfire on already dedicated and passionate workers and students (e.g., Kohn, 1993). One application of this general principle, by the way, is how to train your dog not to bark. If your dog barks a lot and you want her to stop, start rewarding the barking behavior. Dog barks, give her a biscuit. Dog barks, give her another biscuit. Your dog will eventually be trained that she should get a biscuit for barking, and she will slowly stop giving you the barking behavior for free. Little does she know, however, that you have again proved your intellectual dominance and fooled her (although your dog does know where you keep the cheese; she's just slowly waiting for the right opportunity to embezzle said cheese and move to Guam, under the mistaken illusion that Guam has a cheese-based economy).

So we have intrinsic motivation and learning goals on one side and extrinsic motivation and performance goals on the other side. It will likely not come as a surprise that creativity tends to be associated with the intrinsic-learning side. Indeed, the idea that feeling passionately about something leads you to be more creative seems almost simplistic. One time, I was being interviewed for Spanish television about creativity. Right as the segment was ending, the journalist summed up (very nicely, actually) everything I had just said, and then asked me for any final thoughts. I was a bit stymied—anything that came to mind was something that he had just said. The only thing that popped into my brain was "Love what you do." Afterward, I was kicking myself for how corny it sounded (although nothing new entered my head), but the basic mantra holds true.

Much of the research on this area has been conducted by Teresa Amabile and her colleagues (Amabile, 1979, 1982, 1983, 1996; Amabile & Gitomer, 1984; Amabile, Hennessey, & Grossman, 1986; Amabile, Hill, Hennessey, & Tighe, 1994). I will highlight a few of the key studies here. Amabile (1985) studied the effects of an intrinsic versus extrinsic motivational orientation on creative-writing graduate and undergraduate students. She asked the students to first write a poem to establish a baseline of creative writing. She then gave them a list of reasons for writing. One group received lists that stressed extrinsic motivation (i.e., "You want your writing teachers to be favorably impressed with your writing talent," "You know that many of the best jobs available require good writing skills"), while another group received lists that emphasized intrinsic motivation (i.e., "You enjoy the opportunity for self expression," "You like to play with words"). Amabile then had the students rank-order these reasons, and then write a second poem. The poems were rated according to the Consensual Assessment Technique (CAT) described earlier. The students who were given the list of intrinsic reasons to rank, as well as a control group that received no lists, showed no significant difference in the ratings of creativity. The students given the extrinsic list, however, were rated significantly lower on their second poem.

If extrinsic motivation can possibly hurt creativity, intrinsic motivation can specifically enhance creativity. Greer and Levine

(1991) found that students given an intrinsic motivation introduction wrote poems that were judged to be more creative than those produced by a control group. One explanation for why intrinsic motivation may be so beneficial is that it frees people from concerns about the context of a situation (Amabile, Goldfarb, & Brackfield, 1990). This freedom then allows people to focus on the primary task at hand—whether writing a poem or developing a new product.

A more recent study examined intrinsic vs. extrinsic motivation in relationship to personality. Prabhu et al. (2008) found (consistent with past research) that intrinsic motivation was positively associated with creativity, and extrinsic motivation was negatively associated. They also found that intrinsic motivation helped mediate the relationship between openness to experience and creativity. This relationship makes sense given the common ground between intrinsic motivation and openness to experience (liking challenges, being emotional, having many interests).

One contextual factor incorporated into Amabile's and others' research is the depth of interest. For example, Ruscio, Whitney, and Amabile (1998) examined which task behaviors best predicted creativity in three domains (problem solving, art, and writing). The most important indicator was found to be a participant's involvement in the task, as measured through behavioral coding and think-aloud protocol analysis. Involvement in a task is a crucial component of intrinsic motivation. Like many of these studies, these aren't shocking concepts—if you're more involved in a task, it makes sense that you'd be more creative.

A third factor that can decrease creativity is the threat of evaluation. In general, if people are expecting that their creativity output is going to be judged or evaluated, they are less creative (Amabile, 1979; Amabile, et al., 1990), and they feel less competent (King & Gurland, 2007). Work by Shalley (1995) suggests the relationship may be more complex; she found that if people worked alone with the goal of being creative, then the expectation of evaluation led to more creative work. She hypothesizes that if people know that they are expected to be creative (and that their work will be judged), then they may be able to focus better on a creative task. Chamorro-Premuzic and Reichenbacher (2008) looked at the interaction between personality and threat of evaluation; they found that both openness to experience and extraversion predicted creativity regardless of whether the participants thought they would be evaluated. People who were low on emotional stability did worse in the evaluation threat condition, although much of this correlation was due to introversion (i.e., neurotic, introverted people did particularly poorly when they thought their work would be evaluated).

In addition, Amabile et al. (1986) looked at the effect of reward on student creative performance. They had a "reward" and a "no reward" condition and then another condition as to how the task was presented—"work," "play," or no label. In the "reward" condition, the children were offered the use of a Polaroid camera, a desirable activity for these children, if they would promise to tell a story later. In the "no reward" condition, the children were also allowed the use of a Polaroid camera, but this was presented as merely another task, not as a reward for future activity. After the children in all conditions took photographs, they were then asked to tell a story, based on a picture book. In the "work" condition, the story-telling task was labeled "work," while in the "play" task it was labeled "play." The "no label" condition did not use a label for the storytelling activity. These stories were then judged by outside raters. Amabile et al. (1986) found that children told more creative stories if they were in the "no reward" condition, while no significant effect was found for the task labeling condition.

The effect of rewards on creativity may, however, be more complex. In one study, participants received intrinsic motivation training (such as directed discussion sessions that focused on intrinsic reasons for performing the task in question) before performing a task and receiving a reward. For these trained people, receiving a reward did not have a negative effect on creativity (Hennessey, Amabile, & Martinage, 1989). Others, however, have found that even with tasks set in a context that emphasized intrinsic motivation, rewards had a negative impact on performance (Cooper, Clasen, Silva-Jalonen, & Butler, 1999).

THE OTHER SIDE GETS TO SPEAK

Recently, however, some reviews of the motivation research have challenged the assertion that intrinsic motivation is linked to higher performance (and increased creativity). Cameron and Pierce (1994) conducted a meta-analysis of 96 experimental studies involving the effects of reward on intrinsic motivation and found that the only negative effect came from a reward being tangible, expected, and given for the performance of a simple task. Eisenberger and Cameron (1996) argued that rewards (which result in extrinsic motivation) are not necessarily detrimental to performance. They stated that the detrimental effects occur under restricted and avoidable conditions and that reward can often have a positive effect on creativity.

Further studies have shown that intrinsic motivation and creativity were not negatively affected by a reward (particularly a verbal reward) and could actually be improved if the reward was presented in a less salient manner, especially in tasks requiring divergent thinking (Eisenberger & Selbst, 1994). Eisenberger, Armeli, and Pretz (1998) found that a promised reward increased creativity if individuals received training in divergent thinking or if instructions emphasized the need for creativity, while Eisenberger, Haskins, and Gambleton (1999) found that rewards increased creativity if the students had prior experience with creative acts. Eisenberger and Rhoades (2001) found that employees offered more creative suggestions at work with the promise of a reward—if an intrinsic interest in the activity was already present. Eisenberger and Shanock (2003), in reviewing the many studies on the harm or benefits of reward, conclude that much of the debate is surrounding methodological issues. Rewarding creative performance, they argue, increases both intrinsic motivation and creativity; rewarding conventional performance decreases both intrinsic motivation and creativity.

There may be a gender-related effect in the role of extrinsic motivation, although these studies have been limited to samples of school-age children. Baer (1997) asked eighth-grade subjects (66 girls, 62 boys) to write original poems and stories under conditions favoring both intrinsic and extrinsic motivation. In the intrinsic motivation conditions, subjects were told that their poems and stories would not be evaluated; in the extrinsic condition, subjects were led to expect evaluation, and the importance of the evaluation was made highly salient. The poems and stories were judged for creativity by experts. There was a significant gender by motivational interaction effect. For boys, there was virtually no difference in creativity ratings under intrinsic and extrinsic conditions, but for the girls these differences were quite large. This was confirmed in a follow-up study using students of the same age (Baer, 1998b), in which the negative impact of both rewards and anticipated evaluation was shown to be largely confined to female subjects. More recently, Conti, Collins, and Picariello (2001) found that girls were less creative in competitive situations, and boys were more creative in competitive situations.

So where does all of this seemingly conflicting research leave us? The prevalence of studies by Eisenberger and his colleagues make it clear that the issue is a nuanced and complicated one. There are clearly situations where rewards and extrinsic motivation may, in fact, help creativity. But the overall trend suggests that intrinsic motivation is the best path to creativity.

CREATIVITY AND INTELLIGENCE

Creativity and intelligence, like bacon and eggs, certainly seem like they should go together (with less cholesterol). But exactly how they do, or whether intelligence is part of creativity or creativity is part of intelligence, is still debated. I have already discussed models of creativity (such as the Investment model and the Componential model) that include intelligence as an aspect of creativity. There have also been many intelligence theories that include creativity as a component, although most theories do not place high importance on creativity. As I described in the historical section of this book, Guilford's work on divergent thinking was part of his Structure of Intellect model (1967).

Many subsequent theories of intelligence incorporated creativity-related abilities into their structures. Undoubtedly, the theory of intelligence that is most used in IQ tests is the Cattell-Horn-Carroll (CHC) theory, a combination of the Cattell-Horn theory of fluid and crystallized intelligence (Horn & Cattell, 1966; Horn & Hofer, 1992; Horn & Noll, 1997) and Carroll's (1993) Three-Stratum Theory. The CHC model proposes 10 different broad factors of intelligence: Gf (fluid intelligence; the ability to solve novel problems, ones that don't benefit from past learning or experience), Gq (quantitative knowledge, typically math-related), Gc (crystallized intelligence; the breadth and depth of a person's accumulated knowledge of a culture and the ability to use that knowledge to solve problems), Grw (reading and writing), Gsm (short-term memory), Gv (visual processing), Ga (auditory processing), Glr (long-term storage and retrieval), Gs (processing speed), and Gt (decision speed/reaction time). Of these 10, only 7 are measured by today's IQ tests: Gq and Grw are in the domain of academic achievement, and, therefore, measured by individually administered achievement tests, and Gt is not measured by any standardized test. The Stanford-Binet IV (Thorndike, Hagen, & Sattler, 1986) and the Woodcock-Johnson-Revised (WJ-R; Woodcock & Johnson, 1989) were the first IQ tests to be built on Gf-Gc theory. Today, nearly every major IQ test is founded either explicitly or implicitly on the current version of the theory, namely CHC.

In the early stages of the Cattell-Horn Gf-Gc theory, Gf (fluid intelligence) was hypothesized to be strongly linked to creativity (Cattell & Butcher, 1968); such a relationship is no longer explicitly part of the model. Currently, creativity/originality is considered one of the components of Glr (long-term storage and retrieval). Specific components of Glr and their relationship to creativity are discussed in more detail in J. C. Kaufman and S. B. Kaufman (2008).

Martindale (1999) proposed a differential relationship between Gs (processing speed) and creativity, and his theory has been tested out (Dorfman, Martindale, Gassimova, & Vartanian, 2008; Vartanian, Martindale, & Kwiatkowski, 2007). According to Martindale's model, people who are creative are selective with their speed of information processing. Early in the creative problem-solving stage, they widen their breadth of attention, allowing a larger amount of information to be processed (and thereby lowering their speediness). Later, when the problem is better understood, their attention span is shortened and their reaction time is quicker. To test this theory, Dorfman et al. (2008) and Vartanian et al. (2007) created two different types of reaction time tasks. One task included potentially distracting information, whereas the other task did not. In both studies, creative potential and Gs were negatively correlated for interference tasks and positively correlated for noninterference tasks, supporting Martindale's theory.

However, the CHC model seems to shortchange creativity a bit. According to this model, the only real way that creativity is related to intelligence is as part of long-term memory. Certainly, the ability to selectively draw on past experiences is essential for creating something new. But creativity would seem to be a primary component of fluid intelligence.

Luria's (1966, 1970, 1973) neuropsychological model, which features three blocks or functional units, has also been applied extensively to IQ tests. According to this model, the first functional unit is responsible for focused and sustained attention. The second functional unit receives and stores information with both simultaneous and successive (or sequential) processing. Simultaneous processing is integrating information together; pieces are synthesized together much as one might appreciate a painting all at once. Successive processing is interpreting each piece of individual separately, in sequential fashion. Think about how you would want to get directions to an unknown place. If you want someone to draw you a map, then you prefer simultaneous processing—seeing everything together. If you want someone to write out line-by-line directions ("Turn right on Outer Highway 10, then turn left in front of the monster truck dealership"), then you prefer successive processing. If you prefer to have a GPS use maps, directions, and vocal instructions to tell you what to do, then you're simply lazy.

The third functional unit is responsible for planning, decision-making, and self-monitoring behavior. It is this last ability, planning, that has been hypothesized to be related to creativity (Naglieri & Kaufman, 2001). For example, in a study of cognitive styles and creativity, the cognitive style emphasizing planning (called, appropriately enough, "the planner") was strongly linked to creative productivity (Guastello, Shissler, Driscoll, & Hyde, 1998). Also, people who spent time planning and replanning a project were more productive and more creative (Redmond, Mumford, & Teach, 1993).

Luria's model was the theoretical basis of the Kaufman Assessment Battery for Children (K-ABC; A. S. Kaufman & N. L. Kaufman, 1983), specifically, Luria's Block 2 distinction between Sequential and Simultaneous Processing. The key contributions of the K-ABC were, first, to finally produce an IQ test built on theory and, second, to switch the emphasis from the *content* of the items (verbal vs. nonverbal) to the *process* that children use to solve problems (sequential vs. simultaneous). The PASS (Planning, Attention, Simultaneous, and Successive) theory is a cognitive processing theory based on the works of Luria that represents an important expansion of Luria's model to emphasize all three of the blocks and functional units, not just Block 2 (see Das, Naglieri, & Kirby, 1994, for an overview). The PASS theory is the basis for the Cognitive Assessment System (Naglieri & Das, 1997).

Sternberg's theory of successful intelligence (1996, 1999b) includes creative abilities as one of three essential components, along with analytical and practical abilities. Although not currently adapted into a major IQ test, this theory is the basis for exciting work in college admissions. Sternberg and his colleagues at Tufts University have added an explicit assessment of creativity as a nonrequired component for college admittance. His measures of successful intelligence (including creativity) predict college success more accurately than standard admissions tests, and differences by ethnicity are significantly reduced (Stemler, Grigorenko, Jarvin, & Sternberg, 2006; Sternberg, 2006; Sternberg & The Rainbow Project Collaborators, 2006). I will discuss these and similar findings later in the book.

Gardner's well-known theory of multiple intelligences (1999) does not specifically address creativity. However, his eight intelligences (interpersonal, intrapersonal, spatial, naturalistic, language, logical-mathematical, bodily-kinesthetic, and musical) certainly seem to require varying levels of creativity. Gardner (1993) has also written books with case studies of eminent creative individuals who embody his intelligences (Freud, Einstein, Picasso, Stravinsky, T. S. Eliot, Martha Graham, and Gandhi).

Most studies that look at creativity and intelligence use divergent thinking tests (such as the TTCT) or other related paper-and-pencil tests also scored for fluency, originality, or other divergent thinking-related methods of scoring. They have generally found that creativity is significantly associated with psychometric measures of intelligence (especially verbally oriented measures). This relationship is typically not a particularly strong one (Barron & Harrington, 1981; Kim, 2005; Wallach & Kogan, 1965), although Silvia (2008a, 2008b) argues that the relationship is underestimated because we are limited by looking at observable scores (i.e., performance on an intelligence test).

Creativity's correlation with IQ is maintained up to a certain level of performance on a traditional individual intelligence test. Traditional research has argued for a "threshold theory," in which creativity and intelligence are positively correlated up until an IQ of approximately 120; in people with higher IQs, the two constructs show little relationship (e.g., Barron, 1963;

Fuchs-Beauchamp, Karnes, & Johnson, 1993; Getzels & Jackson, 1962; Richards, 1976). More recently, however, the threshold theory has come under fire. Runco and Albert (1986) found that the nature of the relationship was dependent on the measures used and the populations tested. Preckel, Holling, and Wiese (2006) looked at measures of fluid intelligence and creativity (as measured through divergent thinking tests) and found modest correlations across all levels of intellectual abilities. Wai et al. (2005), in a longitudinal study of gifted (top 1%) 13-year-olds, found that differences in SAT scores—even within such an elite group—predicted creative accomplishments 20 years later. Kim (2005), in a meta-analysis of 21 studies, found virtually no support for the threshold theory, with small positive correlations found between measures of ability and measures of creativity and divergent thinking.

It is notable, however, that nearly all of these studies do not use traditional, individually administered intelligence tests. In Kim's (2005) meta-analysis, many of the studies were more than 30 years old and, therefore, were conducted using IQ tests that do not reflect current IQ theory. In addition, most of the studies used group IQ tests. Although group IQ tests serve a strong purpose in research studies, they are not used by most school psychologists for psychoeducational assessment (A. S. Kaufman & Lichtenberger, 2006). One of the few research studies to use an individually administered, modern IQ test was Sligh, Conners, and Roskos-Ewoldsen (2005), who used the Kaufman Adolescent and Adult Intelligence Scale (A. S. Kaufman & N. L. Kaufman, 1993) and a creative invention task (in which people would use shapes to create a possible object, and then name and describe their invention; see Finke, 1990). Sligh et al. (2005) delved deeper into the intelligence–creativity relationship by specifically examining the relationship between Gf (novel problem solving) and Gc (acquired knowledge) and a measure of actual creative innovation. Gc showed the same moderate and positive relationship to creativity as past studies, mentioned previously; in contrast, Gf showed the opposite pattern. IQ and creativity were significantly correlated for the high IQ group, but they were not significantly correlated for people with average IQs. This finding implies that students who receive high Gf scores may be more likely to be creative than students who receive high Gc scores.

An interesting suggestion posed by Batey and Furnham (2006) is that the role of Gf and Gc to creativity may shift across the lifespan of a creative person. Gf, they argue, might be more important in early stages, such as mini-c and little-c (e.g., Beghetto & Kaufman, 2007; J. C. Kaufman & Beghetto, in press). Conversely, a later-career creator (who might be in Pro-c) may rely more on Gc—and, I would add, Glr.

What do all of these results mean? Certainly, nothing specifically contradicts the idea that creative people tend to be fairly smart, and smart people are usually somewhat creative. But some of the tested-and-true ideas about the specific relationship are still unclear. If the threshold theory is correct, then there may be a certain point at which being smart stops helping creativity. Recent evidence calls the theory into question, however.

WHERE CREATIVITY FITS

There are other individual constructs I could have discussed. Emotional intelligence (EI), for example, would seem to have a link with creativity. One factor in the initial conception of EI was "Utilizing Emotional Intelligence," and it included creative thinking as one of its key four components (Salovey & Mayer, 1990). Current models downplay the role of creativity, although using one's emotions to think more creatively is still a component (Salovey, Woolery, & Mayer, 2001). However, emotional creativity and emotional intelligence are not the same thing. Ivcevic, Brackett, and Mayer (2007) examined EI, creativity, and emotional creativity. Emotional creativity is being able to experience and express combinations of emotions that are new, appropriate, and genuine (Averill, 2004). They found that self-reported emotional creativity correlated with self-reported and measured creativity; an ability measure of emotional creativity correlated only with one self-report measure of emotional creativity. Also, EI was not related to any of the creativity measures.

Another construct that plays some role in creativity is thinking styles, which are ways that people tend to solve problems and interpret information; rather than representing cognitive ability, they are supposed to indicate how people use their ability (Messick, 1989; Sternberg, 1997). Perhaps the most well-known theory of cognitive styles is field dependence versus independence (see Witkin & Goodenough, 1981). People who rely on the context of a situation, or external cues, are called field dependent, while people who rely more on internal cues and focus on specific details are called field independent (Anderson & Adams, 1992). Although there are indications that people who are more field independent are also more creative (Brophy, 2000; Miller, 2007), this theory is not heavily studied today. One reason is that some have argued that field independence is too similar to fluid intelligence (Sternberg & Grigorenko, 1997).

A different theory, Sternberg's (1988, 1997) Mental Self Government, has three primary functional components: Legislative, Executive, and Judicial. Legislative thinkers prefer to create things and to be self-directed. Executive thinkers prefer to follow directions, to carry out orders, and to work under a great deal of structure. Judicial thinkers like to judge and evaluate things. Indeed, legislative thinkers do tend to be more creative (J. C. Kaufman, 2002; O'Hara & Sternberg, 2001; S.-K. Park, Park, & Choe, 2005).

Despite the presence of some research on these topics and creativity, the three central individual difference areas are personality, motivation, and intelligence. Creativity is related to these constructs in certain, obvious ways—people high on openness to experience tend to be more creative; people who love what they do tend to be more creative; and people who are bright tend to also be creative. But the exact relationship of creativity to other dimensions of these constructs is still open for debate. Are creative people more likely to be conscientious? It appears to depend on what type of creativity. Will being driven by dollar signs lead you to be less creative? Results are pending.

The one part of the personality–creativity literature that I did not discuss, the relationship of neuroticism (or low emotional stability) and creativity, is the area with the most debate. As promised, I will tackle this question in the next chapter.

Does Creativity
Have a Dark Side?

T he other "hot topics" I've described are interesting, but people tend not to fight about them (indeed, picture a bar brawl over whether creativity is domain-specific). The dark side of creativity, however, can get folks riled up. Some people believe that creativity and mental illness are not connected at all; others argue that there is a particular connection between manic depression and creativity or schizophrenia and creativity; still others just prefer their creative geniuses to be stark-raving, ear-cutting, cackling-out-loud mad. Robert Downey, Jr., an Oscar-nominated actor, has been arrested countless times for prescription and illegal drug abuse and gun possession (among other things). He has now conquered his demons and is drug- and alcohol-free; as he is quick to point out, though: "My vice, it seems now, is creativity" (Stoynoff, 2008).

As usual, the truth is both less sensational and more complex than the quick stereotypes, which is why people are usually quite happy to stop at stereotypes. The first questions that must be addressed, however, are: (a) What do we mean by creativity, and (b) What do we mean by mental illness? It is a different argument that creative genius is more likely to be associated with manic depression than to say that your brother who writes stories is likely to end up a little weird.

Ideally, this question could be addressed by giving in-depth clinical interviews and assessments to a large sample of a wide range of creative individuals, from Nobel Prize–winning chemists to published poets to a group of graduate students recommended by their advisors as being particularly creative. In the real world, however, famous people don't like psychologists, and often with good reason. We ask a lot of questions and take up a lot of time, and we usually don't have good things to offer, like money or candy. The kinds of questions that would need to be asked for this type of a study would be intrusive, embarrassing, and generally unappealing. It may not be surprising that most studies of creative genius are conducted on dead people, who complain less.

Before we start a survey of the research that has been done, some basic facts: Approximately 1 in 5 people in America (18 years or older) suffers from mental illness. Depressive disorders occur in approximately 10% of the population, and approximately 1.2% of Americans have bipolar disorder, or manic depression (National Institute of Mental Health [NIMH], 2001). Without these rates in mind, any comparisons become meaningless. A wonderful Yiddish proverb says that, "For example is not proof." It is easy to anecdotally pick out 10 or 20 or 200 instances of people who are creative and mentally ill. I could just as easily pull out a list of people who are creative and short: Michael J. Fox, Dr. Ruth, Prince, Henri de Toulouse-Lautrec, my wife, Tom Cruise, Peter Dinklage, and so forth. Therefore, I could argue, creative people are short. That doesn't make it true.

SURVEYING THE RESEARCH

Perhaps the most well-known empirical study was conducted by Andreasen (1987), who used structured interviews to analyze 30 creative writers, 30 matched controls, and first-degree relatives of each group. The writers had a higher rate of mental illness, with a particular tendency toward bipolar and other affective disorders. The writers' first-degree relatives were more likely to both be creative and have affective disorders. This study is often used as a cornerstone for demonstrating a connection between creative writing and mental illness. It is worth pointing out, however, that there have been several critiques of the methodology (Lindauer, 1994; Rothenberg, 1990, 1995; Schlesinger, 2003, in press). Rothenberg (1990), for example, argues that Andreasen's control group was not well-matched to the writers chosen; the creative group comprised faculty members from the creative writing department, whereas the control group had a wide mix of people. Andreasen was the sole interviewer, with no corroborating opinions about the mental health of the writers.

Most of the other studies of living, eminent people have also been conducted on writers. Jamison (1989) interviewed 47 British artists and writers and found that a significantly higher percentage of them suffered from some form of mental illness, particularly from affective disorders, than would be expected from population rates. Ludwig (1994) studied 59 female writers and 59 matched controls and found that the writers were more likely to have mental illness, including mood disorders and general anxieties. Staltaro (2003) looked at 43 published poets and found that approximately one-third had a history of at least one psychiatric condition and more than half had been in therapy (this is notably higher than population rates). However, poets did *not* score significantly higher than the norm on a measure of current depression. Nettle (2006) examined poets, mathematicians, visual artists, and average folks, finding higher levels of schizotypy in poets and visual artists and lower levels in mathematicians. Another study that found domain-based differences was Rawlings and Locarnini (2007), who gave measures of low-level psychosis and autism to artists and scientists. In the artist group, creativity was linked to schizotypy and hypomania. In the scientist group, these connections were not found; however, a slight connection was found between creativity and autistic tendencies. However, the relationship between schizotypy and creativity is not uncontested. Miller and Tal (2007) found that although both openness to experience and intelligence predicted creativity, schizotypy did not.

Several studies have used personality measures, such as the Minnesota Multiphasic Personality Inventory (MMPI) or the Eysenck Personality Questionnaire (EPQ), which also measure mental illness. The best-known line of research in this vein is by legendary researcher Frank Barron (1969), who tested many prominent and creative individuals throughout his work with the Institute for Personality Assessment and Research. Most creators scored higher on the pathology-related scales of the MMPI. Other studies have examined creative traits in everyday people and "lesser" mental disorders, such as hypomania (Furnham, Batey, Anand, & Manfield, 2008) and schizotypy (Abraham & Windmann, 2008; Karimi, Windmann, Güntürkün, & Abraham, 2007; Nettle, 2006). Hypomania, as Furnham et al. (2008) and Lloyd-Evans, Batey, and Furnham (2006) argue, is a disorder that is related to bipolar depression (there are periods of elevated mood, but these are less intense and shorter), yet, it does not necessarily lead to a diagnosis of "mentally ill." People with minor hypomania may be more creative, whereas people with extreme bipolar disorder may be less creative (see also Richards & Kinney, 1990).

Similarly, there are several studies on schizotypy, a disorder that is closer to a personality trait than a mental illness. Symptoms of schizotypy, which includes some components of psychoticism, are similar to creativity, specifically, highly original and sudden new thoughts. Burch et al. (2005) found visual artists to be higher on both schizotypy and creativity than nonartists. What I found particularly interesting, though, was that the artists produced more responses designed to shock and provoke (e.g., you could "have sex on" a chair or "snort coke" off a knife). Typical creativity tests (such as those used in this study) reward antisocial or unusual behavior as much as they reward specifically creative behavior. It may not be that bizarre, then, that people who score high on creativity tests also demonstrate antisocial or unusual behavior. Such a finding could be more a statement on the creativity test used than any deeper insights into antisocial behavior and real creativity.

Also related to both schizotypy and creativity is the idea of latent inhibition, which is defined as a person's ability to ignore irrelevant input based on previous experience (Lubow, 1989). Someone with high latent inhibition could ignore distracters in (hey, look, it's a bear!) this sentence. An extensive body of work suggests that people with schizophrenia and those suffering from schizophrenic-like disorders (such as schizotypy) have lower levels of latent inhibition. Peterson and Carson (2000) found that latent inhibition was strongly associated with higher levels of openness to experience. Additionally, they further found that low latent inhibition in highly intelligent individuals is correlated to higher levels of openness to experience (Peterson, Smith, & Carson, 2002) and creative achievement (Carson, Peterson, & Higgins, 2003). They suggest that intelligence may be used as a mechanism to handle the many different stimuli that a person with low levels of latent inhibition may be forced to encounter—intelligence may serve as a coping device, so to speak. A further possibility is that perhaps higher intelligence allows better management of potentially dangerous impulses.

Other investigations use what are called psychological autopsies, which are less grisly than actual autopsies if quite a bit more speculative. Traditional historiometric research involves reading biographies of eminent people and noting life events (marriages, winning prizes, battling sea monsters). A typical historiometric study might analyze the word content of a president's inaugural address or categorize the themes present in Shakespearean sonnets (Simonton, 1990).

Psychological autopsies are different; they involve assessing people's symptoms based on life details (such as suicide attempts or hospitalizations). There are a few problems with this technique. Some argue it is unscientific, in part because any diagnosis is given by the researcher—who knows the hypothesis of the study (e.g., Schlesinger, 2003). In other words, in many cases the same person is planning the study, developing the hypothesis, choosing the sample, and deciding if these people have a mental illness. If such a technique was used in any other type of empirical work, it couldn't get published; most journals would want to see a random sample selected or have the raters be blind to the condition. Similarly, some researchers diagnose eminent creators not based on objective criteria (such as the number of times someone attempted suicide) but instead use subjective criteria (such as the tone of a private letter). I know I wouldn't want my own life to be interpreted so closely. George Carlin once talked about a criminal who had a "history of questionable behavior" and wondered which of us would not qualify as having such a background.

Another problem is that no one ever wrote a biography of a creative person because they were so gosh-darn normal. Indeed, normal people can seem boring, at least as subjects of biographies. If I want to sell books—or get published—I'll write about the most bizarre people I can find. So if a researcher is using biographies to get information about a creator, these biographies may not be perfectly objective. Creative people who are bizarre, weird, or suffer from mental illness make more compelling stories than creative people who are boring, work hard, and have happy marriages. There may be more biographies available for that kind of creative genius than for happy, well-adjusted creative geniuses.

Similarly, it is impossible to compare, let's say, 100 legendary poets and 100 legendary shepherds because no one is writing the biographies of the shepherds. Another problem is sample selection—drawing from a specific, well-defined set of people is great. Picking out 50 poets or 50 musicians and then analyzing their lives begs the question of how these people were chosen. If you're picking out data points (or people) selectively, you can prove anything.

With all of this said, there has been a tremendous amount of work done on dead people. Sometimes (for better or worse) psychological autopsies are used, such as Wills' (2003) investigation of jazz musicians (musicians showed higher rates of psychopathology), Post's (1994) study of 291 eminent men (visual artists and writers suffered from more personality disorders), and Post's (1996) replication with 100 writers (higher rates of affective disorders).

Other studies are more traditionally historiometric, looking at life events without necessarily doing a full psychiatric analysis. Perhaps the most impressive historiometric study was conducted by Ludwig (1995), who investigated over 1,000 eminent individuals who were the subjects of major biographies written between 1960 and 1990. Among many other discoveries, he found a higher incidence of mental illness among people in artistic professions (e.g., writing, art, and theater) than in nonartistic professions (e.g., business, politics, and science), similar to Nettle's (2006) work. In another study, Ludwig (1998) found that visual artists with a more emotive style were more likely to suffer from depression and other disorders than artists with more formal styles.

This line of research may indicate that the issue of domains is more important than the issue of creativity. Given the research on personality differences between artists and scientists I've discussed earlier, is this work simply looking at spurious correlations? Perhaps it's not that creative people are more likely to be mentally ill, but rather, people in the arts are more likely than people not in the arts to suffer from mental illness—regardless of the level of creativity. I've done some work in this area, looking mostly at writers. For example, female poets were significantly more likely to suffer from mental illness (as measured by suicide attempts, hospitalizations, or specific periods of depression that warranted discussion in a brief biography) than other types of women writers (fiction writers, playwrights, and nonfiction writers) and male writers (fiction writers, poets, playwrights, and nonfiction writers; J. C. Kaufman, 2001a, 2001b). An additional study looked only at women and compared poets with journalists, politicians, actresses, novelists, and visual artists. Again, poets were significantly more likely to have mental illness than any other group (J. C. Kaufman, 2001b). This finding was dubbed the "Sylvia Plath effect."

Other studies have also explored writers. J. C. Kaufman (2005) studied 826 writers from Eastern Europe from the 4th century to the present day. I found that poets were significantly more likely to suffer from mental illness than any other type of writer (fiction writer, playwright, nonfiction writer). Similarly, Thomas and Duke (2007) found that eminent poets showed significantly more cognitive distortion than fiction writers; they hypothesized that poets were more apt to accept depressive thinking. Stirman and Pennebaker (2001) found that suicidal poets were likely to use words associated with the self (as opposed to the collective) in their poetry, as opposed to nonsuicidal poets. The authors of the study suggested that this tendency revealed an inward focus and lack of social integration. Forgeard (2008) examined the linguistic patterns of eminent writers who were either bipolar, unipolar, or neither; bipolar writers used more death-related words than unipolar, whereas unipolar writers were less likely to use self-related words than the controls. Her findings are somewhat consistent with Stirman and Pennebaker in that unipolar depressives are less likely to commit suicide than bipolar depressives (who used more self-associated words). Djikic, Oatley, and Peterson (2006) did a neat study that explored linguistic patterns of creative writers and physicists; the writers used more emotion-related words and—specifically—more negative-emotion words (i.e., related to anger, anxiety, or depression). This finding doesn't necessarily mean that writers feel these emotions more, just that they are more likely to use these words.

Another finding that bears mention is that writers have a shorter lifespan than people in other occupations, including other artistic-related occupations (Cassandro, 1998; Kaun, 1991; Ludwig, 1995; Simonton, 1975). A large-scale study of almost 2,000 American, Chinese, Turkish, and Eastern European writers found that, on average, poets died younger than fiction writers and nonfiction writers across all four cultures (J. C. Kaufman,

2003). Earlier studies also found poets to die the youngest of all writers (e.g., Ludwig, 1995; Simonton, 1975). It is important to note that general creativity (as associated with openness to experience) is *not* associated with earlier mortality (see Roberts, Kuncel, Shiner, Caspi, & Goldberg, 2007).

A completely different approach to this work is to look at the type of mental illness and less at the type of creativity. One way to do this is to study people with mental illness and see if they are creative. Richards, Kinney, Lunde, Benet, and Merzel (1988) looked at 17 people with manic depression, 16 people with severe mood swings (cyclothymes), 11 normal first-degree relatives, and 33 controls. They found higher creativity levels (as measured by the Lifetime Creativity Scale) in the 33 people with mental illness and their relatives, as compared to the controls. Kinney, Richards, Lowing, LeBlanc, and Zimbalist (2001) tested adults who were born to schizophrenic parents and adopted by non-schizophrenic parents and compared them to adults born to and adopted by nonschizophrenic parents. They found that (consistent with other studies), people with schizoid or schizotypal disorders were more creative than those without the disorder—but the presence of schizophrenia in biological parents did not have an impact on creativity.

Keefe and Magaro (1980) gave measures of divergent thinking to 10 paranoid schizophrenics, 10 nonparanoid schizophrenics, 10 nonpsychotic psychiatric patients, and 10 controls. The nonparanoid schizophrenics were found to get higher divergent thinking scores than the other three groups. Wadeson (1980) found that bipolar patients going through depression and unipolar depressive patients had similar painting styles, with fewer colors; bipolar patients in a manic stage used more colors and were more expressive. Strong et al. (2007) studied creativity and personality in bipolar and unipolar depressives, as well as controls from creative and noncreative disciplines. They found two distinct factors; one was strongly based in neuroticism and mood disorders (cyclothymia and dysthymia), whereas the other was comprised mostly of openness to experience and creativity. Although both factors were related to self-report measures of creativity, neither factor was related to scores on the Torrance Tests. Santosa, Strong, Nowakowska, Wang, Rennicke, and Ketter (2007) examined bipolar and unipolar depressives along with nondepressives and a group of people from creative disciplines (although, as you may remember from chapter 3, *any* discipline can be creative). They found that bipolar (but not unipolar) depressives outperformed nondepressives on the Barron-Walsh Art Scale (a scale that is used less often in current creativity research) but found the only difference on the Torrance Tests was that those in creative domains outperformed unipolar depressives. As is consistent with much research in this area (including my own), it is easy to emphasize the mental illness–creativity connection. Santosa et al.'s (2007) paper is titled "Enhanced creativity in bipolar disorders." Couldn't it just as easily be called "Lowered creativity in unipolar disorders"?

Certainly, there are obvious ways that both manic depression and schizophrenia mirror creativity. The extreme highs of mania can result in creative output, and it is easy to compile a long list of individuals with manic depression (e.g., Jamison, 1993); however, remember the list of people who were short and creative. Or, if you prefer, think of the marvelous argument advanced by Lott (2002), who contended that the Eagles were responsible for world tragedy. He pointed out that the dates at which their hit singles (such as "Hotel California") peaked coincided with terrible events, such as the prime minister of Tunisia having a stroke, Nixon making budget cuts, or the spillage of a Liberian oil tanker. Clearly, you can take any series of dates (or lists of creative people) and argue *anything*. These examples are not to call into question all data analysis, of course—but one needs to be an informed consumer. Just as if you didn't know how to pick out a good grapefruit, you would ask someone, so, too, if you don't know anything about statistics (and it is okay if you don't), then you should at least seek out an expert opinion if you want to truly consider past research in this area. So many of the debates and discussions about manic depression and creativity give example upon example upon example; such tactics do not make my inner scientist believe.

It is also interesting, incidentally, to note that Ghadirian, Gregoire, and Kosmidis (2001) studied a total of 44 psychiatric patients with and without bipolar illness and found no difference between the two groups in creative abilities. Eisenman (1990) tested 37 individuals with schizophrenia, manic depression, or psychotic depression and found them to be *less* creative than controls.

ARE CREATIVE GENIUSES MAD? THOUGHTS AND PERCEPTIONS

As the last few pages may have made clear, I don't know. This next discussion will be mostly my own synthesis of the existing research. There are certainly many arguments and evidence for a mental illness–creativity connection. Yet, I feel like whenever I am reading a paper or book on the topic, the author always goes into anecdote at the exact moment that real data are needed. When I reviewed Nettle's book *Strong Imagination* (2001; see J. C. Kaufman, 2003), I noted his clear and systematic discussion of the genetics of mental illness. I became more leery as he discussed creativity and mental illness, noting that he gave a great deal of focus to Andreasen, Jamison, and other "pro-mad-genius" crowds, whereas the opposing point of view received virtually no attention. By the time that Nettle began discussing his genetic-creativity theory, in which psychoses are mostly genetic and also associated with creativity, he was limited to almost entirely anecdotal support. His discussion of an Inuit singer named Opingalik was certainly interesting—but I wasn't convinced it meant anything. Why not discuss a Nebraskan singer named Doug who plays jazz, is happily married, has three children, and enjoys playing miniature golf on weekends?

I had earlier been asked to review *Emotional Illness and Creativity* and was mostly struck by its psychoanalytic and philosophical approach...and virtually complete lack of empirical

121

support (Chessick, 1999; see J. C. Kaufman, 2000). I was later asked to review *Divine Madness: Ten Stories of Creative Struggle* and was again underwhelmed by any actual evidence (Kottler, 2005; see J. C. Kaufman & Burgess, 2007).

I don't mean to indicate there is no empirical evidence for a creativity–mental illness connection, but it is certainly often buried in rhetoric, narrative, or anecdotes. For such a controversial topic, there are comparatively few studies that look at the question in a direct manner. As I explained at the beginning of this chapter, the reasons are obvious. I can test 500 college students pretty easily; getting 10 poets is a challenge. However, there are many areas of research that lack a consistent line of replicated studies. Why, then, do so many books, papers, and essays assume a strong connection exists?

It's a sensitive question. Judith Schlesinger, one of few outspoken critics of the mad genius research, asks, "Why are so many people so invested in pathologizing the exceptionally talented among us?" (2002, p. 75). She argues that the myth of the mad genius allows people who are not creative to feel better about their own lives. Such a discussion brings us to the related question of perceptions of creativity. Does the average person want creators to fail and suffer? It's certainly possible. We like watching rich and famous people fail (there's a reason shows such as VH1's *Behind the Music* do so well).

DRUG USE AND CREATIVITY

This same concern has been raised about a related topic: the use of drugs and creativity. Do we feel the need to connect drug use and creativity because we like "punishing" people who are creative (and, by extension, more likely to be successful)? Plucker and Dana (1998a) argue that we want this relationship to exist for these types of reasons. Creativity becomes more mysterious, and therefore, the burden some people may feel to be creative is removed. In adolescents, they also note, the creativity–drug connection may provide a convenient excuse for experimentation. Indeed, Novacek, Raskin, and Hogan (1991) studied adolescent explanations for using illicit drugs, and one of the five reasons was to enhance creativity (for those who need to know the other four reasons, they were belonging, coping, pleasure, and aggression).

What does the research say about creativity and drug use? Most studies have found little or no connection. Plucker and Dana (1998b) found that past histories of alcohol, marijuana, and tobacco usage were not correlated with creative achievements; familial drug and alcohol use also were not significantly associated with creative accomplishments (Plucker & Dana, 1998a). Bourassa and Vaugeois (2001) studied the effect of marijuana on creativity. They found that those who smoked marijuana before a divergent thinking task showed no beneficial effects if they were new users and a negative effect if they were experienced users.

Norlander and Gustafson conducted a series of studies looking at alcohol consumption during various stages of the creative process, with half the participants being randomly assigned to drink alcohol and the other half placed in the control group. I will discuss a few key studies. First, they looked at three groups— alcohol, control, and a placebo group. Those given alcohol did poorer on creativity tasks, along with measures of persistence and deductive reasoning. In another investigation, they studied alcohol consumption during the incubation stage of the creative process (see chapter two for more information) and found that the alcohol group showed higher originality on a scientific creativity task but no other differences (Norlander & Gustafson, 1996). Next, they had both groups imbibe alcohol during the verification stage and then have their artwork rated by artists and college art professors. They found no differences except that the handicraft in the control group was given a higher rating by the college art professors (Norlander & Gustafson, 1997). Finally, they studied the illumination stage of the creative process and found that the alcohol group scored higher on originality in a divergent thinking test but lower on flexibility than the control group (Norlander & Gustafson, 1998).

Why does the drug–creativity connection persist? There is evidence that creators use more of certain drugs, regardless of whether it helps them. Kerr, Shaffer, Chambers, and Hallowell (1991) looked at writers, artists, musicians, and controls and found that musicians used more cocaine and marijuana than the other groups, and artists used more caffeine. There were no differences for alcohol, narcotics, hallucinogens, and tranquilizers, however. Could the reason for drug use be rooted in social expectancy? Lapp, Collins, and Izzo (1994) gave participants either tonic water or tonic water mixed with vodka and then (randomly) told them that the drinks were either nonalcoholic or alcoholic. They found no pharmacological effects of alcohol on creativity—but they found a strong placebo effect, indicating that the social expectation of alcohol's effect on creativity is more important than the alcohol itself. Janiger and de Rios (1989), in a 7-year study of LSD and artistic creativity, found that artists believed that LSD had improved their perceptions and made a difference in their art—but little aesthetic difference was found in the artwork itself (see also Lang, Verret, & Watt, 1984).

From the studies reviewed, it seems reasonable to conclude that any connection between drug use and creativity is largely one manufactured in the drug user's mind. The actual creative work is likely not impacted. The link between drug use and creativity will likely continue, however, regardless of what the data say—much as in the mental illness–creativity debate.

THE IMPACT OF THE MAD GENIUS STEREOTYPE

The idea of the mad genius (particularly the mad artist) has been prevalent in the research literature for more than one hundred years (e.g., Lombroso, 1891). Simonton (1994) traces its genesis back to Aristotle, arguing that by 1800, "the notion of the mad genius had become virtual dogma" (p. 284). Regardless of empirical evidence, most people believe in the mad genius theory (Plucker, in press). The image of the mad genius or tormented artist persists in media, popular culture, and psychology. Some have dubbed this concept the "lone nut" view of creativity (Plucker et al., 2004).

The results of such beliefs can be seen in many forms. Teachers have been found to value creative students less than they value bright students, in part because they associate creativity with nonconformity, impulsivity, and disruptive behavior. This finding was discussed by Torrance (1963) and has been repeatedly confirmed by other studies (e.g., Cropley, 1992; Dawson, 1997; Scott, 1999). Bachtold (1974, 1976), in a survey of teachers, parents, and students, found that creativity was not considered to be important; there was a high discrepancy between creative descriptors and traits that were highly valued. All groups preferred people with a good sense of humor, consideration for others, health, and self-confidence (which are perfectly fine attributes, of course).

Some of this association may be legitimate; creative students *can* be a pain in the ass (certainly, I know I was an annoying kid; I just hope I was also creative). Brandau et al. (2007) found that students who were rated by teachers as being hyperactive, impulsive, and disruptive scored higher on a test of creative fluency. An extreme case can be seen in a lawsuit filed by Priya Venkatesan, a former Dartmouth lecturer, who accused her English class of representing a hostile working environment. The class's crime, apparently, was disagreeing with Venkatesan's opinions and questioning her knowledge (Rago, 2008). Some of us dream about getting classes filled with students like that.

There are other studies that do show that teachers feel favorably about creative students (e.g., Runco, Johnson, & Bear, 1993). However, subsequent studies have indicated that many teachers who view creative children favorably are not fully clear on what creativity means. For example, in one study, teachers reported liking creative students yet then defined creativity with adjectives such as well-behaved or conforming. When the same teachers were given adjectives that were more typically used to describe creative people, they said they disliked students who possessed those adjectives (Westby & Dawson, 1995; see also Aljughaiman & Mowrer-Reynolds, 2005).

These findings have also been found in Eastern cultures. Teachers and parents in America and India reported favorable views of creativity but also linked several words associated with mental illness (e.g., emotional, impulsive) with creativity (Runco & Johnson, 2002). Tan (2003) found that student teachers in Singapore favored students who had pleasant dispositions (such as kind or friendly) over students who were more creative and risk-taking. Chan and Chan (1999) found that Chinese teachers associated socially undesirable traits with student creativity; they argue that in Chinese culture, nonconforming or expressive behavior can be interpreted as arrogant or rebellious; similar findings have been found in Turkish teachers (Güncer & Oral, 1993). Similar to the studies that found that even people who like creativity may not understand exactly what it is, Lau and Li (1996) found that students who were the most popular were also the most likely to be rated as the most creative.

It is important to note, however, that despite cautions of potential misuse (e.g., Pearlman, 1983), teacher ratings of creativity are quite popular (such as J. S. Renzulli et al., 2004). Such ratings are often a key determinant in admittance into gifted and talented programs (Bracken & Brown, 2006). Runco (1984) found that teacher ratings were significantly associated with student scores on divergent thinking tests, indicating that such ratings do have some validity. An interesting dissertation by Whitelaw (2007) found that a teacher's own creativity (assessed through the TTCT-Figural and self-ratings) was not associated with how well that teacher could identify creative student characteristics, reinforcing past results that teacher creativity was not associated with their rating patterns of student creativity (Baker, 1978). Similarly, Baker (1979) found that although the students of creative teachers were more verbally creative, they were sometimes less creative on figural measures.

It is reasonable to assume that creative students might be harmed by negative impressions and thoughts from their teachers. If the mad genius stereotype has a trickle-down effect and hurts children or teenagers, there's no excuse; indeed, virtually no one would argue that creative kids are crazy (I hope). Certainly, Terman's (1954) extensive long-term studies of gifted children found *lower* rates of mental illness, alcoholism, and criminal behavior.

Does the mad genius stereotype hurt adults? It's not as clear. What do creative people think about creativity in the first place? Runco and Bahleda (1986) compared the implicit theories of creativity held by artists and nonartists and found that both groups agreed that artists were imaginative and expressive. However, artists also believed that artistically creative people were emotional. Similarly, Sternberg (1985) found that art professors believed that creativity entailed originality and taking risks, whereas professors in nonart areas (such as business, philosophy, and physics) emphasized traits such as problem solving and being insightful. Glück, Ernst, and Unger (2002) found that artists themselves can differ based on their format; "free" artists (such as painters and sculptors) embraced the idea of the "artistic personality" and believed strongly in the importance of originality, but "constrained" artists (such as designers and architects) focused more on the importance of functionality.

The relationship that artists have to the mad genius hypothesis is unclear. Schlesinger (2003) contends that creative people (in her sample, jazz musicians) are aware of the myth but choose to not focus on it. Yet, Romo and Alfonso (2003) studied Spanish painters and found that one of the implicit theories that the painters held about creativity involved the role of psychological disorders. This theory stated that isolation and personal conflicts were at the heart of art. These associations do not necessarily mean that artists *desire* such a connection. Indeed, others have suggested that creators use their art as a form of self-therapy, trying to heal themselves as they express their feelings (e.g., Spaniol, 2001).

Kaufman, Bromley, and Cole (2006) investigated how everyday people react to the mad genius hypothesis. They asked 772 college students to answer a series of questions about the mad genius stereotype and then gave a problem-solving measure of creativity and a creative personality scale. Both high endorsers and low endorsers rated themselves as more creative than did people with a neutral opinion. On the problem-solving measure, those with higher creativity were more likely to endorse the stereotype. What does this finding mean? It may explain the extensive debates; more creative people tend to have a stronger opinion about the topic. Yet, their opinion may not be negative; some everyday creative people may accept such a connection and romanticize mental illness.

PERSONAL EXPERIENCES WITH THE TOPIC

Richards (2007) makes an interesting point as she discusses her Richards, Kinney, Lunde et al. (1988) study, which found higher levels of creativity in patients with mental illness: "It is ironic that work I have done . . . has been cited to support this negativity, although we, the researchers, think it is quite the opposite. We investigated the possibility that everyday creativity might carry a compensatory advantage" (Richards, 2007, p. 28).

My own work is often cited as evidence that creative people are more likely to be mentally ill, even though I never actually said that, nor would I say that today (J. C. Kaufman, 2001a, 2001b, 2003; Kaufman & Baer, 2002). I began my own work being interested in writers; I entered information initially on 1,987 writers using many different categories—mentors, best works, age of first publication, as well as mental illness. I didn't (and don't) claim to be a diagnostician; I only entered basic information focused on a yes–no dichotomy for the presence of possible mental illness. What I actually found was that poets, especially female poets, were more likely to be mentally ill *than other types of writers*. I thought this was interesting, and I didn't see how it could be potentially inflammatory. So I published it. Unexpectedly, the media caught on to my finding that poets die young (Lee, 2004), and I wasted some of my 15 minutes of fame trying to explain this odd finding in the world press. Even an anonymous caption-writer at CNN.com got into the act, writing, "This study found this/ Haiku holds the threat of death/ Write prose live longer."

What struck me most was that people don't understand anything about psychological research—that I wasn't saying that *all* poets die young, or *all* poets were mentally ill, and that I only studied very eminent poets. People posted online comments about how poetry was hazardous to your health, and so-and-so wrote poetry so she or he would die soon, and so on. Some people wondered who was funding me (and why); one Web site began critiquing my posted photo on the department Web site, and a former college classmate then posted that I always had seemed creepy. No one actually bothered to read the original work (of course). Regardless, it surprised me how much it struck a nerve—some people were genuinely upset and felt stigmatized, and I felt bad. Especially because the main comparison I made was between poets, novelists, playwrights, and nonfiction writers. I was surprised there weren't an equal number of journalists gloating online. Most people, either to prove a point or to help them react in fury, assumed I was arguing that all poets were nuts, and therefore, creative people in general were more crazy than less creative people.

What many people (both in the press and on the Internet) responded to was the tone. As I briefly alluded to earlier in the book, phrases such as the "Sylvia Plath effect" or the "Cost of the Muse" are a little salacious, if not downright inflammatory. One blogger wrote of my study:

> A paper's findings are often less important than, or deferent to, the rhetoric used…The phrasing of Kaufman's title, "The Cost of the Muse," for example, encourages the idea, unexamined in Kaufman's

paper, that mental illness functions as a commodity, with a high exchange value in the marketplace of creativity and social recognition. But, if we think of mental illness as an exchange or acquisition, we may be at risk of dehumanizing the subjective experience (or, more precisely: the pain) of mental illness. (Chica, 2004)

Although I was initially annoyed at reading this blog (and a bit defensive), I see her point now. Throughout my career, I have been driven by what I call the WGASA factor, which is named after the (now defunct) WGASA Bush Line at the Wild Animal Park in San Diego. The park was trying to figure out what to call the monorail, which takes visitors on a tour of most of the animals and is a key part of the park experience. After a long time of debating and getting nowhere, one zoo executive wrote down in frustration, "WGASA." If you ask workers at the park today, they will either say they don't know what it stands for, or that it's an African word that means something like "happiness," or that it's for "World's Greatest Animal Show Anywhere." In fact, the acronym stands for something quite different: "Who gives a spit anyhow?" (the actual word is a little coarser). I have often felt that a lot of psychology—a lot of life, really—can suffer from the WGASA sentiment. It is easy to do research on any topic and lose sight of the purpose or the point; I can't be the only professor to be stumped by a student asking me why a particular study or theory is important. I think there is a corollary to the WGASA factor, which states that research should ideally lead to more potential positive outcomes than negative outcomes. Obviously, this rule can't always be true—but there are certainly areas of research (such as the countless studies that emphasize one group's superiority to another) that seem destined to cause harm and to hurt people, with little benefit. I think that some research on creativity and mental illness can certainly help—but psychologists who are interested in these areas should make sure they are not glorifying illness, stigmatizing creative people, or generally causing havoc in the name of truth or headlines, whichever comes first.

CREATIVITY AND MOOD

There's more to the "dark side of creativity" literature than the question of mental illness. Another debate is whether being in a bad mood (officially known as "negative affect") will get you to be more creative. Some studies have found results that support this connection. A few studies have found that positive mood inhibits creative performance (e.g., Kaufmann & Vosburg, 1997; see Kaufmann, 2003, for a review), while other studies have found that negative mood either has no effect on creativity or can enhance creative performance (e.g., Grawitch, Munz, & Kramer, 2003). Kaufmann and Vosburg (2002) looked at positive and negative mood in creative problem solving. Interestingly, they found that a positive mood led to better scores in early idea production (similar to past findings, most recently Gasper, 2004). But a negative mood led to better scores in later idea production. George and Zhou (2002) found that negative moods were related to higher levels of creativity (as measured by supervisor ratings) when rewards and recognition for creative work were salient.

An equally large body of research, however, has found that positive emotions and a good mood can have beneficial influences on creative performance. Several studies, many led by Alice Isen (Estrada, Isen, & Young, 1994; Isen, Daubman, & Nowicki, 1987; Isen, Johnson, Mertz, & Robinson, 1985; Isen, Labroo, & Durlach, 2004; Montgomery, Hodges, & Kaufman, 2004), have conducted a series of studies in which they induced participants into a good mood (typically through watching a comedic movie or receiving a small gift of candy) and then measured innovation/creativity (typically through problem-solving tasks or verbal creativity measures). People in good moods tended to show higher creativity than those in neutral or negative moods.

Similarly, Lynton and Salovey (1997) found that students in a good mood wrote better-constructed fiction and nonfiction than students in a bad mood; unfortunately, they were unable to get reliable ratings for the creativity of the pieces. Schere (1998)

131

found that both writers and artists showed improved mood after being creative within their own domain (there was no effect when writers created art or artists wrote). Locher, Frens, and Overbeeke (2008) found that students in a good mood (induced by giving candy) rated a digital camera as having strong visual appeal.

Still other studies have found no relationship. Verhaeghen, Joormann, and Khan (2005) found that rumination served as a mediating variable between depression and creativity in college undergraduates. Self-reflective rumination was connected to both creative interests and behavior and depression—yet, being in a current depressed mood was not associated with creativity. Consistent with their findings, as discussed earlier, is Forgeard's (2008) finding that writers with unipolar depression were more likely to use words associated with cognitive thought (such as *know* or *understand*) than either bipolar writers or the control group.

One new study looks at the interaction between mood and more trait-based affect. Akinola and Mendes (in press) created positive or negative emotional responses by enabling students to experience either social rejection (bad) or social approval (good) or neither. They also measured participants' levels of an adrenal steroid that has been traditionally linked to depression. What they found was that people in the social rejection condition created collages considered more creative than those produced by participants in other conditions. There was an interaction between the steroid and the condition; there was an additive effect such that those more prone to depression who were placed in the "bad" social situation produced the most creative work.

One criticism of this research could be that in nearly all studies, mood was induced. In other words, the moods were triggered by being asked to remember a happy or sad memory or being shown a funny or upsetting scene from a movie. Yet, typically, people experience moods based on their own thoughts, emotions, or spontaneously occurring life events. Amabile, Barsade, Mueller, and Staw (2005) studied the relationship of creativity and mood in organizational employees working on potentially creative products. They used the Electronic Event Sampling

Methodology based on earlier work by Csikszentmihalyi and Larson (1987), in which participants were e-mailed daily questionnaires about the day's events. These narratives were then coded for both affective and creative thought. In addition, the creative performances of these employees were rated by their peers on a monthly basis. Amabile et al. (2005) found significant results across their multiple measures that creative performance (self and peer evaluated) was positively related to being in a good mood. There was no relationship between creative performance and being in a bad mood.

You may remember the idea of Flow, proposed by Csikszentmihalyi (1990), in which participating in a creative event can be seen as an optimal experience. Perry's (1999) interviews with well-known writers found that creative writers consistently described writing in flow as being exhilarating, extraordinary, an out-of-body experience, and at times almost orgasmic. Most of the writers she interviewed saw their creative process as a markedly good thing.

Hirt, Levine, McDonald, Melton, and Martin (1997) argue for a hedonic contingency theory explanation for the positive mood–creativity relationship. People in a happy mood want to maintain their happy mood and are conscientious of behaving in a way to stay happy. People in a sad mood, however, are not so careful, because most activities are likely to improve their mood (Wegener & Petty, 2001). Therefore, people in a happy mood, when faced with a divergent thinking–type task, try to make the task as fun and enjoyable as possible by being more creative. Hirt, Devers, and McCrea (2008) manipulated people's beliefs in whether or not their moods could be changed. People typically believe moods are changeable, which makes sense. If you're generally in a good mood and someone kicks you in the shins or makes fun of your hair, you typically become in a bad mood. Indeed, with no manipulation, people generally were more creative if they were in a good mood. However, when people were convinced that their moods could be frozen, Hirt et al. (2008) found no connection between mood and creativity.

Related to a positive or negative mood is the idea of stress and anxiety. Several studies have found that higher stress and anxiety is related to lower creativity (Carlsson, 2002; Eysenck, 1995). Carson and Runco (1999) found that students with better coping skills were more likely to be better creative problem solvers.

MALEVOLENT CREATIVITY

Another way of looking at the dark side of creativity is to actually examine malevolent creativity, which is a creative act that is purposely planned to hurt other people (Cropley, Kaufman, & Cropley, 2008; see also the idea of negative creativity, Clark & James, 1999). Creativity is typically assumed to be benevolent creativity—think about the many examples of creativity I discussed in the beginning of the book. Only one of them (the scam e-mail from Nigeria) was not basically benevolent. Ask 10 friends to talk about creative activities, and see if any of them mention "Thinking of ways to commit the perfect murder." If they do, that's a nice cue to stop being friends with them.

One of the few times I've seen this question raised was in a journal of business ethics (Baucus, Norton, Baucus, & Human, 2008). They made a solid argument that many of the "Be more creative" suggestions may violate some basic standards of ethical behavior. They specifically mention rule breaking, challenging authority, taking risks, and creating conflict and stress. As I have discussed, a psychologically safe workplace is likely more conducive to creativity (and, hence, would be less likely to increase conflict and stress). Yet couldn't the first three points refer just as easily to my description of being open to experience? Some domains allow one to be creative in an ideal environment; others may not. In my own current role I am both teacher/scholar and an administrator. It's one thing for me to take risks in the classroom or challenge conventional wisdom in my research area. But if I try the same bag of tricks with running my institute, it goes from being creative to being irresponsible. It's easy to assume that abilities will be used for good. Think of the construct of emotional intelligence (Mayer, Caruso, & Salovey, 2000; Mayer & Salovey, 1997; Mayer, Salovey, & Caruso, 2000). Is Dr. Hannibal Lecter an emotionally intelligent person? It is hard to answer no when you actually examine the definition of emotional intelligence. The concept traditionally has four abilities: (1) perceiving, appraising, and expressing emotions; (2) accessing and producing feelings in aid of cognition; (3) comprehending information on affect and using emotional knowledge; and (4) regulating emotions for growth and contentment (Mayer & Salovey, 1997; Mayer, Salovey, & Caruso, 2000). Hannibal Lecter has all four of these abilities: He is terrific at understanding other people's feelings (and exploiting this knowledge); he uses his own feelings to help him think (such as his ability to concentrate and listen to music to prepare for killing the two guards); he understands quite a bit about emotion and affect itself (as is clear from his "reading" of Clarice); and he can certainly regulate his emotions toward outcomes that are useful to him (such as escaping from jail).

Is Hannibal Lecter creative? Was Adolf Hitler creative? How about Ted Bundy, Voldemort, Charles Manson, Vito Corleone, Jesse James, Dexter, Lizzie Borden, or that guy who used to pick on you in the sixth grade? If creativity is seen as having an inherent moral component to it (as in Gardner, 1993), then these people cannot be creative. If to be a creative person is to be a good person, then it's hard to argue that Josef Stalin or John Wilkes Booth were particularly creative. Indeed, Sternberg (in press) discussed how both Stalin and Hitler still have followers today, showing that their ideas have "lived on" and borne the test of time—one hallmark for determining if someone is "Big C." It is the lack of morality needed for lasting creativity that has led Sternberg (2003, in press) to argue for the equal importance of wisdom.

The idea of malevolent creativity is still being explored empirically. In one of the few recent studies, Walczyk, Runco, Tripp,

135

and Smith (2008) just found some evidence that creative liars may score higher on measures of divergent thinking. Even if the idea is in its scientific infancy, the concept is an interesting contrast to most approaches. When discussing mental illness and creativity, the "creativity" part is often assumed to be good—indeed, some of the evolutionary work argues that creativity is the reason why mental illness persists; being imaginative is supposedly enough of an advantage to outweigh the detriments of mental illness. Yet, malevolent creativity can be harmful and evil in its own right. It is certainly a poor assumption to believe that creativity is always a good thing.

THE HEALING POWER OF CREATIVITY

I've discussed in some depth the literature surrounding mental illness and creativity ("the dark side"); the flip side of the coin is that there are arrays of studies that show the healing powers of expressive forms of creativity (particularly writing). The arts can be used as a coping mechanism or as a distraction against physical pain (Zausner, 2007). Indeed, if there is a genuine connection between creative genius and mental illness, it could easily be the creativity in their lives that kept some of the geniuses afloat and as healthy as possible.

The research on expressive writing and mental and physical health, often measured by doctor visits, self-assessments, risk-taking, and life success, has been propelled by the work of James Pennebaker and colleagues (Pennebaker, 1997; Pennebaker & Beall, 1986; Pennebaker, Mayne, & Francis, 1997). Expressive writing can help people cope more effectively with traumas (Frisina, Borod, & Lepore, 2004). People who are randomly assigned to write 15–20 minutes a day on an emotional topic—even if for only 3 days—still show benefits. These populations include first-year college students (Pennebaker, Colder, & Sharp, 1990), survivors of sexual assault (Brown & Heimberg, 2001), laid-off engineers (Spera, Buhrfeind, & Pennebaker, 1994), and psychiatric prison inmates (Richards, Beal, Seagal, & Pennebaker, 2000). Writing topics have included coming to college (Pennebaker et al., 1990), the most traumatic experience of one's life (Pennebaker, 1997), job loss (Spera et al., 1994), and one's goals in life (King, 2001).

One of the central components to expressive writing having a positive effect is the need for a narrative (Pennebaker & Seagal, 1999). When people retell the story of a traumatic event, they organize it in their mind. This act enables them to manage and store away the event, thereby reducing excessive rumination (which is often linked to depression; Nolen-Hoeksema, Larson, & Grayson, 1999). The narrative acts as part of the healing process. Writing in a more fragmented fashion helps people much less (Smyth, True, & Souto, 2001).

Another finding is that writers who shift their use of the first-person singular (e.g., I, me, my) to third person (e.g., he, she, they) are better off than those who continue to use the first-person singular (Stirman & Pennebaker, 2001). This suggests that a shift in perspective is an important element and is consistent with the idea of story telling. This concept is similar to the belief that one of the critical ingredients in psychotherapy is to tell a coherent story or a narrative about important life events that one can embrace and accept as one's own (Mahoney, 1995). Story-making has long been thought to contribute to good mental health, not only in times of trauma, but also through the lifespan (McAdams, 1999; Sexton & Pennebaker, 2004).

J. C. Kaufman and Sexton (2006) argue that it is the healing power of the narrative that may be responsible for the Sylvia Plath effect. The formation of a story has been identified as a key component in the health effects of writing. Yet, poems do not carry the same narrative structure that stories do. Poems are less likely than short stories, novels, or plays to tell a story with a beginning, middle, and end. Many poems do not have narratives; most stories and plays do. It is not evident that writing poetry would have the same benefits as other kinds of writing. Therefore, we argue, it is *not* that writing poetry causes mental illness, but rather that poets may not reap the same mental health benefits from writing that other writers experience.

THE DARK SIDE OF CREATIVITY

Does creativity have a dark side? Sure. Everything has a dark side. Pizza can burn the roof of your mouth, and people can drown in Jacuzzis. So, yes, there are some creative people who are mentally ill, and there have been a tremendous amount of resources spent detailing those eminent geniuses who have also been mad. But I am not convinced by the highly inconsistent research literature that a strong and steady connection exists between creativity and mental illness. I am not denying that such a connection *may* exist; I have certainly seen evidence that certain types of creators or people of a high level of eminence may be more at risk. But I believe that the vast majority of studies on the topic are flawed in either their definition or measurement of creativity, mental illness, or both.

I understand the need to want to answer these questions. People who are creative are often reflective and introspective; I've certainly been impressed with the many sensitive and thoughtful blogs and posts about my research on the "Sylvia Plath effect." People who are not successful creatively may well vicariously enjoy reading about the troubles that successful creative people endure. Creative writers and artists were the legends of their time, and it is from these stories that the myth of the tortured creator first emerged. Perhaps future generations, raised on Britney Spears, Paris Hilton, and Lindsay Lohan, will have entirely different associations with creativity and fame.

It is important to re-emphasize that even if all of the "mad genius" literature is true (and I would hope that most readers will not assume this point), it is a further leap to think that the average person who is creative is more likely to be mentally ill.

138

Whether or not creative genius is connected to illness will likely have no impact on most people's lives.

The fabled "dark side" of creativity has, at times, made it seem to be a less-than-desirable trait. These stereotypes don't help the cause of those who would like creativity to be better valued in society, and in fact, they can help squelch people's everyday creativity through stigmatization. One way that creativity could play a stronger role in life today would be if its worth was readily acknowledged by the gatekeepers of the world. In other words, all it would take to make creativity a key component of American life would be to have admissions committees and employers include creativity as a factor in admittance or hiring. Whether such a shift could (or should) take place will be discussed in the next chapter.

Should Creativity Be Included in School Admissions?

n some situations, college admissions are straightforward to the point of simplicity (or idiocy) itself. Many colleges use a formula. Multiply your GPA by your SAT score; if you're above a specific line, you're in, and if you're below the line, you're out. Certainly, many programs look beyond GPA and test scores; examples of other commonly used tools include letters of recommendation, personal statements, or statements of goals (Briel et al., 2000). But GPAs and SATs or GREs tend to be the key. You might think that the criteria get more in depth as you advance through the academic system, but that's not necessarily true. Surveys of psychology graduate admissions committees have found the two most important criteria for graduate admissions are undergraduate GPA and Graduate Record

Examination (GRE) scores (Keith-Spiegel, Tabachnick, & Spiegel, 1994; Landrum, Jeglum, & Cashin, 1994).

Does this focus on test scores work? It's a tricky question. Sternberg and Williams (1997) found that GRE scores predicted first-year grades, just as they are designed to do—but they did not predict other, arguably more important variables. GRE scores did not, for example, predict advisor ratings of the quality of a student's teaching, research, or dissertation (it is worth pointing out, however, that the study suffered from a restriction of range problem). It is also interesting to remember back to Chamorro-Premuzic's (2006) study that associated creativity with both dissertation quality and preference. Other studies (many of them) have shown that the GREs are a perfectly good predictor (e.g., House & Johnson, 2002; Kuncel & Hezlett, 2007; Kuncel, Hezlett, & Ones, 2001), although grades in graduate school are typically (but not always) used as the dependent variable.

It is tempting to argue that the GREs and SATs are unnecessarily narrow or not indicative of full student potential. But the people who make these tests are not stupid; if it were easy to add a construct such as creativity to a standardized test, it would be done. The impact of environment on creativity (discussed in the second chapter) and the noncognitive components to creativity (discussed in the fourth chapter) make it difficult to measure. One other major deterring factor is that creativity is susceptible to coaching and faking (Kyllonen, Walters, & Kaufman, 2005). There is a clearly desired outcome (which school would specifically look for an uncreative student?). Any self-report or personality-style item could be coached or faked. If you know that creativity is important, and I ask you whether you have a vivid imagination or like to think complex thoughts, how stupid would you have to be to say that you are dull and enjoy pondering dull and narrow things? What if you spent the majority of your time thinking about noncreative issues ("I am sitting on my bed and looking at my ceiling. There are four walls in this room, and no windows. The ceiling is yellow.")? You would still likely know enough to lie. If you didn't know enough to lie but had money, you could hire someone to tell you to lie.

A measure of divergent thinking could also be coached; just by reading this book, you understand (or may dimly recall) the scoring mechanisms behind the test and could specifically focus on improving your fluency scores (rattle off as much as you can) or originality scores (say the weirdest stuff you can think of). Researchers at the Educational Testing Service (ETS), which create the GREs and are involved in the creation of the SATs, have been considering measures of creativity for over 50 years (Stewart, 1953). Frederiksen developed and tested a measure of scientific creativity to see how many hypotheses someone could generate in response to a graph or chart (1959; Frederiksen & Evans, 1974; Frederiksen, Evans, & Ward, 1975). Although ETS still uses this task in research studies (now adapted for computer use), the measure has yet to make it onto the actual test. One reason is likely its extremely low correlation with the rest of the test (Bennett & Rock, 1995).

It's a safe bet that the last Number 2 pencil will have been ground to nub by a nervous test-taker before creativity sneaks its way onto a big bucks group test. The ETS would likely argue that the two are not mutually exclusive—and, indeed, I helped them argue this point in a study that showed that people who were more creative (as measured by a personality-style test) also scored higher on the GRE (Powers & Kaufman, 2004). Wang (2007) found that CBEST scores (an achievement test for teachers) were strongly related to creativity. Kuncel et al. (2001) used a meta-analysis to argue that the Miller Analogies Test not only predicts academic performance but also creativity (and job performance, career potential, and perhaps the ability to regenerate limbs like a newt).

These results should not be shocking to those who are aware of the creativity–intelligence research (or those who read chapter 4). Regardless, seeking a measure of creativity from the people who grind out the standardized exams may be like seeking an emotional commitment from a warthog—you are left heartbroken, and the warthog is vaguely aware that something important has happened. How else might creativity enter the admissions field?

One school admissions area that already uses creativity is gifted admissions—which students are chosen to enter gifted classes, programs, or after-school activities. The federal government has actually proposed its own definition of giftedness, the Marland definition, which about half of all schools use (which makes it the most commonly used definition; Callahan, Hunsaker, Adams, Moore, & Bland, 1995). This view argues that giftedness and talent are most present in six areas: general intellectual ability, specific academic aptitude, creative or productive thinking, leadership ability, visual and performing arts, and psychomotor ability (Marland, 1972). The second most commonly used definition is simply using an IQ cut-off score, which is a fine measure of IQ but not a particularly good measure of creativity (Hunsaker & Callahan, 1995).

The third most commonly used definition is Renzulli's three-ring definition. J. S. Renzulli (1978) proposed that there are two types of giftedness: *schoolhouse* and *creative–productive*. Schoolhouse giftedness is more analytic in nature; someone with high schoolhouse giftedness would be a good test-taker. Creative–productive giftedness emphasizes generation and production (similar to Guilford's ideas discussed earlier in the book).

Most schools that use the Marland or Renzulli definitions include some kind of creativity measure, often the Torrance or Guilford tests or a ratings checklist, such as the Scales for Rating the Behavioral Characteristics of Superior Students (SRBCSS; J. S. Renzulli et al., 2004). Other schools use the CAT methodology of expert ratings; such schools include the Governor's School of the Arts and Gifted and Talented programs in Washington County, Maryland (Baer & McKool, in press). Unfortunately, not all schools are careful in their creativity assessment. Some schools use group-based intelligence or achievement tests to score student creativity, which seems a rather poor choice (Callahan et al., 1995; see longer discussion in Kaufman, Plucker et al., 2008).

Beyond gifted programs, it is possible to use creativity assessment as part of university admissions. Most arts-based schools, such as Juilliard, or art-related departments (such as NYU's Tisch School of the Arts) often incorporate rated creativity, artistic portfolios, or performance as a major part of their admissions. Most schools that do not focus on the arts do not look at creativity, although there are some exceptions. As mentioned earlier, Sternberg and his colleagues have studied how college admissions would be impacted by supplemental measures of successful intelligence (such as practical intelligence and creativity). These assessments are based on Sternberg's work on open-ended creativity assessments. Specifically, Sternberg and colleagues used three types of open-ended measures (Sternberg, 2008; Sternberg & The Rainbow Project Collaborators, 2006). Students are asked to write captions to a cartoon, write short stories based on titles such as "The Octopus's Sneakers," and tell stories based on a selected series of images. These responses are then evaluated using a similar methodology as the CAT. Performance was then rated by trained judges for cleverness, humor, originality, and task appropriateness (for the cartoons); and originality, complexity, emotional evocativeness, and descriptiveness for both written and oral stories (Sternberg & Lubart, 1995, 1996; Sternberg & The Rainbow Project Collaborators, 2006).

Sternberg dubs his work with these new measures (including creativity) at Tufts University the "Kaleidoscope Project." Similar to earlier work, students write stories (with titles such as "Confessions of a Middle School Bully"), describe an alternate history in which Rosa Parks gave up her seat on the bus, and design and advertise new products. These measures were included (optionally) in the 2006–2007 application for the 15,000 students who applied to arts, sciences, and engineering at Tufts.

The results from Sternberg's earlier work and his current work at Tufts are encouraging. His measures (not only of creativity, but for all components of successful intelligence) predict college success more accurately than standard admissions tests; in addition, ethnic differences are significantly reduced (Stemler,

Grigorenko, Jarvin, & Sternberg, 2006; Sternberg, 2006; Sternberg & The Rainbow Project Collaborators, 2006). At Tufts, the quality of applicants rose (indeed, despite de-emphasizing SAT scores, the average SAT scores of applicants increased), and minority admissions went up (Sternberg, 2008).

It is interesting to note that even in the creativity realm, there are critics of the Tufts approach despite their improved results. These essays are "probably not the right way to assess...creativity, in my view," Howard Gardner told NPR (Smith, 2007). Gardner goes on to argue that personal, one-on-one interviews would be the best way to get such information. Yet, it would be hard to imagine an interview having any real scientific rigor, and personal interviews would represent an enormous investment in assessing creativity—could any nonelite private school afford to interview 10,000 applicants? I worry that such a criticism may make it that much less likely that any school would actually take such an initiative and try to measure creativity at all.

Creativity is popping up as an admissions "extra credit" possibility around the country. The Boulder Leeds School of Business is just one example of a school that encourages students to submit offbeat inclusions to their application package. Students baked cakes, stuck ice picks through computers, drew self-portraits, and sent in 50-pound bags of concrete; another school received a box of homemade sushi—which unfortunately was delayed substantially by the post office (Anas, 2007; Damast, 2007). Although the Leeds question/component was optional, between 60% and 75% of applicants responded. The high response rate doesn't mean that all students loved it; one admissions counselor told *BusinessWeek*, "There is very little neutrality. Usually, some say, 'Hey, I'm going to have some fun with this,' while others react with just one big, 'Oh no'" (Damast, 2007).

So, what can we conclude? With enough effort, creativity *can* be part of the admissions process. Yet, *should* creativity be part of the admissions process? Certainly, most graduate schools that ask letters of recommendation to rate or describe different traits in prospective students include creativity as one of the many variables (Walters, Plante, Kyllonen, Kaufman, & Gallagher, 2004). In a proposed Standardized Letter of Recommendation project being considered by ETS (which I initially helped develop), letter writers would use a Web portal to rate students on seven specific qualities; one of these seven qualities is creativity (Walters, Kyllonen, & Plante, 2006). Similarly, when faculty members are asked which factors are important for success in graduate school, creativity invariably is included (Enright & Gitomer, 1989; Powers & Fowles, 2000; Walpole, Burton, Kanyi, & Jackenthal, 2001). Many schools specify on their admissions Web sites that they may look for creativity either in the entire application packet or in specific essay responses.

Yet, it is interesting to note that some schools that do not specifically seek creative applications (unlike Tufts or Leeds) may be turned off by such quirky demonstrations. "Does this help the student get in?... No," Debra Shaver, Smith College director of admission, told the *Boston Globe*. "It certainly entertains the staff, but it doesn't help the student get in" (Wertheimer, 2008). In a discussion with different admissions officers such as Shaver, the consensus was that most clever and uncommon additions to the traditional application may be amusing but will not help students. It may even backfire, as in the student who sent in a photograph of herself riding a bicycle naked; the committee felt it reflected poor judgment.

Indeed, some admissions officers noted that there were fewer of these displays in recent years, perhaps because of the fear of seeming too unusual. "I regret that sense that an applicant has to come across as a perfectly polished product at the age of 17," Duke University director of undergraduate admissions Christoph Guttentag told the *Boston Globe*, "because they're not" (Wertheimer, 2008). As the competition for college acceptance becomes fiercer, some researchers worry that there may be a backlash against the standardized tests routinely used for admissions (if there is not already). Larry Litten, former director of institutional research at Dartmouth, argued that students may feel that such requirements overshadow their creativity (Hoover, 2007).

Do students think that creativity should be part of the admissions process? I teach a regular course at California State University at San Bernardino called Intelligence and Creativity. I'm unabashedly procreativity (which is not a terribly controversial position to take). Near the end of the class, I do an exercise where I split the class into five or six groups. I appoint each group to be the admissions committee of a different university—one group is CSUSB, another is usually an elite Ivy League school (such as Harvard or Yale), another is a huge public school (such as the University of Michigan or the University of Texas at Austin), another is an arts school (such as Juilliard), and another is a smaller, elite, private school (such as Bennington or Bryn Mawr). I then ask them to decide how they would admit students to their school. The first time I did this exercise, I was surprised to find that no "committee" except for Juilliard included creativity. They all included GPAs and SATs; some suggested an interview process to see if someone was motivated; others suggested personality tests; a few suggested an actual IQ test. Only the arts school said they would incorporate creativity (via performance and portfolios, much as the actual schools do). Each class since tends to do the same thing. I wonder, then, about what the average student would choose to have as part of the admissions process. After all, if students who have been subject to intense preaching about the wonders of creativity still don't choose to have it as part of the admissions process, what would an average student think?

The workforce has already included creativity (or openness to experience) as part of a broad spectrum of valued abilities (Moy & Lam, 2004). Even if other personality attributes are valued more (such as conscientiousness; Schmidt & Hunter, 1998), creativity at least plays a role. I'd love to see creativity become a regular supplement to IQ and achievement tests, as well. Obviously, I've outlined in this book hundreds of things I think are interesting and cool about creativity, but here's what might be the biggest reason: Adding creativity may help address questions of fairness and equity. I'm going to spend the rest of the chapter addressing this issue.

CREATIVITY AND FAIRNESS

You may remember I mentioned previously about how Stern-berg (2008) found that minority admissions went up with the new admissions measures. I think that will just be the beginning. Keep in mind from a few chapters back that creativity is related to and part of intelligence (even if the exact nature or extent is still debated). If you look at most tests of intelligence and academic achievement, they show significant differences in scores by ethnicity. A wide variety of measures of intelligence and ability have shown lower scores for African Americans and Hispanic Americans (see Loehlin, 1999, for an overview). Standardized tests such as the SAT, ACT, GRE, and AP exams show similar results (Camara & Schmidt, 1999; Morgan & Maneckshana, 1996). The reasons behind these differences are well-debated. Some researchers argue that these measures reflect actual differences (e.g., Herrnstein & Murray, 1994; Jensen, 1998). Others point to the discrepancy between socioeconomic status and opportunities across ethnicities (Rogers, 1996; Sternberg, 1996), whereas still others argue that current ability measures do not incorporate enough aspects of intelligence (Sternberg, Kaufman, & Grigorenko, 2008). The presence of these differences, however, regardless of the reason, is well-established.

The differences between males and females are not as large for intelligence tests as the differences found between different ethnic groups, although males tend to obtain higher scores on tasks involving mental rotation (S. B. Kaufman, 2007; Masters & Sanders, 1993), and females tend to obtain higher scores on verbal tests (Hedges & Nowell, 1995). Males tend to outscore females on the SAT, GRE, and GMAT, particularly on the quantitative sections (Coley, 2001).

Simple group differences do not tell the whole story. It is too easy to say that if one ethnicity, gender, or culture scores better on a test, then the test is biased and evil. Indeed, it is possible to create a test that seems fair but is biased. For example, let's say that I want to test your knowledge of cities. I ask you to estimate the population of Birmingham, Tuscaloosa, Decatur, Mobile, Huntsville, Auburn, and Montgomery. As you may realize, all of these cities are in Alabama. People from Alabama would therefore (probably) do better on this test than people from California or New York. If my intention was to measure general knowledge of cities (or American cities), then I have not succeeded.

The problem is not always with the tests, however. Newer psychometric approaches argue that another possibility is that the test may measure different things for different people. A test may measure verbal ability in Whites, for example, but may be measuring something quite different in a Hispanic American population (Reynolds, 2000; Reynolds, Lowe, & Saenz, 1999). Going back to the CHC theory of intelligence, think about Gf (fluid intelligence/solving novel problems). If I want to test Gf, I might present a series of new problems to solve. Maybe I'll ask you to solve a lateral thinking puzzle (e.g., DeBono, 1992). These puzzles are ambiguous or unlikely situations or dilemmas that have a specific answer that can be deduced through a back-and-forth dialogue (Sloane, 1992). Maybe the puzzle I ask you to solve is the first one I ever solved, which my brother asked me 20 years ago:

A man walks into a restaurant and orders albatross soup. He takes one bite, then pulls out a gun and kills himself. Why?

It would take me another 30 pages to present a typical back-and-forth conversation (or it would take you several hours of guessing) so I will cut to the answer—he is a man who was a sailor, and was in a shipwreck. He was blinded, and his brother was killed. Another sailor fed him, telling him he was eating albatross soup. After being rescued, he tried albatross soup and it tasted different—and he realized he had eaten his brother's body. So he kills himself.

Not going into the absurdity of the question or the further questions of whether this actually measures fluid intelligence, let's explore how your response might be affected. Maybe you have read *Rime of the Ancient Mariner* or otherwise know that the albatross is a seafaring bird. In this case, the puzzle might be easier for you—and be tapping more into Gc (crystallized intelligence/acquired knowledge). Or perhaps you have solved other, similar puzzles, in which case the concept would make more sense. In the most extreme situation, maybe you solved the puzzle the day before when someone else asked you, and you are simply remembering the answer. In this case, you are using Glr (long-term storage and retrieval). The same question can produce different results depending on which people are answering it, and the test is not always purely at fault.

Another possibility is stereotype threat. Many studies have suggested that individuals feel stress when placed in a situation where they run the risk of confirming a negative stereotype about their group (e.g., ethnicity). This stress often causes poor performance (Steele, 1997; Steele & Aronson, 1995). Stereotypes about intelligence are widely known, even among people who are targets of the stereotypes and who do not endorse them (Devine, 1989). As a result, for example, an African American test-taker may worry about confirming negative stereotypes, which causes added stress—and, by extension, a lower performance on the test. Schmader and Johns (2003) argue that stereotype threat causes reduced working memory.

What may then occur is that members of ethnicities that have traditionally scored lower on IQ tests may experience "disidentification" in this domain—in other words, they gradually remove this domain (in this case, analytic and other "IQ test" type abilities) from their conception of self (Crocker & Major, 1989; Steele, 1997). Instead of identifying themselves with these types of abilities, some people may instead identify themselves with other important cognitive abilities that are not associated with IQ tests. One of these abilities might be creativity.

CREATIVITY ACROSS ETHNICITIES

What does this discrepancy in intellectual and achievement scores mean for admissions? The ability/achievement tests that are so commonly used may measure disparate things for different people—or groups of people. Some have suggested, for example, that creativity does not benefit African Americans on intelligence tests and may even hurt them. These researchers have proposed that differences on some IQ or achievement subtests, such as those involved in remembering the details of a story, may show larger African American–White differences in part because African Americans approach the task differently (Heath, 1983; see Manly et al., 1998). This theory argues that Whites approach the task as the test-makers intended—by trying to memorize as many appropriate details as possible and stick to the presented story; in contrast, African Americans may put more emphasis on telling the story creatively. Indeed, another possible negative outcome is that African Americans will be penalized for creative behavior in the classroom. Baldwin (1985, 2003) argues that teachers and other authority figures may mistake creativity in African American students as unruly or disruptive behavior.

Baldwin (2001) also analyzed a list of creative traits and abilities. These abilities included well-researched aspects, such as being open to experience or having high divergent thinking ability, and more theoretical aspects, such as being antiauthoritarian, having a "zany" sense of humor, and a low tolerance for boredom (Clark, 1988). Many of these abilities, Baldwin (2001) argued, are sometimes seen as being inappropriate—and often found in African Americans. These ideas are consistent with Shade's (1986) theory of an African American cognitive style. Her research with cognitive style tests found that African Americans were more likely to be spontaneous, flexible, and open-minded. In contrast, Whites were more regulated and structured. Similarly, Crim (2008) found that African American eighth-grade science students responded particularly well to projects that allowed for creativity.

Certainly, the differences that are present between African Americans and Whites on measures of ability and achievement are *not* found, by and large, in creativity, regardless of how it is measured. The Torrance Tests of Creative Thinking (TTCT; Torrance, 1966, 1974a, 1974b), discussed earlier, have been used along with other divergent thinking measures in these studies with both verbal and figural forms (e.g., Glover, 1976; Iscoe & Pierce-Jones, 1964; Kaltsounis, 1974; Knox & Glover, 1978; Torrance, 1971, 1973). Torrance (1971, 1973) found that African American children scored higher on the TTCT than White children on the Figural tests in fluency, flexibility, and originality; Whites scored higher on Figural elaboration and all Verbal subtests. The initial sample compared African American children in Georgia with higher-SES children in Minnesota; when a subsequent study used Whites also from Georgia, all differences were significantly reduced. Kaltsounis (1974) also found that African Americans received higher fluency and originality scores on the TTCT. Troiano and Bracken (1983) gave measures of creative thinking to three kindergarten classes (Dutch Americans, African Americans, and Native Americans). They found that African Americans and Native Americans scored approximately one standard deviation higher on creative thinking, particularly in fluency, than the Dutch Americans.

Other studies that found no differences have utilized biographical questionnaires measuring creative accomplishments (Stricker, Rock, & Bennett, 2001), the ability to be trained on creativity tasks (Moreno & Hogan, 1976), and the development of divergent thinking abilities in adolescents from South Africa and the United States (Ripple & Jacquish, 1982). J. C. Kaufman, Baer, and Gentile (2004) studied poems, stories, and personal narratives written by African American and White eighth-grade students. There were no differences in creativity scores assigned by expert judges.

Although, as discussed earlier, self-reported creativity can be of limited value, it is worth also noting that J. C. Kaufman (2006) asked 3,553 individuals (mostly high school and college students) to rate themselves in 56 different domains of creativity. African Americans rated themselves as significantly higher than at least one other ethnicity on all factors. All ethnicities except for Asian Americans rated themselves higher than another ethnicity on at least one factor.

Not all creativity measures lend such support, however. As I mentioned in chapter four, openness to experience is highly correlated with creativity. Unlike the creativity studies I've mentioned, there are huge personality studies with thousands and thousands of participants. If Baldwin and others are right about African Americans approaching tasks from a more creative perspective, then you would also assume that African Americans would be more open to experience. There generally tend to be no differences on any personality factors across cultures (e.g., Goldberg, Sweeney, Merenda, & Hughes, 1998; Kyllonen, Walters, & Kaufman, 2005; McCrae & Costa, 1997). However, Heuchert, Parker, Stumpf, and Myburgh (2000) found that White South Africans scored higher on openness to experience than Black South Africans (much of this difference was in the openness to feelings subcomponent). Allik and McCrae (2004) found that people from European and White cultures tended to be more open to experience than people from Asian and African cultures. Schmitt, Allik, McCrae, and Benet-Martínez (in press), in a massive study of 17,837 people from 56 nations, found that people from South American and European countries were the most open to experience (Chile was the highest), with people from South Asian countries generally being less open to experience. African countries were in the middle. It is worth pointing out, in addition, that Saucier and Goldberg (2001) studied personality labels in 13 languages (including English) and found that openness to experience was the only one of the Big Five personality factors to *not* be found in all languages. Openness to experience, therefore, can be considered a concept more readily accepted in Anglo cultures (Benet-Martínez & Oishi, in press).

Further research has looked at Hispanic Americans and creativity. The key variable tends to be whether creativity is measured verbally or nonverbally. For example, Argulewicz and Kush (1984) found that Whites scored higher than Hispanic Americans on three of four TTCT Verbal forms, but they found no significant differences on the Figural forms. It is worth pointing out, however, that the TTCT has been translated into Spanish (among many other languages) and has been shown to have validity in many Hispanic cultures (e.g., Wechsler, 2006). Studies using only nonverbal assessments have typically found no differences (e.g., Argulewicz, Elliott, & Hall, 1982) or show a slight advantage for bilingual Hispanic Americans (Kessler & Quinn, 1987; Price-Williams & Ramirez, 1977). However, low-income Hispanic American elementary students scored below the norms on the TTCT (Mitchell, 1988), and teachers rated White students as being more creative than Hispanic American students, with highly accultur-ated Hispanic Americans receiving higher marks than less accul-turated Hispanic Americans (Masten, Plata, Wenglar, & Thedford, 1999).

Some researchers found that White parents had more favor-able perceptions of creativity than Hispanic American parents (Strom & Johnson, 1989; Strom, Johnson, Strom, & Strom, 1992). However, they also found that Hispanic American parents were more likely to engage in play activities with their children and valued play more (Strom & Johnson, 1989). Make-believe play can be a valuable component of a child's developing imagination (Singer & Singer, 1990).

CREATIVITY ACROSS CULTURE: EAST VS. WEST

Studies of the TTCT often show Western cultures outperforming Eastern cultures. Jellen and Urban (1989) administered a mea-sure of creative thinking and drawing to children from several different countries. They found that, in general, Western coun-tries (such as Germany, England, and the United States) scored higher than Eastern countries (such as China and India). American students outperformed Japanese students on the TTCT at the college and elementary school level (Ogawa, Kuehn-Ebert, & De-Vito, 1991; Saeki, Fan, & Van Dusen, 2001); the reverse findings were found, however, in a study of education majors (Torrance & Sato, 1979). Americans from five different age groups scored higher than similar people from Hong Kong (Jaquish & Ripple, 1984), and American schoolchildren outperformed those in Taiwan, Singapore, and Germany on the TTCT-Verbal; the results on the TTCT-Figural were in reverse order. American graduate students outperformed their Chinese counterparts on divergent thinking tests (Zha, Walczyk, Griffith-Ross, Tobacyk, & Walczyk, 2006).

Plucker, Runco, and Lim (2006) found no difference in creative potential (as measured by the Runco Ideational Behavior Scale; Runco, Plucker, & Lim, 2000–2001) between Korean students and American students; similarly, Lim and Plucker (2001) found that Koreans and Americans hold similar concepts about the nature of creativity. Results on comparing Eastern and Western self-assessments were mixed (Palaniappan, 1996). Studies have shown American students producing more creative artwork than Chinese students (Niu & Sternberg, 2001); others have found no differences (Chen et al., 2002; Cox, Perara, & Fan, 1998); a student that compared American and Japanese favored the latter (Cox, Koyasu, Hiranuma, & Perara, 2001). In both studies, American and Chinese judges tended to agree on which products were creative and which products were not creative, although Niu and Sternberg (2001) found that the Chinese judges tended to give higher scores than their American counterparts.

Differences in styles and values in Eastern and Western cultures may explain some of the findings of Westerners receiving higher scores on creativity assessments. Li (1997) proposed a horizontal and vertical tradition of creativity. Horizontal traditions, which are favored by Western cultures, tend toward changing and modifying pre-existing structures—think of an artist such as Picasso, constantly challenging the limits of an art form. In vertical traditions, however, the nature of the work is much more constrained and consistent with past work. A piece's worth depends more on how well the artist is able to capture his or her subject matter (Li, 1997). Similarly, Averill, Chon, and Hahn (2001) propose that both Eastern and Western cultures value the effectiveness of a piece of creativity, the West values the novelty of a piece much more than the East. Of much more interest to the East is whether a piece is authentic, representing the creator's personal values and beliefs.

Why does this difference occur between East and West? One answer may lie in the theory of interdependence (collectivistic) vs. independence (individualistic). This theory argues that Northern Americans and Western Europeans see themselves as independent. Their motivations and goals follow accordingly. In contrast, Asian cultures are more interdependent and have a higher sense of group responsibility. These cultures are motivated by different variables, such as group harmony (Markus & Kitayama, 1991). Ng (2001) has argued that it is this emphasis that is responsible for East–West differences in creativity (see also Ng & Smith, 2004). People who are focused on group cohesiveness and are *nice* (a term Ng uses without specific positive connotations) are less creative; people who are creative are less *nice*. Goncalo and Staw (2006) examined individualistic and collectivistic-oriented people; when given instructions to be creative, individualistic people generated both a higher number of ideas and more creative ideas than collectivistic people. With instructions to be practical, there were nonsignificant trends in the opposite direction.

Indeed, whether a person is part of an independent or interdependent culture can affect his or her personality and style. People from interdependent cultures are more likely to see themselves as fundamentally linked to others and to view themselves in the context of their social relationships (Cross & Markus, 1999). This view translates to a cognitive style; Asians were found to be more field dependent and more holistic than Americans, for example (Ji, Peng, & Nisbett, 2000; Nisbett, Peng, Choi, & Norenzayan, 2001). People who are more field dependent have been found to score lower on tests of creativity (e.g., Chadha, 1985; Noppe, 1985).

There are many studies that compare Asians and Europeans or Americans. Fewer studies have compared Asian *Americans* to Americans of different ethnicities. Rostan, Pariser, and Gruber (2002) studied Chinese American and White students' artwork, with two groups in each culture: students with additional art training and classes and students with no such classes. Each group's artwork (one drawing from life and one drawing from imagination) was judged by both Chinese and American judges. There were no significant differences between cultures from either set of judges, only between art students versus nonart students. Wang (2007) studied Taiwanese and American student teachers and found that Whites outperformed Hispanic Americans, Asian Americans, and Taiwanese on the Torrance tests; however, Asian Americans were more creative than Taiwanese. Differences on fluency, flexibility, and originality were minor, whereas differences on elaboration were larger.

Pornrungroj (1992) administered the Figural form of the TTCT to Thai children and Thai American children and found that Thai children received significantly higher scores than Thai Americans. Yoon (2005) gave the TTCT to European American and Asian American middle school students (the latter being a mix of Chinese American, Korean American, Japanese American, and Southeastern Asian Americans). There were no significant differences either between the European Americans and Asian Americans or between the different subgroups of Asian Americans.

A final note on cultural differences in creativity: Having basic knowledge about other cultures may increase your own creativity. Leung, Maddux, Galinsky, and Chiu (2008) found that when students were given information about another culture (China), they subsequently wrote more creative stories set in a different culture (Turkey) than students who had not been exposed. The authors infer that multicultural experiences enhance creativity. Similarly, studies from the industrial/organizational literature show that work teams that represent diverse backgrounds will be more innovative (Choi, 2007; Yap, Chai, & Lemaire, 2005).

GENDER DIFFERENCES IN CREATIVITY

No simple conclusions can be drawn from examining the many studies that report gender differences (or lack thereof) on creativity tests. Some studies show women do better; other studies show men do better; still other studies show no difference. Baer and Kaufman (2008) reviewed the extensive literature on gender differences and found that most studies found no differences (21) or mixed results (30). Four studies showed males doing better, and nine studies showed females doing better. Generally, there is a trend showing women scoring higher on verbal measures and men scoring higher on figural/mathematical measures (mirroring the larger cognitive findings in achievement tests).

Most large-scale studies of personality do not show gender differences in openness to experience (Collins & Gleaves, 1998; Goldberg et al., 1998). There is a trend, already discussed, for rewards to impact men and women differently (with females being less creative when rewards are present). There is also an interaction with education; women with higher levels of education tend to be more creative than less-educated women—there is no such difference in men (Matud, Rodríguez, & Grande, 2007).

It is important to note that there is a large inconsistency between gender differences on creativity tests and actual creative accomplishment. Although gender differences on creativity tests are minor or nonexistent, differences in real-world creative accomplishment are large and significant (Simonton, 1994). Murray (2003), in a review of human accomplishment, notes that out of 4,002 people he categorized as "significant," only 88 (2%) were female. He further points out that women comprised only 4% of all Nobel Prize winners from 1901–1950—and then only 3% of all winners from 1951–2000. The question is not simply a matter of older sources or accounts being biased; current awards show just as much male dominance.

Why do women not reach the same creative peaks as men? Helson (1990) argued that cultural values, social roles, and sexist thinking are now recognized as key reasons for the comparative lack of creative accomplishment by women. Piirto (1991) notes that girls do not show less creative achievement until *after* high school and college, indicating that a key issue may be a conflict between personal vs. professional demands. It is also important to note Baer's work, discussed earlier, that indicates that women's creativity may be more susceptible to the negative effects of evaluation (and subsequent loss of intrinsic motivation).

Of course, old-time psychologists had quite different opinions. In response to complaints that virtually no women were elected to high administrative positions at APA, E. G. Boring (1951), in an article titled "The Woman Problem," wrote that:

> All along the question of marriage interferes with the woman's assured planning. Can a woman become a fanatic in her profession and still remain marriageable? Yes, she can, for I know some, but I think a woman must be abnormally bright to combine charm with concentration. These women make the synthesis by being charmingly enthusiastic...Some women readers will undoubtedly think me callous to the frustration of others, but I am asking only for realism. (p. 681)

What's frightening is how many men (in academia, in institutions, in most places) still believe Boring's logic.

CREATIVITY AND LEARNING DISABILITIES

In addition to possibly yielding a more balanced assessment for minorities and women, creativity may also benefit learning-disabled students. Enrichment programs have shown creativity improvement in both gifted and learning-disabled students

(Baum, 1988; Nogueira 2006; Olenchak, 1995). Differences in creativity may vary; one study found that elementary school children with learning disabilities engaged in less task persistence than average children and, as a result, scored lower on the TTCT in elaboration. On the other three components of the TTCT, however, the students with learning disabilities scored as well as the group of average children (Argulewicz, Mealor, & Richmond, 1979). Another study of gifted children with and without learning disabilities found that there were no significant differences between the two groups on measures of verbal creativity (Woodrum & Savage, 1994). Conversely, children with learning disabilities produced more original responses than a control group when presented with a typical fluency task (N. L. Kaufman & A. S. Kaufman, 1980).

Cox and Cotgreave (1996) examined human figure drawings by 10-year-old children with mild learning disabilities (MLD) and 6- and 10-year-old children without MLD. They discovered that the drawings by the MLD children were easily distinguished from drawings by the other 10-year-olds but not from the group of 6-year-old children. This finding implies that while the MLD children may be developing artistic and creative abilities at a slower rate, the development still approaches a normal pattern.

Measures of creativity could particularly lend insight into individuals with dyslexia. Everatt (1997) studied dyslexics and controls and found dyslexics scored higher on measures of both verbal and nonverbal measures of creativity. Vail (1990) found dyslexic children excelled at divergent thinking. Indeed, several scholars have suggested creativity as being a way to identify gifted children with dyslexia and to reduce frustration and improve self-perceptions (Burrows & Wolf, 1983; LaFrance, 1997).

Another learning disability with a strong connection to creativity is attention-deficit hyperactivity disorder (ADHD). Gifted and talented students are being diagnosed with ADHD at an increasing rate (Baum & Olenchak, 2002; Silverman, 1998). Several scholars have proposed that the behaviors and characteristics associated with ADHD, such as sensation, stimulation-seeking, and a greater use of imagery, are highly similar to creative behaviors (Cramond, 1994; Shaw, 1992). Studies are inconsistent, however. High IQ children with ADHD scored higher on tests of figural creativity than high IQ children without ADHD (Shaw & Brown, 1990, 1991); another study found that students with ADHD showed specific creativity strengths in fluency, originality, and elaboration on the TTCT (Gollmar, 2000); still another found no differences (Healy & Rucklidge, 2005). Abraham, Windmann, Siefen, Daum, and Güntürkün (2006) found that adolescents with ADHD had creative strengths and weaknesses compared to controls; they were better at overcoming constraints but performed worse when asked to create a functional invention. A study of adults with ADHD found that they performed better than controls on a divergent thinking task and worse on the Remote Associates Test (White & Shah, 2006).

One particular learning disability, Williams Syndrome, is caused by a lack of genetic material that produces the protein elastin. Children with Williams Syndrome are developmentally delayed and often have profound disabilities in spatial cognition (Bellugi, Lichtenberger, Jones, Lai, & St. George, 2000). Yet, children with Williams Syndrome have exceptional narrative skills for their cognitive ability level. Although their syntax was simpler and they were more likely to make errors in morphology than average children, they also used more evaluative devices and—of most interest for creativity studies—used much more elaboration in their narratives (Losh, Bellugi, Reilly, & Anderson, 2000). Between these narrative skills and the hypersociability associated with Williams Syndrome, these children often engage in storytelling (Jones et al., 2000). And while their stories use less complex syntax compared to average children, they are much *more* complex (and more expressive) than children with similar cognitive abilities with Down syndrome (Reilly, Klima, & Bellugi, 1990). There is also some evidence that children with Williams Syndrome have better musical ability than their cognitive patterns would predict. They were able to keep rhythm as well as nonimpaired controls, and their mistakes were more likely to be related to the original beat—in other words, their mistakes could theoretically be considered an act of creative improvisation (Levitan & Bellugi, 1998).

Creativity can even be analyzed with students with much more severe disabilities. Children with autism and Asperger's syndrome were able to generate changes to an object as part of the TTCT. These children made fewer changes than a sample of children without impairment, and their changes were more reality-based than imagination-based (Craig & Baron-Cohen, 1999). But the simple fact that creativity assessment was able to add information about this population's abilities is encouraging. An additional study compared children with autism and children with Asperger's syndrome (Craig & Baron-Cohen, 2000). They found that while both groups showed less imaginative events in a story-telling exercise than children without impairment, children with Asperger's syndrome were better able to demonstrate imagination than children with autism. This finding was also demonstrated with a drawing task (Craig, Baron-Cohen, & Scott, 2001). It is interesting to note that autistic children often participate in creative activities; a recent documentary, *Autism: The Musical*, follows five children with autism who help create and perform an original musical.

In a related fashion, researchers studied human figure drawings in children with Down syndrome (Cox & Maynard, 1998). While Down syndrome children scored lower than both age mates and younger children, it is interesting to note that their drawings did not differ when drawn from a model or drawn from imagination, whereas both groups of non–Down syndrome children improved when drawn from a model. This finding may indicate that creative processes may be a comparative strength for children with Down syndrome.

Dykens, Schwenk, Maxwell, and Myatt (2007) administered semiprojective tests to people with Williams, Down, and Prader-Willi syndromes. They used a sentence completion task (e.g., I like to _____) and a three wishes task (e.g., what would you do with three wishes). Although those were not measures of creativity, these tests did allow participants to display their imagination and self-perceptions (the study itself examined the contents of their responses, not the creativity of these responses).

CAN CREATIVITY HELP?

As I ask at the end of most of these chapters, what does all this mean? Are the patterns of creative abilities different across ethnicity than patterns of intellectual achievement? Might creativity measures allow for a better informed measure of cognitive capabilities for school admissions than the current SAT–GPA formulas typically used? Early results from Sternberg (2008) and the other studies I've highlighted indicate that everyone has some capacity for being creative, and I believe this concept is encouraging. But there's a lot more work to be done. As J. Alfred Prufrock might ask, is it worth it?

When I was discussing the lack of differences found by ethnicity on creativity measures with one colleague, he said that the discrepancies found between intellectual achievement and creativity were simply a matter of error. All IQ or achievement tests, he argued, were really measures of g, and if anyone found different results on tests of creativity, it was simply that these assessments were flawed measures of g, and the findings were therefore worthless.

I am reminded of my father's discussion of maternal effects on intelligence (A. S. Kaufman, 1999), specifically the research on identical twins who either shared or didn't share a placenta (e.g., Rose, Uchida, & Christian, 1981). In brief, twins that shared a placenta were more alike on both verbal and nonverbal measures of intelligence, whereas twins that did not share a placenta were less similar on nonverbal intelligence (if you are interested in more information about this, see A. S. Kaufman & Lichtenberger, 2006, chapter two), his response was what struck me. The findings were unique at the time, and they have been little explored since. Indeed, other scholars in the field have either explained them away or simply ignored them as an aberration. What A. S. Kaufman (1999) wrote was, "the findings are, however, sufficiently provocative to challenge all known heritability estimates pertaining to intelligence and personality" (pp. 627–628). That's toned down, though; what he would say in his talks was that if these findings *might* be true, then how *dare* we not consider their implications (e.g., A. S. Kaufman, 2004)?

So, to return to the question of this chapter, should creativity be used in admissions? Can creativity help improve fairness and equity in these decisions? There is no one obvious, correct answer. I'm not arguing that all of the research supports this contention; it doesn't. The studies are scattered and sometimes sloppily conducted. It may seem like each study uses a different measure of creativity. The findings on gender differences may be encouraging, or they may be identical to the findings on cognitive achievement. The findings on special education may mean nothing at all.

However, I think there's something there. Too many studies indicate that creativity may be a real or perceived intellectual strength for people who may be underserved by achievement or placement tests. I'd like to see more research. I'd like to see more colleges consider creativity as a supplemental or optional admissions tool. But most of all, I'd like to see some outstanding students who might otherwise slip through the cracks be able to go to college or graduate school. If it is within our power to make this happen, then how dare we not explore these issues?

Looking Forward:
What Now?

'I've been studying creativity my entire professional career, and I've had a blast. I love creativity. I love discovering new ways that people can be creative. When I was finishing the last chapter, I got an e-mail forward that took me to a Web site called Improv Everywhere, where I watched a video called "Food Court Musical" (Todd, 2008). It was 16 "undercover" people staging a "spontaneous" musical, starting with a woman who seemed to work for one of the fast-food chains asking for a napkin. Person after person burst into song, when they were suddenly stopped by a security guy—who then began to sing with them. This video made my soul happy. There are people out there who are creative in ways I couldn't dream, and I get enjoyment and pleasure from their creativity.

And always, I want to learn more. I read books that I love—from Ken Grimwood's *Replay* (1986) to Connie Willis's *Passage* (2001) to Tim O'Brien's *The Things They Carried* (1990)—and

I want to know where the ideas came from (and I admit to being a little terrified at admitting my possibly low-brow literary taste). I see theater productions—George Hearn and Audra McDonald in Stephen Sondheim's *Sweeney Todd* or college kids in Thomas Stoppard's *Arcadia*—and I marvel at the group-level creative collaborations that must occur at all levels for the final product to be so perfect. I watch the films of David Mamet, whose characters talk in their own rapid-fire staccato language, or the flamboyant narcissism of Bob Fosse's *All That Jazz,* or the quirky greatness of films that fly under the mainstream radar, such as *Lone Star, Fearless,* or *Stay,* and I marvel that filmmakers and actors don't always take the easy way out and that they continue to struggle to make art. I love reading Roger Ebert's movie reviews and watching Ricky Jay use playing cards to penetrate watermelons and seeing John Cullum still singing on Broadway in his late 70s and checking out Will Shortz's work on the *New York Times* crosswords page.

I'm aware that this past paragraph was heavy on the arts. So turning to science and business and pop culture: I love that Oreos and Chips Ahoy have figured out how to make 100-calorie packages that actually taste like candy. I love that the Internet has produced more random Web sites than I could ever dream and that I can find other people who share my morbid obsession on the VoyForums Celebrity Obituaries board. I love that I can play Scrabble with high school friends on Facebook (until Scrabulous was ended by greedy Hasbro people) and find places to download old '80s video games that I thought were long gone. I love wondering what the next game will look like from Will Wright or Sid Meier. I love that we've developed medicine that has made my high blood pressure go away, and that I can talk to people long-distance on my cell phone (and if I'm able to master it, Skype), and that if I get in one of my moods, I can use my new extra-special juicer to eat my entire dinner in liquid form.

So, if I ever waver about my interest in creativity research, I never question my love of nearly all things creative. However, I do sometimes think back to what the Internet journalist said and which I used to start this book—What does studying creativity do? Does the research help anyone? Does the research even say anything consistently? Many of the studies I've discussed may seem contradictory.

Runco (2007b) argues that many creativity researchers rely too much on superficial Internet searches and miss a lot of groundbreaking work done pre-Guilford; he's right. In my own journey in writing this book, I've been amazed as well at the other end—so much research is currently being done on creativity across so many areas. Whether it's called imagination or innovation or cognitive flexibility or divergent thinking, it's all based on the same core issues. There are dozens of bright young scholars who have chosen to devote their careers to studying creativity. With so many people joining the field, and with the current masters still at the top of their game, it's an exciting time.

So, what do I think about the future of creativity research? There will be some exciting things going on. One of the areas that excited me is computer programming. There are many textual analysis programs, from ETS's E-Rater (e.g., Monaghan & Bridgeman, 2005), to Linguistic Inquiry and Word Count (LIWC; Pennebaker, Francis, & Booth, 2001), to Hyperspace Analogue to Language (HAL; Burgess, 1998, who is my wife's Ph.D. advisor), to Latent Semantic Analysis (LSA; Landauer & Dumais, 1997). It may well be possible to train a computer program to assess an essay or story for creativity, if you input appropriate expert judgments as the target goal. If a computer reads enough essays and is told that these particular essays are rated by experts as less creative, and these particular essays are rated by experts as more creative, then the computer will eventually be able to distinguish. There has already been work in science education on automatically grading creative problem-solving responses; early results show that the computers have a solid level agreement with human raters (Wang, Chang, & Li, 2008).

Just as IQ and achievement tests are slowly becoming computerized, so too can creativity tests. Pretz and Link (in press) have devised the Creative Task Creator, a software program available for free that allows a researcher to create divergent thinking tests and open-ended questions that can be scored using the Consensual Assessment Technique. The software is a Java program that creates HTML forms and stores the data in a MySQL database. If you read that last sentence and are thinking I just began typing random abbreviations, you still don't need to fear—the software is almost foolproof (e.g., I can almost use it). Pretz and Link are on to something big—and by sharing the software, they're letting everyone benefit. As Pretz has said (personal communication, May 8, 2008), by allowing people to use their own ideas to program different creativity tests, "it's not just a creator of creativity tasks, but rather a creator of *creative* creativity tasks."

There's going to be a lot more research done on creativity and the brain. There are already several books that claim to focus on this topic (e.g., Andreasen, 2005; Heilman, 2005), but in general, I agree with reviewers who felt that the books tended to focus on brain research and (a little) creativity research, without particularly integrating the two fields (e.g., Bristol & Viskontas, 2006; A. B. Kaufman, 2007). There's been some great work in this area by Martindale (1999) over his career, but I have yet to see other researchers pick up the torch. I have yet to be bowled over by current work. That could easily change.

Some promising work in neuroscience suggests that taking a beta-blocker, such as propranolol, facilitates creativity and cognitive flexibility better than other drugs, such as adrenergic and dopamine agonists and a peripheral nervous system beta blocker (nadolol; Beversdorf, Hughes, Steinburg, Lewis, & Heilman, 1999; Beversdorf, White, Chever, Hughes, & Bornstein, 2002; Smyth & Beversdorf, 2007). However, propranolol did not raise performance better than a placebo on standard-level RAT items. Campbell, Tivarus, Hillier, and Beversdorf (2008) found that participants tested after taking propranolol demonstrated higher cognitive flexibility performance on harder items (if you got a little confused about the jargon, I'm about to bring it back to mainstream talk!). We already know that drugs such as caffeine and Ritalin boost general alertness and cognition (Childs & de Wit, 2008; Mehta et al., 2000), and propranolol itself has been used to help alleviate test anxiety and improve SAT scores (Faigel, 1991). As with many drugs that have legitimate uses, people already abuse them to improve performance. Might the same writers who currently rail against steroid abuse in athletes someday take different drugs to boost their own creativity?

I also think there's going to be more research on new forms of media. It's only been in the last few decades that research on creativity in the movies has begun in earnest—Simonton (2004b) has led the charge; he has found, for example, that cinematic creativity can be broken down into four clusters (dramatic, visual, technical, and musical). He has also discovered that a film's budget is not associated with winning awards and hypothesized that this discrepancy is because movie screenplays can be broken down into film-as-art and film-as-business (Simonton, 2005a, 2005b). Plucker, Neustadter, and Holden (in press) found that movie reviews were more correlated with later box office success than with early box office success—in other words, a movie's "make or break" opening weekend grosses were not the best predictor of the movie's "legs" (how long it stays in theaters and continues to make money). Meanwhile, there has just started to be some scientific study of how inventing video games is a creative process (Zackariasson, Styhre, & Wilson, 2006). I am hoping that more will follow—as well as studies of video game participating and creativity. A recent dissertation showed no relationship between levels of creativity and time spent playing video games or proficiency at playing these games...but I'd like to see more work done. North (2007) discussed the use of creativity in making online discussions more enjoyable. Khurana (2008) has studied the relationship between creating comic books and increased creativity, whereas Brandt (2007) has made a documentary exploring creativity in independent comic book artists.

I highly anticipate studies on the relationship between creativity and blogging, aesthetic sensibilities and Facebook and MySpace homepage creation, group creativity and Wikipedia entry production, and how imagination is used in creating role-playing game characters. Already you can go to YouTube and see everyday creativity everywhere (I love the trailers, such as *The Shining* recut as a romantic comedy, and the mash-ups, such as Pink Floyd's *The Wall* juxtaposed onto *The Wizard of Oz*).

One of my biggest dreams is to see an individually administered creativity test (much like an IQ test) given by a trained examiner. I've written about this idea before (J. C. Kaufman & Baer, 2006; J. C. Kaufman, Plucker, & Baer, 2008), but I will do it again here, anyway. In essence, I would love to see my father's idea of intelligent testing applied to creativity. The concept of "intelligent testing" is a popular philosophy of IQ testing that disdains global scores; it has had a tremendous influence on the field (A. S. Kaufman, 1979, 1994). Using this system, the tester is elevated above the test. The global scores (such as an overall IQ) mean little by themselves. The key is interpreting the scores in context. The psychologists administering the test are expected to use their qualifications and training and bring their own experience to the testing session. For a creativity test, a qualified tester would be well versed in the fields of social, cognitive, and educational psychology (among others).

In this manner, the tester can help the child or adult being tested by understanding and interpreting a wide range of behaviors, making inferences about any observed problem-solving strategies, and applying the latest theories and research directly to the person's set of scores. Every aspect of psychology is brought into play to interpret a profile of scores in the context of accumulated research, theory, and clinical practice. This profile is used to help solve problems and create solutions for the person tested based on the reasons they have been referred for testing. It does not solely exist to be a label or classification system (A. S. Kaufman, 1979, 1994).

This approach can be applied to creativity research. Let's say, for example, that a test was created using the Amusement Park Theory discussed earlier (Baer & Kaufman 2005; J. C. Kaufman & Baer, 2004). Maybe some of the general thematic areas could be picked and measured with several different tasks. So, for example, artistic–verbal creativity might be measured by having someone write a poem, a brief story, an essay, and a photo caption. Artistic–visual creativity might be measured by having someone draw a picture free-form, make a collage, expand a current shape into a picture, or draw from a model. These subtests could be summed for an overall score.

Such a test could be done online. The drawings, stories, and other creative products could be rated by all of the Web site users, creating a database of thousands of creative products and thousands of creative ratings. I grew less enthusiastic when I realized how poor nonexpert judges can be (e.g., Kaufman, et al., 2008) and how people may not always be accurate judges of their own creativity (Kaufman, Evans, & Baer, in press). Such an online assessment is still possible, but it may be of less value than originally hoped. I am no longer confident of its purpose beyond amusement, which may be a perfectly valid use.

One possibility is to develop rubrics for how these creative products could be rated. I worked on a project like this at ETS (Gentile & Kaufman, 2001, 2002), which eventually resulted in a great deal of research on how raters agree on creative work (e.g., Baer, Kaufman, & Gentile, 2004; Kaufman et al., 2005) but no finished rubric. Certainly, such a thing is possible. Rubrics are frequently used in other types of assessments.

My goal with a creativity test of this kind would be to play to a person's strengths and show a pattern of her or his abilities that could be used. If people show aptitude or interest in one dimension of creative ability, perhaps they would also like to be creative in a related area. I see the eventual process as being like going to Amazon.com. Right now, if I log on, it remembers everything I've ever purchased and makes recommendations based on my past history. It's not perfect, especially if you don't let it know that you're buying gifts for people; Amazon currently thinks that I'm the one (and not my 2-year-old son) with a fierce passion for all things Elmo. But often you learn about new products that you hadn't heard of—and, often, you buy them. In a creativity test, students could discover and validate areas of creative talent in themselves. They might explore new activities, try new things, or simply have their belief in themselves reinforced.

I don't have the whole idea perfected and primed (if I did, I'd be working on it actively and not writing about it). I'm also not convinced there's a market for it. When talking with my best friend from high school, now a successful computer programmer, I discussed one of my ideas for inventing a program that could grade creative writing. He said it was absolutely doable— but it would take a year and cost about a million dollars in labor. That's the problem: There's no huge market for a creativity test that would justify the expense or effort.

There is much to creativity research besides testing, of course, and there is so much more that I am looking forward to seeing happen. There are more outlets for creativity work (such as journals and conferences) than ever. I imagine that the field of creativity—stuck somewhere between psychology, education, business, social work, computer science, engineering, and neuroscience—will continue much in the same way as it always has. There will be bursts of new activity, new methods, and new statistical techniques for shaping our answers. There is unlikely to be any one test or theory, or even one finding, that everyone agrees with, gets behind, and supports. But where's the fun in that, anyway?

It's become a cliché to start a book by quoting Guilford's (1950) presidential address. It may be just as much of a cliché to bring him in near the end, but note how he began: "I discuss the subject of creativity with considerable hesitation, for it represents an area in which psychologists generally... have feared to tread" (p. 444). Indeed, it is, has been, and is still such an area. So bless the researcher who dares to study creativity—and by doing so risks the NSF grant, or tenure, or getting a job in the first place. A big thanks to my colleagues and fellow researchers who are working with me to answer those people who wonder if creativity researchers are trying to dissect the golden goose, or those who ask if creativity is truly a part of education or psychology.

I think it's the best job in the world.

Appendix:
Recommended
Books on Creativity

A brief tour of some other, recent books in the area: Piirto's (2004) *Understanding Creativity* discusses her model of the Seven I's— Inspiration, Imagery, Imagination, Intuition, Insight, Incubation, and Improvisation. Sawyer's (2006) *Explaining Creativity* takes a sociocultural focus, arguing that creativity can be understood only in the social and cultural contexts in which it occurs. According to Sawyer, an idea that is creative in one sociocultural milieu might not be in another. Runco's *Creativity* (2007a) is designed to be a textbook of the field with an emphasis on creativity's rich history. Weisberg (2006), in his book *Creativity*, argues that the thinking processes used by the average person when being creative are the same as those used by geniuses. Even if the final product may not be remembered for generations, we are all capable of productive and creative thought.

Simonton (2004a) emphasizes creativity in the area of science; Perry (1999) discusses creativity in writing; Kaufman and Baer (2006) collect essays on creativity in cognitive development; Dorfman, Locher, and Martindale (2006) offer essays on creativity and aesthetics; and Zhou and Shalley (2007) and Puccio, Murdock, and Mance (2006) focus on creativity in organizations (such as business). Kaufman, Plucker, and Baer (2008) discuss creativity assessment. Two edited books (Kaufman & Baer, 2005a, and Sternberg, Grigorenko, & Singer, 2004) explore whether creativity is one thing or many things. Kaufman and Sternberg (2006), in the *International Handbook of Creativity*, include essays from many international scholars in 15 different countries. Turning from *outcome* to *process,* another edited book (Richards, 2007) addresses *everyday creativity,* yielding 12 integrating themes or "potential benefits," with both personal and social implications.

Sternberg's two handbooks of creativity (1988 and 1999a) are must-reads for a creativity scholar, and I am currently working with him on an updated forthcoming handbook (J. C. Kaufman & Sternberg, in press). His forthcoming handbook of intelligence (S. B. Kaufman & Sternberg, in press) will also likely be of interest. Sternberg has also authored several books exploring different theories of creativity (Sternberg, 2003; Sternberg, Kaufman, & Pretz, 2002; Sternberg & Lubart, 1995). Amabile (1983, 1996); Baer (1993); and Finke, Ward, and Smith (1996) have written books that are now slightly older but still important and relevant to the field.

References

Abraham, A., & Windmann, S. (2008). Selective information processing advantages in creative cognition as a function of schizotypy. *Creativity Research Journal, 20*, 1–6.

Abraham, A., Windmann, S., Siefen, R., Daum, I., & Güntürkün, O. (2006). Creative thinking in adolescents with Attention Deficit Hyperactivity Disorder (ADHD). *Child Neuropsychology, 12*, 111–123.

Adams, S. (1996). *The Dilbert principle.* New York: HarperBusiness.

Adarves-Yorno, I., Postmes, T., & Haslam, S. A. (2007). Creative innovation or crazy irrelevance? The contribution of group norms and social identity to creative behavior. *Journal of Experimental Social Psychology, 43*(3), 410–416.

Akinola, M., & Mendes, W. B. (in press). The dark side of creativity: Biological vulnerability and negative mood lead to greater artistic creativity. *Personality and Social Psychology Bulletin.*

Aljughaiman, A., & Mowrer-Reynolds, E. (2005). Teachers' conceptions of creativity and creative students. *Journal of Creative Behavior, 39*, 17–34.

Allik, J., & McCrae, R. R. (2004). Toward a geography of personality traits: Patterns of profiles across 36 cultures. *Journal of Cross-Cultural Psychology, 35*, 13–28.

Amabile, T. M. (1979). Effects of external evaluation on artistic creativity. *Journal of Personality and Social Psychology, 37*, 221–233.

Amabile, T. M. (1982). Social psychology of creativity: A consensual assessment technique. *Journal of Personality and Social Psychology, 43*, 997–1013.

Amabile, T. M. (1983). *The social psychology of creativity.* New York: Springer Verlag.

Amabile, T. M. (1985). Motivation and creativity: Effects of motivational orientation in creative writers. *Journal of Personality and Social Psychology, 48,* 393–397.

Amabile, T. M. (1996). *Creativity in context: Update to "The Social Psychology of Creativity."* Boulder, CO: Westview Press.

Amabile, T. M., Barsade, S. G., Mueller, J. S., & Staw, B. M. (2005). Affect and creativity at work. *Administrative Science Quarterly, 50,* 367–403.

Amabile, T. M., & Conti, R. (1997a). Changes in the work environment for creativity during downsizing. *Academy of Management Journal, 42,* 630–640.

Amabile, T. M., & Conti, R. (1997b). Environmental determinants of work motivation, creativity, and innovation: The case of R&D downsizing. In R. Garud, P. R. Nayyar, & Z. B. Shapira (Eds.), *Technological innovation: Oversights and foresights* (pp. 111–125). New York: Cambridge University Press.

Amabile, T. M., & Conti, R. (1999). Changes in the work environment for creativity during downsizing. *Academy of Management Journal, 42,* 630–640.

Amabile, T. M., & Gitomer, J. (1984). Children's artistic creativity: Effects of choice in task materials. *Personality and Social Psychology Bulletin, 10,* 209–215.

Amabile, T., Goldfarb, P., & Brackfield, S. (1990). Social influences on creativity: Evaluation, coaction and surveillance. *Creativity Research Journal, 3,* 6–21.

Amabile, T. M., & Gryskiewicz, N. D. (1989). The creative environment scales: Work environment inventory. *Creativity Research Journal, 2,* 231–253.

Amabile, T. M., Hennessey, B. A., & Grossman, B. S. (1986). Social influences on creativity: The effects of contracted-for reward. *Journal of Personality and Social Psychology, 50,* 14–23.

Amabile, T. M., Hill, K. G., Hennessey, B. A., & Tighe, E. M. (1994). The Work Preference Inventory: Assessing intrinsic and extrinsic motivational orientations. *Journal of Personality and Social Psychology, 66,* 950–967.

Amabile, T. M., Schatzel, E. A., Moneta, G. B., & Kramer, S. J. (2004). Leader behaviors and the work environment for creativity: Perceived leader support. *Leadership Quarterly, 15,* 5–32.

Anas, B. (2007). CU MBA applicants get creative: Business school challenges hopefuls to add personal element for extra credit. Retrieved

July 24, 2008, from http://www.dailycamera.com/news/2007/oct/20/cu-applicants-get-creative/

Anderson, J. A., & Adams, M. (1992). Acknowledging the learning styles of diverse student populations: Implications for instructional design. *New Directions for Teaching and Learning, 49,* 19–33.

Andreasen, N. C. (1987) Creativity and mental illness: Prevalence rates in writers and their first-degree relatives. *American Journal of Psychiatry, 144,* 1288–1292.

Andreasen, N. C. (2005). *The neuroscience of genius.* New York: Dana Press.

Argulewicz, E. N., Elliott, S. N., & Hall, R. (1982). Comparison of behavioral ratings of Anglo-American and Mexican-American gifted children. *Psychology in the Schools, 19,* 469–472.

Argulewicz, E. N., & Kush, J. C. (1984). Concurrent validity of the SRBCSS Creativity Scale for Anglo-American and Mexican-American gifted students. *Educational & Psychological Research, 4,* 81–89.

Argulewicz, E. N., Mealor, D. J., & Richmond, B. D. (1979). Creative abilities of learning disabled children. *Journal of Learning Disabilities, 12,* 21–24.

Augier, M., & March, J. G. (Eds.). (2004). *Models of a man: Essays in memory of Herbert A. Simon.* Cambridge: The MIT Press.

Averill, J. R. (2004). A tale of two snarks: Emotional intelligence and emotional creativity compared. *Psychological Inquiry, 15*(3), 228–233.

Averill, J. R., Chon, K. K., & Hahn, D. W. (2001). Emotions and creativity: East and West. *Asian Journal of Social Psychology, 4,* 165–184.

Bachtold, L. M. (1974). The creative personality and the ideal pupil revisited. *Journal of Creative Behavior, 8,* 47–54.

Bachtold, L. M. (1976). The creative personality and the ideal pupil revisited. *School Psychology Review, 5*(2), 35–39.

Baer, J. (1991). Generality of creativity across performance domains. *Creativity Research Journal, 4,* 23–39.

Baer, J. (1993). *Creativity and divergent thinking: A task-specific approach.* Hillsdale, NJ: Lawrence Erlbaum Associates.

Baer, J. (1994). Divergent thinking is not a general trait: A multi-domain training experiment. *Creativity Research Journal, 7,* 35–46.

Baer, J. (1997). Gender differences in the effects of anticipated evaluation on creativity. *Creativity Research Journal, 10,* 25–31.

Baer, J. (1998a). The case for domain specificity in creativity. *Creativity Research Journal, 11,* 173–177.

Baer, J. (1998b). Gender differences in the effects of extrinsic motivation on creativity. *Journal of Creative Behavior, 32,* 18–37.

Baer, J., & Kaufman, J. C. (2005). Bridging generality and specificity: The Amusement Park Theoretical (APT) model of creativity. *Roeper Review, 27,* 158–163.

Baer, J., & Kaufman, J. C. (2008). Gender differences in creativity. *Journal of Creative Behavior, 42,* 75–106.

Baer, J., Kaufman, J. C., & Gentile, C. A. (2004). Extension of the consensual assessment technique to nonparallel creative products. *Creativity Research Journal, 16,* 113–117.

Baer, J., & McKool, S. (in press). Assessing creativity using the consensual assessment. In C. Schreiner (Ed.), *Assessment technologies, methods, and applications in higher education.* Hershey, PA: IGI Global.

Baker, M. (1978). Teacher creativity and its relationship to the recognition of student creativity. *Creative Child & Adult Quarterly, 3,* 106–115.

Baker, M. (1979). Teacher creativity and its effect on student creativity. *Creative Child & Adult Quarterly, 4,* 20–29.

Baldwin, A. Y. (1985). Programs for the gifted and talented: Issues concerning minority populations. In F. D. Horowitz & M. M. O'Brien (Eds.), *The gifted and talented: Developmental perspectives* (pp. 223–249). Washington, DC: American Psychological Association.

Baldwin, A. Y. (2001). Understanding the challenge of creativity among African Americans. *Journal of Secondary Gifted Education, 12,* 121–125.

Bandura, A. (1997). *Self-efficacy: The exercise of control.* New York: Freeman.

Barron, F. (1955). The disposition toward originality. *Journal of Abnormal and Social Psychology, 51,* 478–485.

Barron, F. (1963). *Creativity and psychological health.* Princeton, NJ: D. Van Nostrand Company.

Barron, F. (1965). The psychology of creativity. In T. Newcomb (Ed.), *New directions in psychology, II* (pp. 3–134). New York: Holt, Rinehart & Winston.

Barron, F. (1969). *Creative person and creative process.* New York: Holt, Rinehart & Winston.

Barron, F. (1995). *No rootless flower: An ecology of creativity.* Creskill, NJ: Hampton.

Barron, F., & Harrington, D. M. (1981). Creativity, intelligence, and personality. *Annual Review of Psychology, 32,* 439–476.

Basadur, M. S., Runco, M. A., & Vega, L. A. (2000). Understanding how creative thinking skills, attitudes and behaviors work together: A causal process model. *The Journal of Creative Behavior, 34*, 77–100.

Batey, M., & Furnham, A. (2006). Creativity, intelligence and personality: A critical review of the scattered literature. *Genetic, Social, and General Psychology Monographs, 132*, 355–429.

Baucus, M. S., Norton, W. I., Jr., Baucus, D. A., & Human, S. E. (2008). Fostering creativity and innovation without encouraging unethical behavior. *Journal of Business Ethics, 81*, 97–115.

Baum, S. (1988). An enrichment program for gifted learning disabled students. *Gifted Child Quarterly, 32*, 226–230.

Baum, S. M., & Olenchak, F. R. (2002). The alphabet children: GT, AD/HD, and more. *Exceptionality, 10*, 77–91.

Becker, M. (1995). Nineteenth-century foundations of creativity research. *Creativity Research Journal, 8*, 219–229.

Beghetto, R. A., & Kaufman, J. C. (2007). Toward a broader conception of creativity: A case for "mini-c" creativity. *Psychology of Aesthetics, Creativity, and the Arts, 1*, 73–79.

Bellugi, U., Lichtenberger, E. O., Jones, W., Lai, Z., & St. George, M. (2000). The neurocognitive profile of Williams syndrome: A complex pattern of strengths and weaknesses. *Journal of Cognitive Neuroscience, 12*, 7–29.

Benet-Martínez, V., & Oishi, S. (2008). Culture and personality. In O. P. John, R. W. Robins, & L. A. Pervin (Eds.), *Handbook of personality: Theory and research* (pp. 542–568). New York: Guildford Press.

Bennett, R. E., & Rock, D. A. (1995). Generalizability, validity, and examinee perceptions of a computer-delivered formulating-hypotheses test. *Journal of Educational Measurement, 32*(1), 19–36.

Beversdorf, D. Q., Hughes, J. D., Steinburg, B. A., Lewis, L. D., & Heilman, K. M. (1999). Noradrenergic modulation of cognitive flexibility in problem solving. *NeuroReport, 10*, 2763–2767.

Beversdorf, D. Q., White, D. M., Chever, D. C., Hughes, J. D., & Bornstein, R. A. (2002). Central betaadrenergic modulation of cognitive flexibility. *NeuroReport, 13*, 2505–2507.

Bilalić, M., McLeod, P., & Gobet, F. (2008). Inflexibility of experts—Reality or myth? Quantifying the Einstellung effect in chess masters. *Cognitive Psychology, 56*, 73–102.

Blair, C. S., & Mumford, M. D. (2007). Errors in idea evaluation: Preference for the unoriginal? *Journal of Creative Behavior, 41*, 197–222.

Bloom, B. S. (Ed.). (1985). *Developing talent in young people.* New York: Ballantine Books.

Boden, M. A. (1999). Computer models of creativity. In R. J. Sternberg (Ed.), *Handbook of creativity* (pp. 351–372). New York: Cambridge University Press.

Boller, P. F., Jr. (1988). *Presidential wives.* New York: Oxford University Press.

Borgia, G. (1985). Bower quality, number of decorations and mating success of male Satin Bowerbirds (*Ptilonorhynchus violaceus*): An experimental analysis. *Animal Behaviour, 33,* 266–271.

Boring, E. G. (1951). The women problem. *American Psychologist, 6,* 679–682.

Boswell, T. (1989). *The heart of the order.* New York: Doubleday.

Bourassa, M., & Vaugeois, P. (2001). Effects of marijuana use on divergent thinking. *Creativity Research Journal, 13,* 411–416.

Bowden, E. M., & Jung-Beeman, M. (2003). One hundred forty-four compound remote associate problems: Short insight-like problems with one-word solutions. *Behavioral Research, Methods, Instruments, and Computers, 35,* 634–639.

Bracken, B. A., & Brown, E. F. (2006). Behavioral identification and assessment of gifted and talented students. *Journal of Psychoeducational Assessment, 24,* 112–122.

"Brady leads Patriots to 30-26 comeback win." *NFL.com.* Retrieved on February 15, 2006, from http://sports.yahoo.com/nfl/recap?gid= 20031103007

Brandau, H., Daghofer, F., Hollerer, L., Kaschnitz, W., Kellner, K., Kitchmair, G., et al. (2007). The relationship between creativity, teacher ratings on behavior, age, and gender in pupils from seven to ten years. *Journal of Creative Behavior, 41,* 91–113.

Brandt, C. (Producer/Director). (2007). *Independents* [Motion picture]. (Available from Brain Street Productions, http://www.independents doc.com/shop.html).

Briel, J., Bejar, I., Chandler, M., Powell, G., Manning, K., Robinson, D., et al. (2000). *GRE Horizons Planning Initiative* (Graduate Record Examination). A research project funded by the GRE Board Research Committee, the GRE Program, and the Educational Testing Service Research Division. Princeton, NJ: Educational Testing Service.

Brinkman, D. J. (1999). Problem finding, creativity style and musical compositions of high school students. *Journal of Creative Behavior, 33,* 62–68.

Bristol, A. S., & Viskontas, I. V. (2005). Review of *The creating brain: The neuroscience of genius. Psychology of Aesthetics, Creativity and the Arts, 1*, 51–52.

Brophy, D. R. (2000). Comparing the attributes, activities, and performance of divergent, convergent, and combination thinkers. *Creativity Research Journal, 13*, 439–455.

Brown, E. J., & Heimberg, R. G. (2001). Effects of writing about rape: Evaluating Pennebaker's paradigm with a severe trauma. *Journal of Traumatic Stress, 14*, 781–790.

Buck, L. A., Kardeman, E., & Goldstein, F. (1985). Artistic talent in "autistic" adolescents and young adults. *Empirical Studies of the Arts, 3*, 81–104.

Burch, G., Pavelis., C., Hemsley, D. R., & Corr, P. J. (2005). Schizotypy and creativity in visual artists. *British Journal of Psychology, 97*, 177–190.

Burgess, C. (1998). From simple associations to the building blocks of language: Modeling meaning in memory with the HAL model. *Behavior Research Methods, Instruments, & Computers, 30*, 188–198.

Burrows, D., & Wolf, B. (1983). Creativity and the dyslexic child: A classroom view. *Annals of Dyslexia, 33*, 269–274.

Cage, J. (1961). *Silence.* Middletown, CT: Wesleyan University Press.

Calaprice, A. (Ed.). (2000). *The expanded quotable Einstein.* Princeton, NJ: Princeton University Press.

Callahan, C. M., Hunsaker, S. L., Adams, C. M., Moore, S. D., & Bland, L. C. (1995). Instruments used in the identification of gifted and talented students. *American Educational Research Journal, 45*, 150–165.

Camara, W., & Schmidt, A. E. (1999). *Group differences in standardized testing and social stratification.* (College Board Rep. No. 99-5). New York: College Board.

Cameron, J., & Pierce, W. D. (1994). Reinforcement, reward, and intrinsic motivation: A meta-analysis. *Review of Educational Research, 64*, 363–423.

Campbell, H. L., Tivarus, M. E., Hillier, A., & Beversdorf, D. Q. (2008). Increased task difficulty results in greater impact of noradrenergic modulation of cognitive flexibility. *Pharmacology, Biochemistry, and Behavior, 88*, 222–229.

Carlsson, I. (2002). Anxiety and flexibility of defense related to creative functioning. *Creativity Research Journal, 14*, 341–349.

Carroll, J. B. (1993). *Human cognitive abilities: A survey of factor-analytic studies.* New York: Cambridge University Press.

Carson, D. K., & Runco, M. A. (1999). Creative problem solving and problem finding in young adults: Interconnections with stress, hassles, and coping abilities. *Journal of Creative Behavior, 33,* 167–190.

Carson, S. H., Peterson J. B., & Higgins, D. M. (2003). Decreased latent inhibition is associated with increased creative achievement in high-functioning individuals. *Journal of Personality and Social Psychology, 85,* 499–506.

Carson, S., Peterson, J. B., & Higgins, D. M. (2005). Reliability, validity and factor structure of the creative achievement questionnaire. *Creativity Research Journal, 17,* 37–50.

Cassandro, V. J. (1998). Explaining premature mortality across fields of creative endeavor. *Journal of Personality, 66,* 805–833.

Cattell, J., Glascock, J., & Washburn, M. F. (1918). Experiments on a possible test of aesthetic judgment of pictures. *American Journal of Psychology, 29,* 333–336.

Cattell, R. B., & Butcher, H. (1968). *The prediction of achievement and creativity.* Indianapolis, IN: Bobbs-Merrill.

Chadha, N. K. (1985). Creativity and cognitive style. *Psycho Lingua, 15,* 81–88.

Chamorro-Premuzic, T. (2006). Creativity versus conscientiousness: Which is a better predictor of student performance? *Applied Cognitive Psychology, 20,* 521–531.

Chamorro-Premuzic, T., & Reichenbacher, L. (2008). Effects of personality and threat of evaluation on divergent and convergent thinking. *Journal of Research in Personality, 42,* 1095–1101.

Chan, D. W., & Chan, L. K. (1999). Implicit theories of creativity: Teachers' perception of student characteristics in Hong Kong. *Creativity Research Journal, 12,* 185–195.

Chassell, L. M. (1916). Test for originality. *Journal of Educational Psychology, 7,* 317–328.

Chen, C., Kasof, J., Himsel, A., Dmitrieva, J., Dong, Q., & Xue, G. (2005). Effects of explicit instruction to "be creative" across domains and cultures. *Journal of Creative Behavior, 39,* 89–110.

Chen, C., Kasof, J., Himsel, A. J., Greenberger, E., Dong, Q., & Xue, G. (2002). Creativity in drawing of geometric shapes: A cross-cultural examination with the consensual assessment technique. *Journal of Cross-cultural Psychology, 33,* 171–187.

Chessick, R. D. (1999). *Emotional illness and creativity.* Madison, CT: International Universities Press.

Chica, N. R. (2004). "Does one have to be insane to be creative?" *Cup of Chica*. Retrieved March 24, 2007, from http://www.nchicha.com/other/archives/002774.html#002774

Child, I. L., & Iwao, S. (1968). Personality and esthetic sensitivity: Extension of findings to younger age and to different culture. *Journal of Personality and Social Psychology, 8,* 308–312.

Childs, E., & de Wit, H. (2008). Enhanced mood and psychomotor performance by a caffeine-containing energy capsule in fatigued individuals. *Clinical Psychopharmacology, 16,* 13–21.

Choi, J. N. (2007). Group composition and employee creative behaviour in a Korean electronics company: Distinct effects of relational demography and group diversity. *Journal of Occupational and Organizational Psychology, 80,* 213–234.

Clapham, M. M. (2004). The convergent validity of the Torrance Tests of Creative Thinking and Creativity Interest Inventories. *Educational and Psychological Measurement, 64,* 828–841.

Clark, B. (1988). *Growing up gifted* (3rd ed.). Columbus, OH: Merrill.

Clark, K., & James, K. (1999). Justice and positive and negative creativity. *Creativity Research Journal, 12,* 311–320.

CNN.com. (2002). Composer pays price for silence. Retrieved January 17, 2006, from http://archives.cnn.com/2002/SHOWBIZ/Music/09/23/uk.silence

Coley, R. J. (2001). *Differences in the gender gap: Comparisons across racial/ethnic groups in education and work.* Princeton, NJ: Education Testing Service.

Collins, A. J., & Gleaves, D. (1998). Race, job applicants, and the Five-Factor Model of personality: Implications for Black psychology, industrial/organizational psychology, and the Five-Factor Theory. *Journal of Applied Psychology, 83,* 531–544.

Connell, M. W., Sheridan, K., & Gardner, H. (2003). On abilities and domains. In R. Sternberg (Ed.), *Psychology of abilities, competencies and expertise* (pp. 126–155). New York: Cambridge University Press.

Conti, R., Collins, M., & Picariello, M. (2001). The impact of competition on intrinsic motivation and creativity: Considering gender, gender segregation, and gender role orientation. *Personality and Individual Differences, 30,* 1273–1289.

Cooper, B. L., Clasen, P., Silva-Jalonen, D. E., & Butler, M. (1999). Creative performance on an inbasket exercise: Effects of inoculation against extrinsic reward. *Journal of Managerial Psychology, 14,* 39–56.

Cox, M. V., & Cotgreave, S. (1996). The human figure drawings of normal children and those with mild learning difficulties. *Educational Psychology, 16*, 433–438.

Cox, M. V., Koyasu, M., Hiranuma, H., & Perara, J. (2001). Children's human figure drawings in the UK and Japan: The effects of age, sex, and culture. *British Education, 16*, 47–56.

Cox, M. V., & Maynard, S. (1998). The human figure drawings of children with Down syndrome. *British Journal of Developmental Psychology, 16*, 133–137.

Cox, M. V., Perara, J., & Fan, X. (1998). Children's drawing ability in the UK and China. *Psychologia Society, 41*, 171–182.

Craig, J., & Baron-Cohen, S. (1999). Creativity and imagination in autism and Asperger syndrome. *Journal of Autism and Developmental Disorders, 29*, 319–326.

Craig, J., & Baron-Cohen, S. (2000). Story-telling ability in children with autism or Asperger syndrome: A window into the imagination. *Israel Journal of Psychiatry, 37*, 64–70.

Craig, J., Baron-Cohen, S., & Scott, F. (2001). Drawing ability in autism: A window into the imagination. *Israel Journal of Psychiatry, 38*, 242–253.

Cramond, B. (1994). Attention-deficit hyperactivity disorder and creativity: What is the connection? *Journal of Creative Behavior, 28*, 193–210.

Cramond, B., Matthews-Morgan, J., Torrance, E. P., & Zuo, L. (1999). Why should the Torrance Tests of Creative Thinking be used to access creativity? *Korean Journal of Thinking and Problem Solving, 9*, 77–101.

Crim, S. R. (2008). African American eighth-grade female students' perceptions and experiences as learners of science literacy. *Dissertation Abstracts International Section A: Humanities and Social Sciences, 68*, 3331.

Crocker, J., & Major, B. (1989). Social stigma and self-esteem: The self-protective properties of stigma. *Psychological Review, 96*(4), 608–630.

Cropley, A. J. (1992). *More ways than one: Fostering creativity.* Norwood, NJ: Ablex.

Cropley, D. H., Kaufman, J. C., & Cropley, A. J. (2008). Malevolent creativity: A functional model of creativity in terrorism and crime. *Creativity Research Journal, 20*, 105–115.

Cross, S. E., & Markus H. R. (1999). The cultural constitution of personality. In L. Pervin & O. John (Eds.), *Handbook of personality* (2nd ed.). (pp. 378–396). New York: Guilford Press.

Csikszentmihalyi, M. (1990). *Flow: The psychology of optimal experience.* New York: Harper & Row.

Csikszentmihalyi, M. (1996). *Creativity: Flow and the psychology of discovery and invention.* New York: HarperCollins.

Csikszentmihalyi, M. (1999). Implications of a systems perspective for the study of creativity. In R. J. Sternberg (Ed.), *Handbook of creativity* (pp. 313–335). Cambridge: Cambridge University Press.

Csikszentmihalyi, M., & Csikszentmihalyi, I. (1988). Introduction to Part IV. In M. Csikszentmihalyi & I. Csikszentmihalyi (Eds.), *Optimal experience: Psychological studies of flow in consciousness* (pp. 251–265). New York: Cambridge University Press.

Csikszentmihalyi, M., & Larson, R. (1987). The Experience Sampling Method. *Journal of Nervous and Mental Disease, 175,* 526–536.

Csikszentmihalyi, M., Rathunde, K., & Whalen, S. (1993). *Talented teenagers: The roots of success and failure.* New York: Cambridge University Press.

Dalek, M. (1995). The conservative 1960's: From the perspective of the 1990's, it's the big political story of the era. *The Atlantic Monthly, 276,* 130–135.

Damast, A. (2007). Applying oneself, creativity. *BusinessWeek.* Retrieved April 14, 2008, from http://www.businessweek.com/bschools/content/jul2007/ bs20070727_140974.htm

The darker side of the lighter side. (2008, March). *Mad Magazine, 487,* 16–17.

Das, J. P., Naglieri, J. A., & Kirby, J. R. (1994). *Assessment of cognitive processes: The PASS theory of intelligence.* Boston: Allyn & Bacon.

D'Aulaire, I., & D'Aulaire, E. P. (1992). *D'Aulaires book of Greek myths* (reprint ed.). New York: Delacorte.

Davidson, J. E, & Sternberg, R. (1998). Smart problem solving: How metacognition helps. In D. J. Hacker, A. C. Graesser, and J. Dunlosky (Eds.), *Metacognition in educational theory and practice* (pp. 47–69). Mahwah, NJ: Lawrence Erlbaum Associates.

Dawson, V. L. (1997). In search of the Wild Bohemian: Challenges in the identification of the creatively gifted. *Roeper Review, 19,* 148–152.

De Bono, E. (1992). *Teach your child how to think.* London: Penguin.

Detert, J. R., & Burris, E. R. (2007). Leadership behavior and employee voice: Is the door really open? *Academy of Management Journal, 50,* 869–884.

Devine, P. G. (1989). Stereotypes and prejudice: Their automatic and controlled components. *Journal of Personality and Social Psychology, 56,* 5–18.

Devlin, D. (2006). You can write the next American Idol single. *Mad Magazine, 466*, 47–51.

De Young, C. G., Quilty, L. C., & Peterson, J. B. (2007). Between facets and domains: 10 aspects of the Big-Five. *Journal of Personality and Social Psychology, 93*, 880–896.

Dixon, J. (1979). Quality versus quantity: The need to control for the fluency factor in originality scores from the Torrance Tests. *Journal for the Education of the Gifted, 2*, 70–79.

Djikic, M., Oatley, K., & Peterson, J. B. (2006). The bitter-sweet labor of emoting: The linguistic comparison of writers and physicists. *Creativity Research Journal, 18*, 191–197.

Dollinger, S. J. (2007). Creativity and conservatism. *Personality and Individual Differences, 43*, 1025–1035.

Dollinger, S. J., & Clancy, S. M. (1993). Identity, self, and personality 2. Glimpses through the autophotographic eye. *Journal of Personality and Social Psychology, 64*, 1064–1071.

Domino, G. (1974). Assessment of cinematographic creativity. *Journal of Personality and Social Psychology, 30*, 150–154.

Dorfman, L., Locher, P., & Martindale, C. (Eds.). (2006). *New directions in aesthetics, creativity, and the arts (Foundations and Frontiers in Aesthetics)*. Amityville, NY: Baywood Press.

Dorfman, L., Martindale, C., Gassimova, V., & Vartanian, O. (2008). Creativity and speed of information processing: A double dissociation involving elementary versus inhibitory cognitive tasks. *Personality and Individual Differences, 44*, 1382–1390.

Dunbar, K. (1995). How scientists really reason: Scientific reasoning in real-world laboratories. In R. J. Sternberg & J. E. Davidson (Eds.), *The nature of insight* (pp. 365–395). Cambridge, MA: The MIT Press.

Dunning, D., Johnson, K., Ehrlinger, J., & Kruger, J. (2003). Why people fail to recognize their own incompetence. *Current Directions in Psychological Science, 12*, 83–86.

Dykens, E., Schwenk, M., Maxwell, M., & Myatt, B. (2007). The Sentence Completion and Three Wishes tasks: Windows into the inner lives of people with intellectual disabilities. *Journal of Intellectual Disability Research, 51*, 588–597.

Edmondson, A. C. (1999). Psychological safety and learning behavior in work teams. *Administrative Science Quarterly, 44*, 350–383.

Eisenberger, R., Armeli, S., & Pretz, J. (1998). Can the promise of reward increase creativity? *Journal of Personality and Social Psychology, 74*, 704–714.

Eisenberger, R., & Cameron, J. (1996). Detrimental effects of reward: Reality or myth? *American Psychologist, 51,* 1153–1166.

Eisenberger, R., Haskins, F., & Gambleton, P. (1999). Promised reward and creativity: Effects of prior experience. *Journal of Experimental Social Psychology, 35,* 308–325.

Eisenberger, R., & Rhoades, L. (2001). Incremental effects of reward on creativity. *Journal of Personality and Social Psychology, 81,* 728–741.

Eisenberger, R., & Selbst, M. (1994). Does reward increase or decrease creativity? *Journal of Personality and Social Psychology, 66,* 1116–1127.

Eisenberger, R., & Shanock, L. (2003). Rewards, intrinsic motivation, and creativity: A case study of conceptual and methodological isolation. *Creativity Research Journal, 15,* 121–130.

Eisenman, R. (1990). Creativity, preference for complexity, and physical and mental illness. *Creativity Research Journal, 3,* 231–236.

Eisenman, R., & Grove, M. S. (1972). Self-ratings of creativity, semantic differential ratings, and preferences for polygons varying in complexity, simplicity, and symmetry. *Journal of Psychology: Interdisciplinary and Applied, 81,* 63–67.

Elliot, A. J., & Church, M. A. (1997). A hierarchical model of approach and avoidance achievement motivation. *Journal of Personality and Social Psychology, 72,* 218–232.

Elliot, S., & Dweck, C. S. (1988). Goals: An approach to motivation and achievement. *Journal of Personality and Social Psychology, 54,* 5–12.

Enright, M. K., & Gitomer, D. H. (1989). *Toward a description of successful graduate students* (GRE Board Professional Rep. No. 89–09, GRE Board Research Rep. 85–17R). Princeton, NJ: Educational Testing Service.

Estrada, C., Isen, A. M., & Young, M. J. (1994). Positive affect influences creative problem solving reported source of practice satisfaction in physicians. *Motivation and Emotion, 18,* 285–299.

Everatt, J. (1997) The abilities and disabilities associated with adult developmental dyslexia. *Journal of Research in Reading, 20,* 13–21.

Everson, H. T., & Tobias, S. (1998). The ability to estimate knowledge and performance in college: A metacognitive analysis. *Instructional Science, 26,* 65–79.

Eysenck, H. J. (1995). *Genius: The natural history of creativity.* Cambridge: Cambridge University Press.

Faigel, H. C. (1991). The effect of beta blockade on stress-induced cognitive dysfunction in adolescents. *Clinical Pediatrics (Phila), 30,* 441–445.

Feist, G. J. (1998). A meta-analysis of personality in scientific and artistic creativity. *Personality and Social Psychology Review, 2*, 290–309.

Feist, G. J. (1999). The influence of personality on artistic and scientific creativity. In R. J. Sternberg (Ed.), *Handbook of creativity* (273–296). New York: Cambridge University Press.

Feist, G. J. (2004). The evolved fluid specificity of human creative talent. In R. J. Sternberg, E. L. Grigorenko, & J. L. Singer (Eds.), *Creativity: From potential to realization* (pp. 57–82). Washington, DC: American Psychological Association.

Feist, G. J., & Barron, F. (2003). Predicting creativity from early to late adulthood: Intellect, potential and personality. *Journal of Research in Personality, 37*, 62–88.

Feldhusen, J. F., & Goh, B. E. (1995). Assessing and accessing creativity: An integrative review of theory, research, and development. *Creativity Research Journal, 8*, 231–248.

Finke, R. (1990). *Creative imagery: Discoveries and inventions in visualization.* Hillsdale, NJ: Erlbaum.

Finke, R. A., & Slayton, K. (1988). Explorations of creative visual synthesis in mental imagery. *Memory & Cognition, 16*, 252–257.

Finke, R. A., Ward, T. B., & Smith, S. M. (1992). *Creative cognition: Theory, research, and applications.* Cambridge, MA: MIT Press.

Finke, R. A., Ward, T. B., & Smith, S. M. (1996). *Creative cognition: Theory, research and applications.* Cambridge, MA: The MIT Press.

Flavell, J. (1979). Metacognition and cognitive monitoring: A new area of cognitive developmental inquiry. *American Psychologist, 34*, 906–911.

Fleenor, J. W., & Taylor, S. (1994). Construct validity of three self-report measures of creativity. *Educational and Psychological Measurement, 54*, 464–470.

Ford, C., & Sullivan, D. M. (2004). A time for everything: How timing of novel contributions influences project team outcomes. *Journal of Organizational Behavior, 21*, 163–183.

Forgeard, M. (2008). Linguistic styles of eminent writers suffering from unipolar and bipolar mood disorder. *Creativity Research Journal, 20*, 81–92.

Frederiksen, N. O. (1959). Development of the test "Formulating Hypotheses": A progress report (Office of Naval Research Technical Report, Contract Nonr-2338(00)). Princeton, NJ: Educational Testing Service.

Frederiksen, N. O., & Evans, F. R. (1974). Effects of models of creative performance on ability to formulate hypotheses. *Journal of Educational Psychology, 66*(1), 67–82.

Frederiksen, N. O., Evans, F. R., & Ward, W. C. (1975). Development of provisional criteria for the study of scientific creativity. *Gifted Child Quarterly, 19*, 60–65.

Frensch, P. A., & Sternberg, R. J. (1989). Expertise and intelligence thinking: When is it worse to know better. In R. J. Sternberg (Ed.), *Advances in the psychology of human intelligence* (Vol. 5, pp. 157–188). Hillsdale, NJ: Erlbaum.

Freud, S. (1908/1959). Creative writers and day-dreaming. In J. Strachey (Ed.), *The standard edition of the complete psychological works of Sigmund Freud* (Vol. 9, pp. 141–154). London: The Hogarth Press.

Frisina, P. G., Borod, J. C., & Lepore, S. J. (2004). A meta-analysis of the effects of written emotional disclosure on the health outcomes of clinical populations. *The Journal of Nervous and Mental Disease, 192*, 629–634.

Fuchs-Beauchamp, K. D., Karnes, M. B., & Johnson, L. J. (1993). Creativity and intelligence in preschoolers. *Gifted Child Quarterly, 37*, 113–117.

Furnham, A. (1999). Personality and creativity. *Perceptual and Motor Skills, 88*, 407–408.

Furnham, A., & Bachtiar, V. (2008). Personality and intelligence as predictors of creativity. *Personality & Individual Differences, 45*, 613–617.

Furnham, A., Batey, M., Anand, K., & Manfield, J. (2008). Personality, hypomania, intelligence and creativity. *Personality and Individual Differences, 44*, 1060–1069.

Furnham, A., & Chamorro-Premuzic, T. (2004). Estimating one's own personality and intelligence scores. *British Journal of Psychology, 95*, 145–160.

Furnham, A., Zhang, J., & Chamorro-Premuzic, T. (2006). The relationship between psychometric and self-estimated intelligence, creativity, personality, and academic achievement. *Cognition and Personality, 25*, 119–145.

Galenson, D. W. (2005). *Old masters and young geniuses: The two life cycles of artistic creativity.* Princeton, NJ: Princeton University Press.

Gardner, H. (1993). *Creating minds.* New York: BasicBooks.

Gardner, H. (1999). *Intelligence reframed: Multiple intelligences for the 21st century.* New York: Basic Books.

Gasper, K. (2004). Permission to seek freely? The effect of happy and sad moods on generating old and new ideas. *Creativity Research Journal, 16,* 215–229.

Gelade, G. (1997). Creativity in conflict: The personality of the commercial creative. *Journal of Genetic Psychology, 165,* 67–78.

Gentile, C. A., & Kaufman, J. C. (2001, November). *How to design scoring rubrics from diverse work samples.* Workshop Series for ETS Interns. Princeton, NJ: Educational Testing Service.

Gentile, C. A., & Kaufman, J. C. (2002, January). *Creative writing: "Sacred Cow" or scorable construct?* ETS Workshop Series. Princeton, NJ: Educational Testing Service.

George, J. M., & Zhou, J. (2001). When openness to experience and conscientiousness are related to creative behavior: An interactional approach. *Journal of Applied Psychology, 86,* 513–524.

George, J. M., & Zhou, J. (2002). Understanding when bad moods foster creativity and good ones don't: The role of context and clarity of feelings. *Journal of Applied Psychology, 87,* 687–697.

Getzels, J. W., & Csikszentmihalyi, M. (1976). *The creative vision.* New York: John Wiley & Sons.

Getzels, J. W., & Jackson, P. W. (1962). *Creativity and intelligence: Explorations with gifted students.* New York: John Wiley & Sons.

Ghadirian, A. M., Gregoire, P., & Kosmidis, H. (2001). Creativity and the evolution of psychopathologies. *Creativity Research Journal, 13,* 145–148.

Glover, J. A. (1976). Comparative levels of creative ability in Black and White college students. *Journal of Genetic Psychology, 128,* 95–99.

Glück, J., Ernst, R., & Unger, F. (2002). How creatives define creativity: Definitions reflect different types of creativity. *Creativity Research Journal, 14,* 55–67.

Goldberg, L. R. (1992). The development of markers for the Big Five factor structure. *Psychological Assessment, 4,* 26–42.

Goldberg, L. R., Sweeney, D., Merenda, P. F., & Hughes, J. E., Jr. (1998). Demographic variables and personality: The effects of gender, age, education, and ethnic/racial status on self-descriptions of personality attributes. *Personality and Individual Differences, 24,* 393–403.

Goldsmith, R. E., & Matherly, T. A. (1988). Creativity and self-esteem: A multiple operationalization validity study. *Journal of Psychology, 122,* 47–56.

Goldwater, B. (1960). *The conscience of a conservative.* Shepherdsville, KY: Victor.

Gollmar, S. M. (2000). *An investigation of attention deficit/hyperactivity disorder, creativity, and cognitive style: Interaction and impact on school success.* Unpublished doctoral dissertation, University of Georgia.

Goncalo, J. A., & Staw, B. M. (2006). Individualism-collectivism and group creativity. *Organizational Behavior and Human Decision Processes, 100,* 96–109.

Gordon, J. (1992). *Art isn't easy.* New York: Da Capo Press.

Graef, R., Csikszentmihalyi, M., & Giannino, S. M. (1983). Measuring intrinsic motivation in everyday life. *Leisure Studies, 2,* 155–168.

Grawitch, M. J., Munz, D. C., & Kramer, T. J. (2003). Effects of member mood states on creative performance in temporary workgroups. *Group Dynamics, 7,* 41–54.

Greenwald, A. G., & Banaji, M. R. (1995). Implicit social cognition: Attitudes, self-esteem, and stereotypes. *Psychological Review, 102,* 4–27.

Greer, M., & Levine, E. (1991). Enhancing creative performance in college students. *Journal of Creative Behavior, 25,* 250–255.

Griffin, M., & McDermott, M. R. (1998). Exploring a tripartite relationship between rebelliousness, openness to experience and creativity. *Social Behavior and Personality, 26,* 347–356.

Grimwood, K. (1986). *Replay.* Washington, DC: Arbor House.

Grubb, K. B. (1991). *Razzle dazzle: The life and works of Bob Fosse.* New York: St. Martin's Press.

Guastello, S. J., Shissler, J., Driscoll, J., & Hyde, T. (1998). Are some cognitive styles more creatively productive than others? *Journal of Creative Behavior, 32,* 77–91.

Guilford, J. P. (1950). Creativity. *American Psychologist, 5,* 444–454.

Guilford, J. P. (1967). *The nature of human intelligence.* New York: McGraw-Hill.

Guilford, J. P. (1988). Some changes in the Structure-of-Intellect Model. *Educational and Psychological Measurement, 48,* 1–4.

Güncer, B., & Oral, G. (1993). Relationship between creativity and nonconformity to school discipline as perceived by teachers of Turkish elementary school children, by controlling for their grade and sex. *Journal of Instructional Psychology, 20,* 208–214.

Hamlen, K. R. (2008). *Relationships between video game play and creativity among elementary school students.* Unpublished doctoral dissertation, State University of New York at Buffalo.

Hamm, C. (1980). John Cage. In *The new Grove dictionary of music and musicians* (Vol. 3, pp. 597–603). London: Macmillan.

Han, K. S. (2003). Domain-specificity of creativity in young children: How quantitative and qualitative data support it. *The Journal of Creative Behavior, 37,* 117–129.

Haritos-Fatouros, M., & Child, I. L. (1977). Transcultural similarity in personal significance of esthetic interests. *Journal of Cross-Cultural Psychology, 8,* 285–298.

Harrington, D. M. (1975). Effects of the explicit instructions to "be creative" on the psychological meaning of divergent thinking test scores. *Journal of Personality, 43,* 434–454.

Harrington, D. M., Block, J. H., & Block, J. (1987). Testing aspects of Carl Rogers' theory of creative environments: Child-rearing antecedents of creative potential in young adolescents. *Journal of Personality and Social Psychology, 52,* 851–860.

Hartman, E. (2000). *Dreams and nightmares: The origin and meaning of dreams.* New York: Perseus.

Hayes, J. R. (1989). Cognitive processes in creativity. In J. A. Glover, R. R. Ronning, & C. R. Reynolds (Eds.), *Handbook of creativity* (pp. 135–145). New York: Plenum Press.

Healey, D., & Rucklidge, J. J. (2005). An exploration into the creative abilities of children with ADHD. *Journal of Attention Disorders, 8,* 88–95.

Heath, S. (1983). *Ways with words: Language, life, and work in communities and classrooms.* New York: Cambridge University Press.

Heausler, N. L., & Thompson, B. (1988). Structure of the Torrance Tests of Creative Thinking. *Educational and Psychological Measurement, 48,* 463–468.

Hébert, T. P., Cramond, B., Spiers-Neumeister, K. L., Millar, G., & Silvian, A. F. (2002). *E. Paul Torrance: His life, accomplishments, and legacy.* Storrs, CT: The University of Connecticut, National Research Center on the Gifted and Talented.

Hedges, L. V., & Nowell, A. (1995). Sex differences in mental test scores, variability, and numbers of high-scoring individuals. *Science, 269,* 41–45.

Heilman, K. M. (2005). *Creativity and the brain.* New York: Psychology Press.

Helson, R. (1990). Creativity in women: Outer and inner views over time. In M. A. Runco & R. S. Albert, *Theories of creativity* (pp. 46–58). Newbury Park, CA: Sage.

Hennessey, B. A., & Amabile, T. M. (1999). Consensual assessment. In M. A. Runco & S. R. Pritzker (Eds.), *Encyclopedia of creativity* (Vol. 1, pp. 346–359). San Diego: Academic Press.

Hennessey, B. A., Amabile, T. M., & Martinage, M. (1989). Immunizing children against the negative effects of reward. *Contemporary Educational Psychology, 14,* 212–227.

Hennessey, B. A., Kim, G., Guomin, Z., & Weiwei, S. (in press). A multicultural application of the Consensual Assessment Technique. *International Journal of Creativity and Problem Solving.*

Herrnstein, R. J., & Murray, C. (1994). *The bell curve.* New York: The Free Press.

Heuchert, J. W. P., Parker, W. D., Stumpf, H., & Myburgh, C. P. H. (2000). The Five-Factor Model in South African college students. *American Behavioral Scientist, 44,* 112–125.

Hickey, M. (2001). An application of Amabile's consensual assessment technique for rating the creativity of children's musical compositions. *Journal of Research in Music Education, 49,* 234–244.

Hillier, A., Alexander, J. K., & Beversdorf, D. Q. (2006). The effect of auditory stressors on cognitive flexibility. *Neurocase, 12,* 228–31.

Hirsch, J. B., & Peterson, J. B. (2008). Predicting creativity and academic success with a "Fake-Proof" measure of the Big Five. *Journal of Research in Personality, 42,* 1323–1333.

Hirt, E. R., Devers, E. E., & McCrea, S. M. (2008). I want to be creative: Exploring the role of hedonic contingency theory in the positive mood-cognitive flexibility link. *Journal of Personality and Social Psychology, 94,* 214–230.

Hirt, E. R., Levine, G. M., McDonald, H. E., & Melton, R. J. (1997). The role of mood in qualitative aspects of performance. *Journal of Experimental Social Psychology, 33,* 602–629.

Hocevar, D. (1976). Dimensionality of creativity. *Psychological Reports, 39,* 869–870.

Hofstee, W. K. B., de Raad, B., & Goldberg, L. R. (1992). Integration of the big five and circumplex approaches to trait structure. *Journal of Personality and Social Psychology, 63,* 146–163.

Holland, J. L. (1997). *Making vocational choices: A theory of vocational personalities and work environments* (3rd ed.). Odessa, FL: Psychological Assessment Resources.

Hoover, E. (2002, May 31). SAT is set for an overhaul, but questions linger about the test. *Chronicle of Higher Education,* A35–36.

Hoover, E. (2007). How applying to college shapes students: Study finds "Formative Experience," frustration, for brightest applicants. *Chronicle of Higher Education*, pA1.

Horn, J. L., & Cattell, R. B. (1966). Refinement and test of the theory of fluid and crystallized intelligence. *Journal of Educational Psychology, 57*, 253–270.

Horn, J. L., & Hofer, S. M. (1992). *Major abilities and development in the adult period.* New York: Cambridge University Press.

Horn, J. L., & Noll, J. (1997). Human cognitive capacities: Gf-Gc theory. In D. P. Flanagan, J. L. Genshaft, & P. L. Harrison (Eds.), *Life-span developmental psychology: Research and theory* (pp. 423–466). New York: Academic Press.

House, J. D., & Johnson, J. J. (2002). Predictive validity of the graduate record examination advanced psychology test for grade performance in graduate psychology courses. *College Student Journal, 36*, 32–37.

Hunsaker, S. L., & Callahan, C. M. (1995). Creativity and giftedness: Published instrument uses and abuses. *Gifted Child Quarterly, 39*, 110–114.

Hutchinson, E. D. (1931). Materials for study of creative thinking. *Psychological Bulletin, 28*, 392–410.

Hutton, E. L., & Bassett, M. (1948). The effect of leucotomy on creative personality. *Journal of Mental Science, 94*, 332–350.

Iscoe, I., & Pierce-Jones, J. (1964). Divergent thinking, age, and intelligence in white and Negro children. *Child Development, 35*, 785–797.

Isen, A. M., Daubman, K. A., & Nowicki, G. P. (1987). Positive affect facilitates creative problem solving. *Journal of Personality and Social Psychology, 52*, 1122–1131.

Isen, A. M., Johnson, M. M., Mertz, E., & Robinson, G. F. (1985). The influence of positive affect on the unusualness of word associations. *Journal of Personality and Social Psychology, 48*, 1413–1426.

Isen, A. M., Labroo, A. A., & Durlach, P. (2004). An influence of product and brand name on positive affect: Implicit and explicit measures. *Motivation and Emotion, 28*, 43–63.

Ivcevic, Z. (in press). Artistic and everyday creativity: An act-frequency approach. *Journal of Creative Behavior.*

Ivcevic, Z., Brackett, M. A., & Mayer, J. D. (2007). Emotional intelligence and emotional creativity. *Journal of Personality, 75*, 199–235.

Ivcevic, Z., & Mayer, J. D. (2007). Creative types and personality. *Imagination, Cognition, and Personality, 26*, 65–86.

Ivcevic, Z., & Mayer, J. D. (in press). Mapping dimensions of creativity. *Creativity Research Journal.*

Iwao, S., Child, I. L., & Garcia, M. (1969). Further evidence of agreement between Japanese and American esthetic evaluations. *Journal of Social Psychology, 78,* 11–15.

Jamison, K. R. (1989). Mood disorders and patterns of creativity in British writers and artists. *Psychiatry, 52,* 125–134.

Jamison, K. R. (1993). *Touched with fire: Manic-depressive illness and the artistic temperament.* New York: Free Press.

Janiger, O., & de Rios, M. D. (1989). LSD and creativity. *Journal of Psychoactive Drugs, 21,* 129–134.

Jaquish, G. A., & Ripple, R. E. (1984). A life-span developmental cross-cultural study of divergent thinking abilities. *International Journal of Aging & Human Development, 20,* 1–11.

Jausovec, N. (1994). *Flexible thinking: An explanation for individual differences in ability.* Cresskill, NJ: Hampton Press.

Jaussi, K. S., Randel, A. E., & Dionne, S. D. (2007). I am, I think I can, and I do: The role of personal identity, self-efficacy, and cross-application of experiences in creativity at work. *Creativity Research Journal, 19,* 247–258.

Jellen, H. G., & Urban, K. K. (1989). Assessing creative potential world-wide: The first cross-cultural application for the Test of Creative Thinking—Drawing Production. *Gifted Education International, 6,* 78–86.

Jensen, A. R. (1998). *The g factor: The science of mental ability.* Westport, CT: Greenwood Publishing.

Ji, L., Peng, K., & Nisbett, R. E. (2000). Culture, control, and perception of relationships in the environment. *Journal of Personality and Social Psychology, 78,* 943–955.

Johnson-Laird, P. N. (1988). Freedom and constraint in creativity. In R. J. Sternberg (Ed.), *The nature of creativity* (pp. 202–219). New York: Cambridge University Press.

Johnson-Laird, P. N. (1991). Jazz improvisation: A theory at the computational level. In P. Howell, R. West, & I. J. Cross (Eds.), *Representing musical structure* (pp. 291–326). London: Academic.

Jones, W., Bellugi, U., Lai, Z., Chiles, M., Reilly, J., Lincoln, A., et al. (2000). Hypersociability in Williams syndrome. *Journal of Cognitive Neuroscience, 12,* 30–46.

Kaltsounis, B. (1974). Race, socioeconomic status and creativity. *Psychological Reports, 35,* 164–166.

Karimi, Z., Windmann, S., Güntürkün, O., & Abraham, A. (2007). Insight problem solving in individuals with high versus low schizotypy. *Journal of Research in Personality, 41*, 473–480.

Kasof, J. (1997). Creativity and breadth of attention. *Creativity Research Journal, 10*, 303–315.

Katz, A. N., & Poag, J. R. (1979). Sex differences in instructions to "be creative" on divergent and nondivergent test scores. *Journal of Personality, 47*, 518–530.

Kaufman, A. B. (2007). An overview of the neuroscience of creativity: Review of *Creativity and the Brain* by Kenneth M. Heilman. *Psychology of Aesthetics, Creativity, and the Arts, 1*, 250–251.

Kaufman, A. S. (1979). *Intelligent testing with the WISC-R*. New York: John Wiley & Sons.

Kaufman, A. S. (1994). *Intelligent testing with the WISC-III*. New York: John Wiley & Sons.

Kaufman, A. S. (1999). Genetics of childhood disorders: Genetics and intelligence II. *Journal of the American Academy of Child and Adolescent Psychiatry, 38*, 626–628.

Kaufman, A. S. (2000). Seven questions about the WAIS-III regarding differences in abilities across the 16 to 89 year life span. *School Psychology Quarterly, 15*, 3–29.

Kaufman, A. S. (2001). WAIS-III IQs, Horn's theory, and generational changes from young adulthood to old age. *Intelligence, 29*, 131–167.

Kaufman, A. S. (2004). *Profile analysis, process deficits, and other provocative puzzles*. Invited Division 16 address presented at the meeting of the American Psychological Association, Honolulu, HI.

Kaufman, A. S., & Kaufman, N. L. (1983). *K-ABC interpretive manual*. Circle Pines, MN: American Guidance Service.

Kaufman, A. S., & Kaufman, N. L. (1993). *Kaufman Adolescent and Adult Intelligence Test (KAIT)*. Circle Pines, MN: American Guidance Service.

Kaufman, A. S., & Lichtenberger, E. O. (2006). *Assessing adolescent and adult intelligence* (3rd ed.). New York: John Wiley & Sons.

Kaufman, J. C. (2000). The tragic muse. [Review of Emotional illness and creativity]. *Contemporary Psychology, 45*, 620–621.

Kaufman, J. C. (2001a). Genius, lunatics, and poets: Mental illness in prize-winning authors. *Imagination, Cognition, and Personality, 20*, 305–314.

Kaufman, J. C. (2001b). The Sylvia Plath effect: Mental illness in eminent creative writers. *Journal of Creative Behavior, 35*, 37–50.

Kaufman, J. C. (2002). Narrative and paradigmatic thinking styles in creative writing and journalism students. *Journal of Creative Behavior, 36*, 201–220.

Kaufman, J. C. (2003). The cost of the muse: Poets die young. *Death Studies, 27*, 813–822.

Kaufman, J. C. (2005). The door that leads into madness: Eastern European poets and mental illness. *Creativity Research Journal, 17*, 99–103.

Kaufman, J. C. (2006). Self-reported differences in creativity by gender and ethnicity. *Journal of Applied Cognitive Psychology, 20*, 1065–1082.

Kaufman, J. C., & Baer, J. (2002). I bask in dreams of suicide: Mental illness and poetry. *Review of General Psychology, 6*, 271–286.

Kaufman, J. C., & Baer, J. (2004). The Amusement Park Theoretical (APT) Model of creativity. *Korean Journal of Thinking and Problem Solving, 14*, 15–25.

Kaufman, J. C., & Baer, J. (Eds). (2005a). *Creativity across domains: Faces of the muse.* Mahwah, NJ: Lawrence Erlbaum.

Kaufman, J. C., & Baer, J. (2005b). The amusement park theory of creativity. In J. C. Kaufman & J. Baer (Eds.), *Creativity across domains: Faces of the muse* (pp. 321–328). Hillsdale, NJ: Lawrence Erlbaum Associates.

Kaufman, J. C., & Baer, J. (Eds). (2006). *Creativity and reason in cognitive development.* New York: Cambridge University Press.

Kaufman, J. C., & Baer, J. (2008, August). *Rater expertise and the Consensual Assessment Technique.* In J. C. Kaufman (Chair), *New thoughts on creativity assessment.* Symposium presented at the American Psychological Association, Boston.

Kaufman, J. C., Baer, J., Cole, J. C., & Sexton, J. D. (2008). A comparison of expert and nonexpert raters using the Consensual Assessment Technique. *Creativity Research Journal, 20*, 171–178.

Kaufman, J. C., Baer, J., & Gentile, C. A. (2004). Differences in gender and ethnicity as measured by ratings of three writing tasks. *Journal of Creative Behavior, 39*, 56–69.

Kaufman, J. C., & Beghetto, R. A. (in press). Beyond big and little: The Four C Model of Creativity. *Review of General Psychology.*

Kaufman, J. C., Bromley, M. L., & Cole, J. C. (2006). Insane, poetic, lovable: Creativity and endorsement of the "Mad Genius" stereotype. *Imagination, Cognition, and Personality, 26*, 149–161.

Kaufman, J. C., & Burgess, S. A. (2007). To create is human, but are genius creators divinely mad? [Review of Divine madness]. *PsycCRITIQUES.*

Kaufman, J. C., Cole, J. C., & Baer, J. (in press). The construct of creativity: A structural model for self-reported creativity ratings. *Journal of Creative Behavior.*

Kaufman, J. C., Evans, M. L., & Baer, J. (in press) The American Idol Effect: Are students good judges of their creativity across domains? *Empirical Studies of the Arts.*

Kaufman, J. C., & Gentile, C. A. (2002). The will, the wit, the judgment: The importance of an early start in productive and successful creative writing. *High Ability Studies, 13,* 115–123.

Kaufman, J. C., Gentile, C. A., & Baer, J. (2005). Do gifted student writers and creative writing experts rate creativity the same way? *Gifted Child Quarterly, 49,* 260–265.

Kaufman, J. C., & Kaufman, A. B. (2004). Applying a creativity framework to animal cognition. *New Ideas in Psychology, 22,* 143–155.

Kaufman, J. C., & Kaufman, S. B. (2008). *Using intelligent testing to find creativity: Searching for divergent production in IQ tests.* Manuscript in preparation.

Kaufman, J. C., Lee, J., Baer, J., & Lee, S. (2007). Captions, consistency, creativity, and the consensual assessment technique: New evidence of validity. *Thinking Skills and Creativity, 2,* 96–106.

Kaufman, J. C., Plucker, J. A., & Baer, J. (2008). *Essentials of creativity assessment.* New York: John Wiley & Sons.

Kaufman, J. C., & Sexton, J. D. (2006). Why doesn't the writing cure help poets? *Review of General Psychology, 10,* 268–282.

Kaufman, J. C., & Sternberg, R. J. (Eds.). (2006). *The international handbook of creativity.* New York: Cambridge University Press.

Kaufman, J. C., & Sternberg, R. J. (in press). *Cambridge handbook of creativity.* New York: Cambridge University Press.

Kaufman, N. L., & Kaufman, A. S. (1980). Creativity in children with minimal brain dysfunction. *Journal of Creative Behavior, 14,* 73.

Kaufman, S. B. (2007). Sex differences in mental rotation and spatial visualization ability: Can they be accounted for by differences in working memory capacity? *Intelligence, 35,* 211–223.

Kaufman, S. B., Christopher, E. M., & Kaufman, J. C. (in press). The genius portfolio: How do poets earn their creative reputations from multiple products? *Empirical Studies of the Arts.*

Kaufman, S. B., & Kaufman, J. C. (2007). Ten years to expertise, many more to greatness: An investigation of modern writers. *Journal of Creative Behavior, 41,* 114–124.

Kaufman, S. B., & Sternberg, R. J. (in press). Conceptions of giftedness. In S. Pfeiffer (Ed.), *Handbook of the gifted and talented: A psychological approach.* New York: Plenum.

Kaufmann, G. (2003). Expanding the mood–creativity equation. *Creativity Research Journal, 15,* 131–135.

Kaufmann, G., & Vosburg, S. K. (1997). "Paradoxical" mood effects on creative problem-solving. *Cognition and Emotion, 11,* 151–170.

Kaufmann, G., & Vosburg, S. K. (2002). The effects of mood on early and late idea production. *Creativity Research Journal, 14,* 317–330.

Kaun, D. E. (1991). Writers die young: The impact of work and leisure on longevity. *Journal of Economic Psychology, 12,* 381–399.

Keefe, J. A., & Magaro, P. A. (1980). Creativity and schizophrenia: An equivalence of cognitive processing. *Journal of Abnormal Psychology, 89,* 390–398.

Keinänen, M., & Gardner, H. (2004). Vertical and horizontal mentoring for creativity. In R. J. Sternberg, E. L. Grigorenko, & J. L. Singer (Eds.), *Creativity: From potential to realization* (pp. 169–193). Washington, DC: American Psychological Association.

Keinänen, M., Sheridan, K., & Gardner, H. (2006). Opening up creativity: The lenses of axis and focus. In J. C. Kaufman & J. Baer (Eds.), *Creativity and reason in cognitive development* (pp. 202–218). New York: Cambridge University Press.

Keith-Spiegel, P., Tabachnick, B. G., & Spiegel, G. B. (1994). When demand exceeds supply: Second-order criteria used by graduate school selection committees. *Teaching of Psychology, 21,* 79–81.

Kerr, B., Shaffer, J., Chambers, C., & Hallowell, K. (1991). Substance use of creatively talented adults. *Journal of Creative Behavior, 25,* 145–153.

Kessler, C., & Quinn, M. E. (1987). Language minority children's linguistic and cognitive creativity. *Journal of Multilingual and Multicultural Development, 8,* 173–186.

Khurana, S. (2008). So you want to be a superhero?: How the art of making comics in an afterschool setting develops young people's creativity, literacy, and identity. In S. Hill (Ed.), *Afterschool matters: Creative programs that connect youth development and student achievement* (pp. 59–72). Thousand Oaks, CA: Corwin Press.

Kim, K. H. (2005). Can only intelligent people be creative. *Journal of Secondary Gifted Education, 16,* 57–66.

King, L. A. (2001). The health benefits of writing about life goals. *Personality and Social Psychology Bulletin, 27,* 798–807.

King, L. A., & Gurland, S. T. (2007). Creativity and experience of a creative task: Person and environment effects. *Journal of Research in Personality, 41,* 1252–1259.

King, L. A., McKee-Walker, L., & Broyles, S. J. (1996). Creativity and the five factor model. *Journal of Research in Personality, 30,* 189–203.

Kinney, D. K., Richards, R., Lowing, P. A., LeBlanc, D., & Zimbalist, M. E. (2001). Creativity in offspring of schizophrenic and control parents: An adoption study. *Creativity Research Journal, 13,* 17–25.

Knox, B. J., & Glover, J. A. (1978). A note on preschool experience effects on achievement, readiness, and creativity. *Journal of Genetic Psychology, 132,* 151–152.

Kohn, A. (1993). *Punished by rewards.* Boston: Houghton Mifflin.

Kottler, J. A. (2005). *Divine madness: Ten stories of creative struggle.* New York: Jossey-Bass.

Kozbelt, A. (2007). A quantitative analysis of Beethoven as self-critic: Implications for psychological theories of musical creativity. *Psychology of Music, 35,* 147–172.

Kozbelt, A., & Durmysheva, Y. (2007). Lifespan creativity in a non-Western artistic tradition: A study of Japanese ukiyo-e printmakers. *International Journal of Aging and Human Development, 65,* 23–51.

Kruger, J., & Dunning, D. (1999). Unskilled and unaware of it: How difficulties in recognizing one's own incompetence lead to inflated self-assessments. *Journal of Personality and Social Psychology, 77,* 1121–1134.

Kuncel, N. R., & Hezlett, S. A. (2007). Standardized tests predict graduate students' success. *Science, 315,* 1080–1081.

Kuncel, N. R., Hezlett, S. A., & Ones, D. S. (2004). Academic performance, career potential, creativity, and job performance: Can one construct predict them all? *Journal of Personality and Social Psychology, 86,* 148–161.

Kuncel, N. R., Hezlett, S. A., & Ones, D. S. (2001). A comprehensive meta-analysis of the predictive validity of the Graduate Record Examinations: Implications for graduate student selection and performance. *Psychological Bulletin, 127,* 162–181.

Kurtzberg, T. R., & Amabile, T. M. (2000). From Guilford to creative synergy: Opening the black box of team-level creativity. *Creativity Research Journal, 13,* 285–294.

Kyllonen, P. C., Walters, A. M., & Kaufman, J. C. (2005). Noncognitive constructs and their assessment in graduate education. *Educational Assessment, 10,* 153–184.

LaFrance, E. B. (1997). The gifted/dyslexic child: Characterizing and addressing strengths and weaknesses. *Annals of Dyslexia, 47,* 163–182.

Landauer, T. K., & Dumais, S. T. (1997). A solution to Plato's problem: The latent semantic analysis theory of the acquisition, induction, and representation of knowledge. *Psychological Review, 104,* 211–240.

Landrum, R. E., Jeglum, E. B. & Cashin, J. R. (1994). The decision-making processes of graduate admissions committees in psychology. *Journal of Social Behavior & Personality, 9,* 239–248.

Lang, A. R., Verret, L. D., & Watt, C. (1984). Drinking and creativity: Objective and subjective effects. *Addictive Behaviors, 9,* 395–399.

Langley, P., Simon, H. A., Bradshaw, G. L., & Zytkow, J. M. (1987). *Scientific discovery: Computational explorations of the creative processes.* Cambridge, MA: MIT Press.

Lapp, W. M., Collins, R. L., & Izzo, C. V. (1994). On the enhancement of creativity by alcohol: Pharmacology or expectation? *American Journal of Psychology, 107,* 173–206.

Larson, R., & Csikszentmihalyi, M. (1983). The experience sampling method. In H. T. Reiss (Ed.), *Naturalistic approaches to studying social interaction. New directions for methodology of social and behavioral sciences* (pp. 41–56). San Francisco: Jossey-Bass.

Lau, S., & Li, W. L. (1996). Peer status and perceived creativity: Are popular children viewed by peers and teachers as creative? *Creativity Research Journal, 9,* 347–352.

Lee, F. R. (2004, April 24). Going early into that good night. *New York Times,* Arts pp. 1, 4.

Lee, J., Day, J. D., Meara, N. M., & Maxwell, S. E. (2002). Discrimination of social knowledge and its flexible application from creativity: A multitrait-multimethod approach. *Personality and Individual Differences, 32,* 913–928.

Leith, G. (1972). The relationships between intelligence, personality, and creativity under two conditions of stress. *British Journal of Educational Psychology, 42,* 240–247.

Leith, S. (2007). Penguin should be ashamed of itself. *Telegraph.co.uk.* Retrieved April 17, 2008, from http://www.telegraphy.co.uk/opinion/main.jhtml?xml=/opinion/2007/11/17/do1704.xml

Lepper, M. R., & Greene, D. (1978). *The hidden costs of reward.* Hillsdale, NJ: Erlbaum.

Lepper, M. R., & Greene, D. (1975). Turning play into work: Effects of adult surveillance and extrinsic rewards on children's intrinsic motivation. *Journal of Personality and Social Psychology, 31,* 479–486.

Lepper, M. R., Greene, D., & Nisbett, R. E. (1973). Undermining children's intrinsic interest with extrinsic reward: A test of the "overjustification" hypothesis. *Journal of Personality and Social Psychology, 28,* 129–137.

Leung, A. K., Maddux, W. W., Galinsky, A. D., & Chiu, C. (2008). Multicultural experience enhances creativity: The when and how. *American Psychologist, 63,* 169–181.

Levitan, D. J., & Bellugi, U. (1998). Musical abilities in individuals with Williams syndrome. *Music Perception, 15,* 357–398.

Li, J. (1997). Creativity in horizontal and vertical domains. *Creativity Research Journal, 10,* 107–132.

Lim, W., & Plucker, J. (2001). Creativity through a lens of social responsibility: Implicit theories of creativity with Korean samples. *Journal of Creative Behavior, 35,* 115–130.

Lindauer, M. S. (1994). Are creative writers mad? An empirical perspective. In B. M. Rieger (Ed.), *Dionysus in literature: Essays on literary madness.* Bowling Green, OH: Bowling Green State University Popular Press.

Lissitz, R. W., & Willhoft, J. L. (1985). A methodological study of the Torrance Tests of creativity. *Journal of Educational Measurement, 22,* 1–11.

Lloyd-Evans, R., Batey, M., & Furnham, A. (2006). Bipolar disorder and creativity: Investigating a possible link. *Advances in Psychology Research, 40,* 11–142.

Locher, P. J., Frens, J. W., & Overbeeke, C. J. (2008). The influence of induced positive affect and design experience on aesthetic responses to new product designs. *Psychology of Aesthetics, Creativity and the Arts, 2,* 1–7.

Loehlin, J. C. (1999). Group differences in intelligence. In R. J. Sternberg (Ed.), *Handbook of intelligence* (pp. 176–193). New York: Cambridge University Press.

Lombroso, C. (1891). *The man of genius.* New York: Scribner's.

Losh, M., Bellugi, U., Reilly, J., & Anderson, D. (2000). Narrative as a social engagement tool: The excessive use of evaluation in narratives from children with Williams syndrome. *Narrative Inquiry, 10,* 265–290.

Lott, R. (2002). There's gonna be an earthquake tonight: The Eagles as harbingers of doom. In M. J. Rosen (Ed.), *101 damnations* (pp. 141–144). New York: St. Martin's Press.

Lubow, R. E. (1989). *Latent inhibition and conditioned attention theory.* New York: Cambridge University Press.

Ludwig, A. M. (1994). Mental illness and creative activity in female writers. *American Journal of Psychiatry, 151,* 1650–1656.

Ludwig, A. M. (1995). *The price of greatness.* New York: Guilford Press.

Ludwig, A. M. (1998). Method and madness in the arts and sciences. *Creativity Research Journal, 11,* 93–101.

Luria, A. R. (1966). *Human brain and psychological processes.* New York: Harper & Row.

Luria, A. R. (1970). The functional organization of the brain. *Scientific American, 222,* 66–78.

Luria, A. R. (1973). *The working brain: An introduction to neuropsychology.* London: Penguin.

Lynton, H., & Salovey, P. (1997). The effects of mood on expository writing. *Imagination, Cognition, and Personality, 17,* 95–110.

Mahoney, M. J. (1995). *Cognitive and constructive psychotherapies: Theory, research, and practice.* New York: Springer.

Manly, J. J., Miller, S. W., Heaton, R. K., Byrd, D., Reilly, J., Velasquez, R. J., et al. (1998). The effect of Black acculturation on neuropsychological test performance in normal and HIV positive individuals. *Journal of the International Neuropsychological Society, 4,* 291–302.

Markus, H., & Kitayama, S. (1991). Culture and the self: Implications for cognition, emotion, and motivation. *Psychological Review, 98,* 224–253.

Marland, S. (1972). *Education of the gifted and talented.* Report to the Congress of the United States by the U.S. Commissioner of Education. Washington, DC: Department of Health, Education and Welfare.

Martindale, C. (1999). Biological bases of creativity. In R. J. Sternberg (Ed.), *Handbook of creativity* (pp. 137–152). New York: Cambridge University Press.

Martindale, C., & Dailey, A. (1996). Creativity, primary process cognition and personality. *Personality and Individual Differences, 20,* 409–414.

Masten, W. G., Plata, M., Wenglar, K., & Thedford, J. (1999). Acculturation and teacher ratings of Hispanic and Anglo-American students. *Roeper Review, 22,* 64–65.

Masters, M. S., & Sanders, B. (1993). Is the gender difference in mental rotation disappearing? *Behavior Genetics, 23,* 337–341.

Matthews, G. (1986). The interactive effects of extraversion and arousal on performance: Are creativity tests anomalous? *Personality and Individual Differences, 7,* 751–761.

Matud, M. P., Rodríguez, C., & Grande, J. (2007). Gender differences in creative thinking. *Personality and Individual Differences, 43,* 1137–1147.

May, B., Moore, P., & Lintott, C. (2008, April 10). *Bang!: The Complete History of the Universe.* Baltimore: Johns Hopkins University Press.

Maybin, J., & Swann, J. (2007). Everyday creativity in language: Textuality, contextuality and critique. *Applied Linguistics, 28,* 497–517.

Mayer, J. D., Caruso, D., & Salovey, P. (2000). Emotional intelligence meets traditional standards for an intelligence. *Intelligence, 27,* 267–298.

Mayer, J. D., & Salovey, P. (1997). What is emotional intelligence? In P. Salovey & D. J. Sluyter (Eds.), *Emotional development and emotional intelligence: Educational implications* (pp. 3–34). New York: Basic Books.

Mayer, J. D., Salovey, P., & Caruso, D. R. (2000). Models of emotional intelligence. In R. J. Sternberg (Ed.), *Handbook of intelligence* (pp. 396–420). New York: Cambridge University Press.

McAdams, D. P. (1999). Personal narratives and the life story. In L. A. Pervin, O. P. John, et al. (Eds.), *Handbook of personality: Theory and research* (Vol. 2, pp. 478–500). New York: The Guilford Press.

McCrae, R. R. (1987). Creativity, divergent thinking, and openness to experience. *Journal of Personality and Social Psychology, 52,* 1258–1265.

McCrae, R. R., & Costa, P. T., Jr. (1997). Personality trait structure as a human universal. *American Psychologist, 52,* 509–516.

McKellar, D. (2007). *Math doesn't suck: How to survive middle-school math without losing your mind or breaking a nail.* New York: Hudson Street Press.

Mednick, S. A. (1962). The associative basis of the creative process. *Psychological Review, 69,* 220–232.

Mednick, S. A. (1968). The Remote Associates Test. *Journal of Creative Behavior, 2,* 213–214.

Mehta, M. A., Owen, A. M., Sahakian, B. J., et al. (2000). Methylphenidate enhances working memory by modulating discrete frontal and parietal lobe regions in the human brain. *Journal of Neuroscience, 20,* 1–6.

Messick, S. (1989). *Cognitive style and personality: Scanning and orientation toward affect.* (ETS Research Rep. No. 89–16). Princeton, NJ: Educational Testing Service.

Middleton, M. J., & Midgley, C. (1997). Avoiding the demonstration of lack of ability: An underexplored aspect of goal theory. *Journal of Educational Psychology, 89,* 710–718.

Mikkelson, B., & Mikkelson, D. P. (2006). Political podiatry. *Snopes.* Retrieved February 16, 2006, from http://www.snopes.com/politics/ballot/footpowder.asp

Miller, A. L. (2007). Creativity and cognitive style: The relationship between field dependence-independence, expected evaluation, and creative performance. *Psychology of Aesthetics, Creativity, and the Arts, 1,* 243–246.

Miller, G. F., & Tal, I. R. (2007). Schizotypy versus openness and intelligence as predictors of creativity. *Schizophrenia Research, 93,* 317–324.

Mitchell, B. M. (1988). Hemisphericity and creativity: A look at the relationships among elementary-age low-income Hispanic children. *Educational Research Quarterly, 2–5.*

Mobley, M. I., Doares, L. M., & Mumford, M. D. (1992). Process analytic models of creative capacities: Evidence for the combination and reorganization process. *Creativity Research Journal, 5,* 125–155.

Mohan, J., & Tiwana, M. (1987). Personality and alienation of creative writers: A brief report. *Personality and Individual Differences, 8,* 449.

Monaghan, W., & Bridgeman, B. (2005, April). E-rater as a quality control on human scorers. *ETS RD Connections.* Retrieved January 7, 2008, from http://www.ets.org/Media/Research/pdf/RD_Connections2.pdf

Montgomery, D., Hodges, P. A., & Kaufman, J. S. (2004). An exploratory study of the relationship between mood states and creativity self-perceptions. *Creativity Research Journal, 16,* 341–344.

Moreno, J. M., & Hogan, J. D. (1976). The influence of race and social-class level on the training of creative thinking and problem-solving abilities. *Journal of Educational Research, 70,* 91–95.

Morgan, R., & Maneckshana, B. (1996). *The psychometric perspective: Lessons learned from 40 years of constructed response testing in the Advanced Placement Program.* Paper presented at the Annual Meeting of the National Council of Measurement in Education, New York.

Mosselmans, B., & White, M. V. (2001). Introduction. In *Economic writings of W. S. Jevons* (pp. v–xxv). London: Palgrave/MacMillan.

Moutafi, J., Furnham, A., & Patiel, L. (2004). Why is conscientiousness negatively correlated with intelligence? *Personality and Individual Differences, 37,* 1013–1022.

Moy, J. W., & Lam, K. F. (2004). Selection criteria and the impact of personality on getting hired. *Personnel Review, 33,* 521–535.

Mumford, M. D., Mobley, M. I., Uhlman, C. E., Reiter-Palmon, R., & Doares, C. (1991). Process-analytic models of creative capabilities. *Creativity Research Journal, 4,* 91–122.

Murray, C. (2003). *Human accomplishment: The pursuit of excellence in the arts and sciences, 800 B.C. to 1950.* New York: HarperCollins.

Myford, C. M. (1989). *The nature of expertise in aesthetic judgment: Beyond inter-judge agreement.* Unpublished doctoral dissertation, University of Georgia, Athens.

Naglieri, J. A., & Das, J. P. (1997). *Cognitive Assessment System (CAS).* Chicago: Riverside.

Naglieri, J. A., & Kaufman, J. C. (2001). Understanding intelligence, giftedness, and creativity using PASS theory. *Roeper Review, 23,* 151–156.

National Institute of Mental Health (NIMH). (2001). *The numbers count: Mental disorders in America.* Washington, DC: Author.

Nettle, D. (2006). Psychological profiles of professional actors. *Personality and Individual Differences, 40,* 375–383.

Nettle, D., & Clegg, H. (2006). Schizotypy, creativity and mating success in humans. *Procedures of Biological Science, 273,* 611–615.

Ng, A. K. (2001). *Why Asians are less creative than Westerners.* Singapore: Prentice-Hall.

Ng, A. K., & Smith, I. (2004). Why is there a paradox in promoting creativity in the Asian classroom? In Sing, L., Hui, A., and Ng, G. (Eds.), *Creativity: When East meets West* (pp. 87–112). Singapore: World Scientific Publishing.

Ng, T. W., & Feldman, D. C. (2008). The relationship of age to ten dimensions of job performance. *The Journal of Applied Psychology, 93,* 392–423.

Nicholls, J. G. (1979). Quality and equality in intellectual development: The role of motivation in education. *American Psychologist, 34,* 1071–1084.

Nisbett, R. E., Peng, K., Choi, I., & Norenzayan, A. (2001). Culture and systems of thought: Holistic vs. analytic cognition. *Psychological Review, 108,* 291–310.

Niu, W., & Sternberg, R. J. (2001). Cultural influence of artistic creativity and its evaluation. *International Journal of Psychology, 36*(4), 225–241.

Niu, W., & Sternberg, R. J. (2002). Contemporary studies on the concept of creativity: The East and the West. *Journal of Creative Behavior, 36,* 269–288.

Niu, W., & Sternberg, X. (2006). The philosophical roots of western and eastern conceptions of creativity. *Journal of Theoretical and Philosophical Psychology, 26,* 1001–1021.

Nogueira, S. M. (2006). MORCEGOS: A Portuguese enrichment program of creativity pilot study with gifted students and students with learning difficulties. *Creativity Research Journal, 18,* 45–54.

Nolen-Hoeksema, S., Larson, J., & Grayson, C. (1999). Explaining the gender difference in depressive symptoms. *Journal of Personality and Social Psychology, 77,* 1061–1072.

Noppe, L. D. (1985). The relationship of formal thought and cognitive style to creativity. *Journal of Creative Behavior, 19,* 88–96.

Norlander, T., & Gustafson, R. (1996). Effects of alcohol on scientific thought during the incubation phase of the creative process. *Journal of Creative Behavior, 30,* 231–248.

Norlander, T., & Gustafson, R. (1997). Effects of alcohol on picture drawing during the verification phase of the creative process. *Creativity Research Journal, 10,* 355–362.

Norlander, T., & Gustafson, R. (1998). Effects of alcohol on a divergent figural fluency test during the illumination phase of the creative process. *Creativity Research Journal, 11,* 265–274.

North, S. (2007). "The voices, the voices": Creativity in online conversation. *Applied Linguistics, 28,* 538–555.

Novacek, J., Raskin, R., & Hogan, R. (1991). Why do adolescents use drugs? Age, sex, and user differences. *Journal of Youth and Adolescence, 20,* 475–492.

O'Brien, T. (1990). *The things they carried.* New York: Macmillan.

Ogawa, M., Kuehn-Ebert, C., & De Vito, A. (1991). Differences in creative thinking between Japanese and American fifth grade children. *Ibaraki University Faculty of Education Bulletin, 40,* 53–59.

O'Hara, L. A., & Sternberg, R. J. (2001). It doesn't hurt to ask: Effects of instructions to be creative, practical, or analytical on essay–writing performance and their interaction with students' thinking styles. *Creativity Research Journal, 13,* 197–210.

Okuda, S. M., Runco, M. A., & Berger, D. E. (1991). Creativity and the finding and solving of real-world problems. *Journal of Psychoeducational Assessment, 9,* 45–53.

Olenchak, F. R. (1995). Effects of enrichment on gifted/learning-disabled students. *Journal for the Education of the Gifted, 18*(4), 385–399.

Oral, G., Kaufman, J. C., & Agars, M. D. (2007). Examining creativity in Turkey: Do Western findings apply? *High Ability Studies, 18,* 235–246.

Palaniappan, A. K. (1996). A cross-cultural study of creative perceptions. *Perceptual and Motor Skills, 82,* 96–98.

Paletz, S. B. F., & Peng, K. (2008). Implicit theories of creativity across cultures: Novelty and appropriateness in two product domains. *Journal of Cross-Cultural Psychology, 39,* 286–302.

Panati, C. (1991). *Panati's parade of fads, follies, and manias.* New York: HarperPerennial.

Park, G., Lubinski, D., & Benbow, C. P. (2007). Contrasting intellectual patterns predict creativity in the arts and sciences: Tracking intellectually precocious youth over 25 years. *Psychological Science, 18,* 948–952.

Park, M., Lee, J., & Hahn, D. W. (2002). *Self-reported creativity, creativity, and intelligence.* Poster presented at the American Psychological Association, Chicago.

Park, S.-K., Park, K-H., & Choe, H-S. (2005). The relationship between thinking styles and scientific giftedness in Korea. *Journal of Secondary Gifted Education, 16,* 87–97.

Parker, P., & Kermode, F. (Eds.). (1996). *A reader's guide to twentieth-century writers.* New York: Oxford University Press.

Patricelli, G. L., Coleman, S. W., & Borgia, G. (2006). Male satin bowerbirds, Ptilonorhynchus violaceus, adjust their display intensity in response to female startling: An experiment with robotic females. *Animal Behaviour, 71,* 49–69.

Paulos, J. A. (1988). *Innumeracy: Mathematical illiteracy and its consequences.* New York: Vintage.

Pearlman, C. (1983). Teachers as an informational resource in identifying and rating student creativity. *Education, 103,* 215–222.

Pennebaker, J. W. (1997). Writing about emotional experiences as a therapeutic process. *Psychological Science, 8,* 162–166.

Pennebaker, J. W., & Beall, S. (1986). Confronting a traumatic event: Toward an understanding of inhibition and disease. *Journal of Abnormal Psychology, 95,* 274–281.

Pennebaker, J. W., Colder, M., & Sharp, L. K. (1990). Accelerating the coping process. *Journal of Personality and Social Psychology, 58,* 528–537.

Pennebaker, J. W., Francis, M. E., & Booth, R. J. (2001). *Linguistic Inquiry and Word Count (LIWC): LIWC 2001.* Mahwah, NJ: Erlbaum Publishers.

Pennebaker, J. W., Mayne, T. J., & Francis, M. E. (1997). Linguistic predictors of adaptive bereavement. *Journal of Personality and Social Psychology, 72,* 166–183.

Pennebaker, J. W., & Seagal, J. D. (1999). Forming a story: The health benefits of narrative. *Journal of Clinical Psychology, 55,* 1243–1254.

Perrine, N. E., & Brodersen, R. M. (2005). Artistic and scientific creative behavior: Openness and the mediating role of interests. *Journal of Creative Behavior, 39,* 217–236.

Perry, S. K. (1999). *Writing in flow.* Cincinnati, OH: Writer's Digest Books.

Peterson, J. B., & Carson, S. (2000). Latent inhibition and openness to experience in a high-achieving student population. *Personality and Individual Differences, 28,* 323–332.

Peterson, J. B., Smith, K. W., & Carson, S. (2002). Openness and extraversion are associated with reduced latent inhibition: Replication and commentary. *Personality and Individual Differences, 33,* 1137–1147.

Phillips, V. K. (1973). Creativity: Performance, profiles, and perceptions. *Journal of Psychology: Interdisciplinary and Applied, 83,* 25–30.

Piirto, J. (1991). Why are there so few? (Creative women: Visual artists, mathematicians, musicians). *Roeper Review, 13,* 142–147.

Piirto, J. (1998). *Understanding those who create* (2nd ed.). Scottsdale, AZ: Gifted Psychology Press.

Piirto, J. A. (2004). *Understanding creativity.* Scottsdale, AZ: Great Potential Press.

Plucker, J. A. (1998). Beware of simple conclusions: The case for the content generality of creativity. *Creativity Research Journal, 11,* 179–182.

Plucker, J. A. (1999). Is the proof in the pudding? Reanalyses of Torrance's (1958 to present) longitudinal study data. *Creativity Research Journal, 12,* 103–114.

Plucker, J. A. (2004). Generalization of creativity across domains: Examination of the method effect hypothesis. *Journal of Creative Behavior, 38,* 1–12.

Plucker, J. A. (in press). Enhancing creativity: Myths, legends, and empirical research. In N. Colangelo (Ed.), *Talent development V: Proceedings of the 2000 Wallace Symposium.* University of Iowa.

Plucker, J. A., & Beghetto, R. A. (2004). Why creativity is domain general, why it looks domain specific, and why the distinction does not matter. In R. J. Sternberg, E. L. Grigorenko, & J. L. Singer (Eds.), *Creativity: From potential to realization*. Washington, DC: American Psychological Association.

Plucker, J., Beghetto, R. A., & Dow, G. (2004). Why isn't creativity more important to educational psychologists? Potential, pitfalls, and future directions in creativity research. *Educational Psychologist, 39*, 83–96.

Plucker, J. A., & Dana, R. Q. (1998a). Alcohol, tobacco, and marijuana use: Relationships to undergraduate students' creative achievement. *Journal of College Student Development, 39*, 483.

Plucker, J. A., & Dana, R. Q. (1998b). Creativity of undergraduates with and without family history of alcohol and other drug problems. *Addictive Behaviors, 23*, 711–714.

Plucker, J. A., Neustadter, D., & Holden, J. (in press). The criterion problem and creativity in film: Psychometric characteristics of various measures. *Psychology of Aesthetics, Creativity, and the Arts*.

Plucker, J., Runco, M., & Lim, W. (2006). Predicting ideational behavior from divergent thinking and discretionary time on task. *Creativity Research Journal, 18*, 55–63.

Pornrungroj, C. (1992). *A comparison of creativity test scores between Thai children in a Thai culture and Thai-American children who were born and reared in an American culture*. Unpublished doctoral dissertation, Illinois State University, Normal.

Post, F. (1994). Creativity and psychopathology: A study of 291 world-famous men. *British Journal of Psychiatry, 165*, 22–34.

Post, F. (1996). Verbal creativity, depression and alcoholism: An investigation of one hundred American and British writers. *British Journal of Psychiatry, 168*, 545–555.

Powell, A. (2001). Warm, fuzzy, weird, funny: The Museum(s) of Natural History spin some tall tales. *Harvard Gazette*. Retrieved May 1, 2008, from http://www.hno.harvard.edu/gazette/2001/07.19/14-talltales.html

Powers, D. E., & Fowles, M. E. (2000). *Likely impact of the GRE writing assessment on graduate admissions decisions*. GRE Board Report No. 97–06R. Princeton, NJ.

Powers, D. E., & Kaufman, J. C. (2004). Do standardized tests penalize deep-thinking, creative, or conscientious students? Some personality correlates of Graduate Record Examinations test scores. *Intelligence, 32*, 145–153.

Prabhu, V., Sutton, C., & Sauser, W. (2008). Creativity and certain personality traits: Understanding the mediating effect of intrinsic motivation. *Creativity Research Journal, 20*, 53–66.

Preckel, F., Holling, H., & Wiese, M. (2006). Relationship of intelligence and creativity in gifted and non-gifted students: An investigation of threshold theory. *Personality and Individual Differences, 40*, 159–170.

Prescott, S., Csikszentmihalyi, M., & Graef, R. (1981). Environmental effects on cognitive and affective states: The experiential time sampling approach. *Social Behavior and Personality, 9*, 23–32.

Pretz, J. E, & Link, J. A. (in press). The Creative Task Creator: A tool for the generation of customized, web-based creativity tasks. *Behavior Research Methods*.

Price-Williams, D. R., & Ramirez III, M. (1977). Divergent thinking, cultural differences, and bilingualism. *The Journal of Social Psychology, 103*, 3–11.

Priest, T. (2006). Self-evaluation, creativity, and musical achievement. *Psychology of Music, 34*, 47–61.

Puccio, G. J., Murdock, M. C., & Mance, M. (2006). *Creative leadership: Skills that drive change.* Thousand Oaks, CA: Sage.

Rago, J. (2008, May 5). Dartmouth's "hostile" environment. *Wall Street Journal.* Retrieved May 6, 2008, from http://online.wsj.com/articl?SB 12099519394666560.htmlmod=ppinionmain commentaries

Randel, A. E., & Jaussi, K. S. (2003). Functional background identity, diversity, and individual performance in cross-functional teams. *Academy of Management Journal, 46*, 763–774.

Rawlings, D., & Locarnini, A. (2007). Dimensional schizotypy, autism, and unusual word associations in artists and scientists. *Journal of Research in Personality, 42*, 465–471.

Redmond, M. R., Mumford, M. D., & Teach, R. (1993). Putting creativity to work: Effects of leader behavior on subordinate creativity. *Organizational Behavior and Human Decision Processes, 55*, 120–151.

Reilly, J., Klima, E. S., & Bellugi, U. (1990). Once more with feeling: Affect and language in atypical populations. *Development and Psychopathology, 2*, 367–391.

Renzulli, J. S. (1978). What makes giftedness? Reexamining a definition. *Phi Delta Kappan, 60*, 180–184, 261.

Renzulli, J. S., Smith, L. H., White, A. J., Callahan, C. M., Hartman, R. K., Westberg, K. L., et al. (2004). *Scales for rating the behavioral characteristics of superior students.* Mansfield Center, CT: Creative Learning Press.

Renzulli, L. A. (2002). Entrepreneurial ambitions in the public sector: A random effects model of the emergence of charter schools in North Carolina. *Education Policy Analysis Archives. 10.* Retrieved February 5, 2008, from http://www.hno.harvard.edu/gazette/2001/07.19/14-talltales.html

Reynolds, C. R. (2000). Methods for detecting and evaluating cultural bias in neuropsychological tests. In F. Strickland & C. R. Reynolds (Eds.), *Handbook of cross-cultural neuropsychology* (pp. 249–285). New York: Plenum.

Reynolds, C. R., Lowe, P. A., & Saenz, A. L. (1999). The problem of bias in psychological assessment. In T. B. Gutkin & C. R. Reynolds (Eds.), *The handbook of school psychology* (3rd ed., pp. 549–595). John Wiley & Sons, New York.

Rhodes, M. (1962). An analysis of creativity. *Phi Delta Kappan, 42,* 305–311.

Richards, J. M., Beal, W. E., Seagal, J., & Pennebaker, J. W. (2000). The effects of disclosure of traumatic events on illness behavior among psychiatric prison inmates. *Journal of Abnormal Psychology, 109,* 156–160.

Richards, R. (1990). Everyday creativity, eminent creativity, and health: "Afterview" for CRJ issues on creativity and health. *Creativity Research Journal, 3,* 300–326.

Richards, R. (2006). Frank Barron and the study of creativity: A voice that lives on. *Journal of Humanistic Psychology, 46,* 352–370.

Richards, R. (2007). Everyday creativity: Our hidden potential. In R. Richards (Ed.), *Everyday creativity and new views of human nature* (pp. 25–54). Washington, DC: American Psychological Association.

Richards, R., & Kinney, D. K. (1990). Mood swings and creativity. *Creativity Research Journal, 3,* 202–217.

Richards, R., Kinney, D. K., Benet, M., & Merzel, A. P. (1988). Assessing everyday creativity: Characteristics of the Lifetime Creativity Scales and validation with three large samples. *Journal of Personality and Social Psychology, 54,* 476–485.

Richards, R. L. (1976). A comparison of selected Guilford and Wallach-Kogan creative thinking tests in conjunction with measures of intelligence. *Journal of Creative Behavior, 10,* 151–164.

Richards, R. L., Kinney, D. K., Lunde, I., Benet, M., & Merzel, A. P. C. (1988). Creativity in manic-depressives, cyclothemes, their normal relatives, and control subjects. *Journal of Abnormal Psychology, 97,* 281–288.

Richardson, A. G. (1985). Sex differences in creativity among a sample of Jamaican adolescents. *Perceptual and Motor Skills, 60,* 424–426.

Ripple, R. E., & Jaquish, G. A. (1982). Developmental aspects of ideational fluency, flexibility, and originality: South Africa and the United States. *South African Journal of Psychology, 12,* 95–100.

Roberts, B. W., Kuncel, N. R., Shiner, R., Caspi, A., & Goldberg, L. R. (2007). The power of personality: The comparative validity of personality traits, socioeconomic status, and cognitive ability for predicting important life outcomes. *Perspectives on Psychological Science, 2*(4), 313–345.

Roe, A. (1952). *The making of a scientist.* New York: Dodd, Mead.

Rogers, R. G. (1996). The effects of family composition, health, and social support linkages on mortality. *Journal of Health and Social Behavior, 37,* 26–338.

Romo, M., & Alfonso, V. (2003). Implicit theories of Spanish painters. *Creativity Research Journal, 15,* 409–415.

Rose, R. J., Uchida, I. A., & Christian, J. C. (1981). Placentation effects on cognitive resemblance of adult monozygotes. *Progress in Clinical and Biological Research, 69,* 35–41.

Roskos-Ewoldsen, B., Black, S. R., & McCown, S. M. (2008). Age-related changes in creative thinking. *Journal of Creative Behavior, 42,* 33–57.

Ross, S. R. (1999). Clarifying the construct of schizotypy: Variability as a marker of subtype. *Dissertation Abstracts International, 60*(06), 3003B.

Rostan, S. M., Pariser, D., & Gruber, H. E. (2002). A cross-cultural study of the development of artistic talent, creativity and giftedness. *High Ability Studies, 13,* 123–155.

Rothenberg, A. (1988). Creativity and the homospatial process: Experimental studies. *Psychiatric Clinics of North America, 11,* 443–459.

Rothenberg, A. (1990). *Creativity and madness: New findings and old stereotypes.* Baltimore: Johns Hopkins University Press.

Rothenberg, A. (1991). The janusian process in psychoanalytic treatment. *Contemporary Psychoanalysis, 27,* 422–453.

Rothenberg, A. (1995). Creativity and mental illness. *American Journal of Psychiatry, 152,* 815–816.

Rothenberg, A. (1996). The janusian process in scientific creativity. *Creativity Research Journal, 9,* 207–232.

Rothenberg, A., & Hausman, C. R. (Eds.). (1976). *The creativity question.* Durham, NC: Duke University Press.

Roussin, C. J. (2008). Increasing trust, psychological safety, and team performance through dyadic leadership discovery. *Small Group Research, 39,* 224–248.

Roy, D. D. (1996). Personality model of fine artists. *Creativity Research Journal, 9,* 391–394.

Rubenson, D. L., & Runco, M. A. (1992). The psychoeconomic approach to creativity. *New Ideas in Psychology, 10,* 131–147.

Rubenson, D. L., & Runco, M. A. (1995). The psychoeconomic view of creative work in groups and organizations. *Creativity and Innovation Management, 4,* 232–241.

Rudowicz, E., & Hui, A. (1997). The creative personality: Hong Kong perspective. *Journal of Social Behavior & Personality. 12,* 139–157.

Rudowicz, E., Lok, D., & Kitto, J. (1995). Use of the Torrance Tests of Creative Thinking in an exploratory study of creativity in Hong Kong primary school children: A cross-cultural comparison. *International Journal of Psychology, 30,* 417–430.

Rudowicz, E., & Yue, X. (2000). Concepts of creativity: Similarities and differences among Mainland, Hong Kong and Taiwanese Chinese. *Journal of Creative Behavior, 34,* 175–192.

Runco, M. A. (1984). Teachers' judgments of creativity and social validation of divergent thinking tests. *Perceptual and Motor Skills, 59,* 711–717.

Runco, M. A. (1989a). Parents' and teachers' ratings of the creativity of children. *Journal of Social Behavior and Personality, 4,* 73–83.

Runco, M. A. (1989b). The creativity of children's art. *Child Study Journal, 19,* 177–190.

Runco, M. A. (Ed.). (1991). *Divergent thinking.* Norwood, NJ: Ablex.

Runco, M. A. (Ed.). (1994). *Problem finding, problem solving, and creativity.* Norwood, NJ: Ablex.

Runco, M. A. (2003). Creativity, cognition, and their education implications. In J. C. Houtz (Ed.), *The educational psychology of creativity* (pp. 25–56). Cresskill, NJ: Hampton Press.

Runco, M. A. (2007a). *Creativity. Theories and themes: Research, development, and practice.* San Diego, CA: Elsevier Academic Press.

Runco, M. A. (2007b). Correcting research on creativity. *Creativity Research Journal, 19,* 321–327.

Runco, M. A., & Albert, R. S. (1986). The threshold theory regarding creativity and intelligence: An empirical test with gifted and nongifted children. *Creative Child & Adult Quarterly, 11,* 212–218.

Runco, M. A., & Bahleda, M. D. (1986). Implicit theories of artistic, scientific and everyday creativity. *The Journal of Creative Behavior, 20,* 93–98.

Runco, M. A., & Chand, I. (1994). Problem finding, evaluative thinking, and creativity. In M. A. Runco (Ed.), *Problem finding, problem solving, and creativity* (pp. 40–76). Norwood, NJ: Ablex Publishing.

Runco, M. A., & Dow, G. T. (2004). Assessing the accuracy of judgments of originality on three divergent thinking tests. *Korean Journal of Thinking & Problem Solving, 14,* 5–14.

Runco, M. A., Illies, J. J., & Eisenman, R. (2005). Creativity, originality, and appropriateness: What do explicit instructions tell us about their relationships? *Journal of Creative Behavior, 39,* 137–148.

Runco, M. A., Illies, J. J., & Reiter-Palmon, R. (2005). Explicit instructions to be creative and original: A comparison of strategies and criteria as targets with three types of divergent thinking tests. *Korean Journal of Thinking & Problem Solving, 15,* 5–15.

Runco, M. A., & Johnson, D. J. (1993). Parents' and teachers' implicit theories on children's creativity. *Child Study Journal, 23*(2), 91–113.

Runco, M. A., & Johnson, D. J. (2002). Parents' and teachers' implicit theories of children's creativity: A cross-cultural perspective. *Creativity Research Journal, 14,* 427–438.

Runco, M. A., Johnson, D. J., & Bear, P. K. (1993). Parents' and teachers' implicit theories of children's creativity. *Child Study Journal, 23,* 91–113.

Runco, M. A., Nemiro, J., & Walberg, H. J. (1998). Personal explicit theories of creativity. *Journal of Creative Behavior, 32,* 1–17.

Runco, M. A., Plucker, J., & Lim, W. (2000–2001). Development and psychometric integrity of a measure of ideational behavior. *Creativity Research Journal, 13,* 393–400.

Runco, M. A., & Smith, W. R. (1992). Interpersonal and intrapersonal evaluations of creative ideas. *Personality and Individual Differences, 13,* 295–302.

Ruscio, J., Whitney, D. M., & Amabile, T. M. (1998). Looking inside the fishbowl of creativity: Verbal and behavioral predictors of creative performance. *Creativity Research Journal, 11,* 243–263.

Saeki, N., Fan, X., & Van Dusen, L. (2001). A comparative study of creative thinking of American and Japanese college students. *Journal of Creative Behavior, 35,* 24–36.

Salovey, P., & Mayer, J. D. (1990). Emotional intelligence. *Imagination, Cognition and Personality, 9,* 185–211.

Salovey, P., Woolery, A., & Mayer, J. D. (2001). Emotional intelligence: Conceptualization and measurement. In G. J. O. Fletcher & M. S. Clark (Eds.), *Blackwell handbook of social psychology: Interpersonal processes* (pp. 279–307). Boston, MA: Blackwell Publishers.

Santosa, C. M., Strong, C. M., Nowakowska, C., Wang, P. W., Rennicke, C. M., & Ketter, T. A. (2007). Enhanced creativity in bipolar disorders: A controlled study. *Journal of Affective Disorders, 100,* 31–39.

Saucier, G., & Goldberg, L. R. (2001). Lexical studies of indigenous personality: Premises, products, and prospects. *Journal of Personality, 69,* 847–879.

Sawyer, R. K. (2006). *Explaining creativity: The science of human innovation.* Oxford: Oxford University Press.

Schere, J. J. (1998). *Effect of engaging in creative activity on the mood of artists and writers: An empirical test of flow theory.* Unpublished doctoral dissertation, California School of Professional Psychology.

Schlesinger, J. (2002). Issues in creativity and madness: Part one, ancient questions and modern answers. *Ethical Human Sciences and Services: An International Journal of Critical Inquiry, 4,* 73–76.

Schlesinger, J. (2003). Issues in creativity and madness, part three: Who cares? *Ethical Human Sciences & Services, 5,* 149–152.

Schlesinger, J. (in press). Creative mythconceptions: A closer look at the evidence for "mad genius" hypothesis. *Psychology of Aesthetics, Creativity, and the Arts.*

Schmader, T., & Johns, M. (2003). Converging evidence that stereotype threat reduces working memory capacity. *Journal of Personality and Social Psychology, 85,* 440–452.

Schmidt, F. L., & Hunter, J. E. (1998). The validity and utility of selection methods in personnel psychology: Practical and theoretical implications of 85 years of research findings. *Psychological Bulletin, 124,* 262–274.

Schmitt, D. P., Allik, J., McCrae, R. R., & Benet-Martínez, V. (in press). The geographic distribution of Big Five personality traits: Patterns and profiles of human self-description across 56 nations. *Journal of Cross-Cultural Psychology.*

Schock, H. (1998). *Becoming remarkable.* Nevada City, CA: Blue Dolphin Publishing.

Schooler, J. W., & Melcher, J. (1995). The ineffability of insight. In S. M. Smith, T. B. Ward, & R. A. Finke (Eds.), *The creative cognition approach* (pp. 97–133). Cambridge, MA: MIT Press.

Schubert, D. S., Wagner, M. E., & Schubert, H. J. (1977). Interest in creativity training by birth order and sex. *Journal of Creative Behavior, 11,* 144–145.

Schuldberg, D. (2005). Eysenck personality questionnaire scales and paper-and-pencil tests related to creativity. *Psychological Reports, 97,* 180–182.

Scott, C. L. (1999). Teachers' biases toward creative children. *Creativity Research Journal, 12,* 321–337.

Sexton, J. D., & Pennebaker, J. W. (2004). Non-expression of emotion and self among members of socially stigmatized groups: Implications for physical and mental health. In I. Nyklicek, L. Temoshok, & A. Vingerhoets (Eds.), *Emotional expression and health* (pp. 321–333). New York: Brunner-Routledge.

Shade, B. J. (1986). Is there an Afro-American cognitive style? An exploratory study. *Journal of Black Psychology, 13,* 13–16.

Shaeffer, C. E. (1969). The self-concept of creative adolescents. *Journal of Psychology, 72,* 233–242.

Shalley, C. (1995). Effects of coaction, expected evaluation, and goal setting on creativity and productivity. *Academy of Management Journal, 38,* 483–503.

Shaw, G. A. (1992). Hyperactivity and creativity: The tacit dimension. *Bulletin of the Psychonomic Society, 30,* 157–160.

Shaw, G. A., & Brown, G. (1990). Laterality and creativity concomitants of attention problems. *Developmental Neuropsychology, 6,* 39–56.

Shaw, G. A., & Brown, G. (1991). Laterality, implicit memory and attention disorder. *Educational Studies, 17,* 15–23.

Silverman, L. K. (1998). Through the lens of the giftedness. *Roeper Review, 20,* 204–210.

Silvia, P. J. (2008a). Another look at creativity and intelligence: Exploring higher-order models and probable confounds. *Personality and Individual Differences, 44,* 1012–1021.

Silvia, P. J. (2008b). Creativity and intelligence revisited: A latent variable analysis of Wallach and Kogan (1965). *Creativity Research Journal, 20,* 34–39.

Silvia, P. J. (2008c). Discernment and creativity: How well can people identify their most creative ideas? *Psychology of Aesthetics, Creativity, and the Arts, 2,* 139–146.

Silvia, P. J., Kaufman, J. C., & Pretz, J. E. (in press). Is creativity domain-specific? Latent class models of creative accomplishments and creative self-descriptions. *Psychology of Aesthetics, Creativity, and the Arts.*

Silvia, P. J., Winterstein, B. P., Willse, J. T., Barona, C. M., Cram, J. T., Hess, K. I., et al. (2008). Assessing creativity with divergent thinking tasks: Exploring the reliability and validity of new subjective scoring methods. *Psychology of Aesthetics, Creativity, and the Arts, 2,* 68–85.

Simonton, D. K. (1975). Age and literary creativity: A cross-cultural and transhistorical survey. *Journal of Cross-Cultural Psychology, 6,* 259–277.

Simonton, D. K. (1977). Creative productivity, age, and stress: A biographical time-series analysis of 10 classical composers. *Journal of Personality and Social Psychology, 35,* 791–804.

Simonton, D. K. (1985). Quality, quantity, and age: The careers of 10 distinguished psychologists. *International Journal of Aging and Human Development, 21,* 241–254.

Simonton, D. K. (1987). Developmental antecedents of achieved eminence. *Annual of Child Development, 5,* 131–169.

Simonton, D. K. (1990). *Psychology, science, and history: An introduction to historiometry.* New Haven, CT: Yale University Press.

Simonton, D. K. (1994). *Greatness: Who makes history and why.* New York: Guilford Press.

Simonton, D. K. (1997). Creative productivity: A predictive and explanatory model of career trajectories and landmarks. *Psychological Review, 104,* 66–89.

Simonton, D. K. (1998). Fickle fashion versus immortal fame: Transhistorical assessments of creative products in the opera house. *Journal of Personality and Social Psychology, 75,* 198–210.

Simonton, D. K. (2000). Creative development as acquired expertise: Theoretical issues and an empirical test. *Developmental Review, 20,* 283–318.

Simonton, D. K. (2004a). *Creativity in science: Chance, logic, genius, and zeitgeist.* New York: Cambridge University Press.

Simonton, D. K. (2004b). Film awards as indicator of cinematic creativity and achievement: A quantitative comparison of the Oscars and six alternatives. *Creativity Research Journal, 16,* 163–172.

Simonton, D. K. (2005a). Cinematic creativity and production budgets: Does money make the movie? *Journal of Creative Behavior, 39,* 1–15.

Simonton, D. K. (2005b). Film as art versus film as business: Differential correlates of screenplay characteristics. *Empirical Studies of the Arts, 23,* 93–117.

Simonton, D. K. (2007). Creative life cycles in literature: Poets versus novelists or conceptualists versus experimentalists? *Psychology of Aesthetics, Creativity, and the Arts, 1,* 133–139.

Singer, D. G., & Singer, J. L. (1990). *The house of make-believe: Children's play and the developing imagination.* Cambridge, MA: Harvard University Press.

Sligh, A. C., Conners, F. A., & Roskos-Ewoldsen, B. (2005). Relation of creativity to fluid and crystallized intelligence. *Journal of Creative Behavior, 39,* 123–136.

Sloane, P. (1992). *Lateral thinking puzzles.* New York: Sterling Publishing.

Smith, T. (2007). Quirky essays a window to future success? *National Public Radio.* Retrieved April 14, 2008, from http://www.npr.org/tem plates/story/story.php?storyId=7384490

Smyth, J., True, N., & Souto, J. (2001). Effects of writing about traumatic experiences: The necessity for narrative structure. *Journal of Social & Clinical Psychology, 20,* 161–172.

Smyth, S. F., & Beversdorf, D. Q. (2007). Lack of dopaminergic modulation of cognitive flexibility. *Cognitive and Behavioral Neurology, 20,* 225–229.

Snyder, A., Mitchell, J., Bossomaier, T., & Pallier, G. (2004). The creativity quotient: An objective scoring of ideational fluency. *Creativity Research Journal, 16,* 415–420.

Soldz, S., & Vaillant, G. E. (1999). The Big Five personality traits and the live course: A 50-year longitudinal study. *Journal of Research in Personality, 33,* 208–232.

Spaniol, S. (2001). Art and mental illness: Where is the link? *The Arts in Psychotherapy, 28,* 221–231.

Spera, S. P., Buhrfeind, E. D., & Pennebaker, J. W. (1994). Expressive writing and coping with job loss. *Academy of Management Journal, 37,* 722–733.

Srinivasan, T. (1984). Originality in relation to extraversion, introversion, neuroticism and psychoticism. *Journal of Psychological Researches, 28,* 65–70.

Staltaro, S. O. (2003). *Contemporary American poets, poetry writing, and depression.* Unpublished doctoral dissertation, Alliant International University at Fresno.

Stedman, E. C. (Ed.). (1900/2001). *An American anthology, 1787–1900.* Boston: Houghton Mifflin. Retrieved February 17, 2004, from http://www.bartleby.com/248/

Steele, C. M. (1997). A threat in the air: How stereotypes shape intellectual identity and performance. *American Psychologist, 52*, 613–629.

Steele, C. M., & Aronson, J. (1995). Contending with a stereotype: African-American intellectual test performance and stereotype threat. *Journal of Personality and Social Psychology, 69*, 797–811.

Stemler, S. E., Grigorenko, E. L., Jarvin, L., & Sternberg, R. J. (2006). Using the theory of successful intelligence as a basis for augmenting AP exams in psychology and statistics. *Contemporary Educational Psychology, 31*, 344–376.

Stern, S. L., & Schoenhaus, T. (1990). *Toyland: The high-stakes game of the toy industry.* New York: Contemporary.

Sternberg, R. J. (1985). *Beyond IQ: A triarchic theory of human intelligence.* New York: Cambridge University Press.

Sternberg, R. J. (1988). A three-facet model of creativity. In R. J. Sternberg (Ed.), *The nature of creativity* (pp. 125–147). New York: Cambridge University Press.

Sternberg, R. J. (1996). *Successful intelligence.* New York: Simon & Schuster.

Sternberg, R. J. (1997). *Successful intelligence.* New York: Plume.

Sternberg, R. J. (Ed.). (1999a). *Handbook of creativity.* Cambridge: Cambridge University Press.

Sternberg, R. J. (1999b). The theory of successful intelligence. *Review of General Psychology, 3*, 292–316.

Sternberg, R. J. (2003). *WICS: Wisdom, Intelligence, and Creativity, Synthesized.* Cambridge: Cambridge University Press.

Sternberg, R. J. (2006). Creating a vision of creativity: The first 25 years. *Psychology of Aesthetics, Creativity, and the Arts, S*, 2–12.

Sternberg, R. J. (2008). Applying psychological theories to educational practice. *American Educational Research Journal, 45*, 150–165.

Sternberg, R. J. (in press). The dark side of creativity and how to combat it. In D. H. Cropley, J. C. Kaufman, A. R. Cropley, & M. A. Runco (Eds.), *The dark side of creativity.* New York: Cambridge University Press.

Sternberg, R. J., & Grigorenko, E. L. (1997). Are cognitive styles still in style? *American Psychologist, 52*, 700–712.

Sternberg, R. J., & Grigorenko, E. L. (2002). *The general factor of intelligence.* Hillsdale, NJ: Erlbaum.

Sternberg, R. J., Grigorenko, E. L., & Singer, J. L. (Eds.). (2004). *Creativity: From potential to realization.* Washington, DC: American Psychological Association.

Sternberg, R. J., Kaufman, J. C., & Grigorenko, E. L. (2008). *Applied intelligence*. Cambridge: Cambridge University Press.

Sternberg, R. J., Kaufman, J. C., & Pretz, J. E. (2001). The propulsion model of creative contributions applied to the arts and letters. *Journal of Creative Behavior, 35*(2), 75–101.

Sternberg, R. J., Kaufman, J. C., & Pretz, J. E. (2002). *The creativity conundrum*. Philadelphia: Psychology Press.

Sternberg, R. J., Kaufman, J. C., & Pretz, J. E. (2003). A propulsion model of creative leadership. *Leadership Quarterly, 14*, 455–473.

Sternberg, R. J., & Lubart, T. I. (1995). *Defying the crowd: Cultivating creativity in a culture of conformity*. New York: Free Press.

Sternberg, R. J., & Lubart, T. I. (1996). *Defying the crowd*. New York: Free Press.

Sternberg, R. J., & Lubart, T. I. (1999). The concepts of creativity: Prospects and paradigms. In R. J. Sternberg (Ed.), *Handbook of creativity* (pp. 3–15). Cambridge, UK: Cambridge University Press.

Sternberg, R. J., & The Rainbow Project Collaborators. (2006). The Rainbow Project: Enhancing the SAT through assessments of analytical, practical and creative skills. *Intelligence, 34*, 321–350.

Sternberg, R. J., & Williams, W. M. (1997). Does the Graduate Record Examination predict meaningful success in the graduate monitoring of psychologists? A case study. *American Psychologist, 52*, 630–641.

Stewart, N. (1953). *Creativity: A literature survey* (ETS Research Report Series: RM 53–08). Princeton, NJ: Educational Testing Service.

Stirman, S. W., & Pennebaker, J. W. (2001). Word use in the poetry of suicidal and non-suicidal poets. *Psychosomatic Medicine, 63*, 517–523.

Stoppard, T. (1993). *Arcadia*. London: Faber and Faber.

Stoynoff, N. (2008, May 19). Robert Downey, Jr. *People*, 81–83.

Stricker, L. J., Rock, D. A., & Bennett, R. E. (2001). Sex and ethnic-group differences on accomplishment measures. *Applied Measurement in Education, 14*, 205–218.

Strom, R., & Johnson, A. (1989). Rural families of gifted preschool and primary grade children. *Journal of Instructional Psychology, 14*, 32–38.

Strom, A., Johnson, A., Strom, S., & Strom, P. (1992). Designing curriculum for parents of gifted children. *Journal for the Education of the Gifted, 15*, 182–200.

Strong, C. M., Nowakowska, C., Santosa, C. M., Wang, P. W., Kraemer, H. C., & Ketter, T. A. (2007). Temperament-creativity relationships

223

in mood disorder patients, healthy controls and highly creative individuals. *Journal of Affective Disorders, 100*(1–3), 41–48.

Subotnik, R. F. (2000). Developing young adolescent performers at Juilliard: An educational prototype for elite level talent development in the arts and sciences. In C. F. Van Lieshout & P. G. Heymans (Eds.), *Talent, resilience, and wisdom across the lifespan* (pp. 249–276). Hove, UK: Psychology Press.

Subotnik, R. F. (2004a). Transforming elite musicians into professional artists: A view of the talent development process at the Juilliard School. In L. V. Shavinina and M. Ferrari (Eds.), *Beyond knowledge: Extra cognitive aspects of developing high ability* (pp. 137–166). Mahwah, NJ: Erlbaum.

Subotnik, R. F. (2004b). A developmental view of giftedness: From being to doing. *Roeper Review.*

Subotnik, R. F., & Jarvin, L. (2005). Beyond expertise: Conceptions of giftedness as great performance. In R. J. Sternberg & J. E. Davidson (Eds.), *Conceptions of giftedness* (2nd ed., pp. 343–357). New York: Cambridge University Press.

Sulloway, F. J. (1996). *Born to rebel.* New York: Vintage.

Tan, A. G. (2003). Student teachers' perceptions of teacher behaviors for fostering creativity: A perspective on the academically low achievers, *Korean Journal of Thinking and Problem Solving, 13,* 59–71.

Tanwar, R. S. (1979). Measurement of creativity thinking and their use in India: An evaluation of Torrance tests of creativity. *Indian Psychological Review, 14,* 59–62.

Taylor, A. (2003). Time travel songs. *Andy's anachronisms.* Retrieved May 6, 2008, from http://www.timetravelreviews.com/music_list.html

Terman, L. M. (1954). Scientists and non-scientists in a group of 800 gifted men. *Psychological Monographs, 68,* 1–44.

Thomas, K., & Duke, M. P. (2007). Depressed writing: Cognitive distortions in the works of depressed and non-depressed. *Psychology of Aesthetics, Creativity, and the Arts, 1,* 204–218.

Thorndike, R. L., Hagen, E. P., & Sattler, J. M. (1986). *The Stanford-Binet Intelligence Scale* (4th ed.). Chicago: Riverside.

Tierney, P., & Farmer, S. M. (2002). Creative self-efficacy: Its potential antecedents and relationship to creative performance. *Academy of Management Journal, 45,* 1137–1148.

Todd, C. (2008). Food court musical. Retrieved May 8, 2008, from http://improveverywhere.com/2008/03/09/food-court-musical

Torrance, E. P. (1963). *Education and the creative potential.* Minneapolis: University of Minnesota.

Torrance, E. P. (1966). *Torrance Tests of Creative Thinking: Directions manual and scoring guide.* Bensenville, IL: Scholastic Testing Service.

Torrance, E. P. (1971). Are the Torrance Tests of Creative Thinking biased against or in favour of disadvantaged groups? *Gifted Child Quarterly, 15,* 75–80.

Torrance, E. P. (1973). Non-test indicators of creative talent among disadvantaged children. *Gifted Child Quarterly, 17,* 3–9.

Torrance, E. P. (1974a). *Torrance Tests of Creative Thinking: Directions manual and scoring guide.* Verbal test booklet A. Bensenville, IL: Scholastic Testing Service.

Torrance, E. P. (1974b). *Torrance Tests of Creative Thinking: Norms-technical manual.* Bensenville, IL: Scholastic Testing Service.

Torrance, E. P. (2008). *The Torrance Tests of Creative Thinking Norms-Technical Manual Figural (Streamlined) Forms A & B.* Bensenville, IL: Scholastic Testing Service.

Torrance, E. P., & Cramond, B. (2002). Needs of creativity programs, training, and research in the schools of the future. *Research in the Schools, 9,* 5–14.

Torrance, E. P., & Safter, H. T. (1989). The long range predictive validity of the Just Suppose Test. *Journal of Creative Behavior, 23,* 219–223.

Torrance, E. P., & Sato, S. (1979). Differences in Japanese and United States styles of thinking. *Creative Child and Adult Quarterly 4,* 145–151.

Troiano, A. B., & Bracken, B. A. (1983). Creative thinking and movement styles of three culturally homogeneous kindergarten groups. *Journal of Psychoeducational Assessment, 1,* 35–46.

Turner, S. R. (1994). *The creative process: A computer model of storytelling and creativity.* Hillsdale, NJ: Lawrence Erlbaum.

Vail, P. L. (1990). Gifts, talents, and the dyslexias: Wellsprings, springboards, and finding Foley's rocks. *Annals of Dyslexia, 40,* 3–17.

Vartanian, O., Martindale, C., & Kwiatkowski, J. (2007). Creative potential, attention, and speed of information processing. *Personality and Individual Differences, 43,* 1470–1480.

Verhaeghen, P., Joormann, J., & Khan, R. (2005). Why we sing the blues: The relation between self-reflective rumination, mood, and creativity. *Emotion, 5,* 226–232.

Wadeson, H. (1980). *Art psychotherapy.* New York: John Wiley & Sons.

Wai, J., Lubinski, D., & Benbow, C. P. (2005). Creativity and occupational accomplishments among intellectually precocious youth: An age 13 to age 33 longitudinal study. *Journal of Educational Psychology, 97*, 484–492.

Walberg, H. J., & Stariha, W. E. (1992). Productive human capital: Learning, creativity, and eminence. *Creativity Research Journal, 5*, 323–340.

Walczyk, J. J., Runco, M. A., Tripp, S. M., & Smith, C. E. (2008). The creativity of lying: Divergent thinking and ideational correlates of the resolution of social dilemmas. *Creativity Research Journal, 20*, 328–342.

Walker, A. M., Koestner, R., & Hum, A. (1995). Personality correlates of depressive style in autobiographies of creative achievers. *Journal of Creative Behavior, 29*, 75–94.

Wallach, M. A., & Kogan, N. (1965). *Modes of thinking in young children: A study of the creativity-intelligence distinction.* New York: Holt, Rinehart and Winston.

Wallas, G. (1926). *The art of thought.* New York: Harcourt, Brace, & World.

Walpole, M. B., Burton, N. W., Kanyi, K., & Jackenthal, A. (2001). *Selecting successful graduate students: In-depth interviews with GRE users* (GRE Board Research Rep. No. 99–11R, ETS Research Rep. 02–8). Princeton, NJ: Educational Testing Service.

Walters, A. M., Kyllonen, P. C., & Plante, J. W. (2006). Developing a standardized letter of recommendation. *Journal of College Admission, 191*, 8–17.

Walters, A. M., Plante, J. A., Kyllonen, P. C., Kaufman, J. C., & Gallagher, A. M. (2004). *System and method for evaluating applicants.* U.S. Patent No. US2004/0053203, March 18, 2004.

Wang, A. Y. (2007). *Contexts of creative thinking: Teaching, learning, and creativity in Taiwan and the United States.* Unpublished doctoral dissertation, The Claremont Graduate University.

Wang, H. C., Chang, C. Y., & Li, T. Y. (2008). Assessing creative problem-solving with automated text grading. *Computers & Education, 51*, 1450–1466.

Ward, T. B. (1994). Structured imagination: The role of category structure in exemplar generation. *Cognitive Psychology, 27*, 1–40.

Ward, T. B. (1995). What's old about new ideas? In S. M. Smith, T. B. Ward, & R. A. Finke (Eds.), *The creative cognition approach* (pp. 157–178). Cambridge, MA: MIT Press.

Ward, T. B., Dodds, R. A., Saunders, K. N., & Sifonis, C. M. (2000). Attribute centrality and imaginative thought. *Memory & Cognition, 28*, 1387–1397.

Ward, T. B., Patterson, M. J., & Sifonis, C. M. (2004). The role of specificity and abstraction in creative idea generation. *Creativity Research Journal, 16*, 1–9.

Ward, T. B., Patterson, M. J., Sifonis, C. M., Dodds, R. A., & Saunders, K. N. (2002). The role of graded category structure in imaginative thought. *Memory & Cognition, 30*, 199–216.

Ward, T. B., & Sifonis, C. M. (1997). Task demands and generative thinking: What changes and what remains the same? *Journal of Creative Behavior, 31*, 245–259.

Wasik, B. (2006). My crowd. *Harper's Magazine, 312*, 56–67.

Wechsler, S. (2006). Validity of the Torrance Tests of Creative Thinking to the Brazilian culture. *Creativity Research Journal, 18*, 15–25.

Wegener, D. T., & Petty, R. E. (2001). Understanding effects of mood through the elaboration likelihood and flexible correction models. In L. L. Martin & G. L. Clore (Eds.), *Theories of mood and cognition: A user's guidebook* (pp. 177–210). Mahwah, NJ: Lawrence Erlbaum Associates.

Weisberg, R. W. (1999). Creativity and knowledge: A challenge to theories. In R. J. Sternberg (Ed.), *Handbook of creativity* (pp. 226–250). Cambridge, UK: Cambridge University Press.

Weisberg, R. W. (2006). *Creativity: Understanding innovation in problem solving, science, invention, and the arts.* New York: John Wiley & Sons.

Wertheimer, L. K. (2008). College applicants get creative to a fault. *The Boston Globe.* Retrieved April 14, 2008, from http://www.boston.com/news/education/higher/articles/2008/01/15/college_hopefuls_get_creative_to_a_fault

Westby, E. L., & Dawson, V. L. (1995). Creativity: Asset or burden in the classroom? *Creativity Research Journal, 8*(1), 1–10.

White, H. A. & Shah, P. (2006). Training attention-switching ability in adults with ADHD. *Journal of Attention Disorders, 10*, 44–53.

Whitelaw, L. A. (2007). *An evaluative study of teacher creativity, use of the heuristic diagnostic teaching process and student mathematics performance.* Unpublished doctoral dissertation, Drexel University, Philadelphia.

Wickes, K. N. S., & Ward, T. B. (2006). Measuring gifted adolescents' implicit theories of creativity. *Roeper Review, 28*, 131–139.

Wiencek, D. (2008). Thirteen writing prompts. In McSweeney's (Eds.), *McSweeney's joke book of book jokes* (pp. 37–39). New York: Vintage.

Willis, C. (2001). *Passage.* New York: Bantam.

Wills, G. I. (2003). A personality study of musicians working in the popular field. *Personality and Individual Differences, 5,* 359–360.

Witkin, H. A., & Goodenough, D. R. (1981). *Cognitive styles: Essence and origins, field dependence and field independence.* New York: International University Press.

Witty, P. A., & Lehman, H. C. (1929). Nervous instability and genius: Poetry and fiction. *The Journal of Abnormal and Social Psychology, 24,* 77–90.

Wolfradt, U., & Pretz, J. E. (2001). Individual differences in creativity: Personality, story writing, and hobbies. *European Journal of Personality, 15,* 297–310.

Woodcock, R. W., & Johnson, M. B. (1989). *Woodcock-Johnson tests of achievement.* Chicago: Riverside.

Woodrum, D. T., & Savage, L. B. (1994). Children who are learning disabled/gifted: Where do they belong. *Educational Research, 36,* 83–89.

Yap, C., Chai, K., & Lemaire, P. (2005). An empirical study on functional diversity and innovation in SMEs. *Creativity and Innovation Management, 14,* 176–190.

Yoon, S. N. (2005). *Comparing the intelligence and creativity scores of Asian American gifted students with Caucasian gifted students.* Unpublished doctoral dissertation, Purdue University, West Lafayette.

Zackariasson, P., Styhre, A., & Wilson, T. L. (2006). Phronesis and creativity: Knowledge work in video game development. *Creativity and Innovation Management, 15,* 419–429.

Zausner, T. (2007). Artist and audience: Everyday creativity and visual art. In R. L. Richards (Ed.), *Everyday creativity and new views of human nature: Psychological, social, and spiritual perspectives* (pp. 75–89). Washington, DC: American Psychological Association.

Zha, P., Walczyk, J. J., Griffith-Ross, D. A., Tobacyk, J. J., & Walczyk, D. F. (2006). The impact of culture and individualism-collectivism on the creative potential and achievement of American and Chinese adults. *Creativity Research Journal, 18,* 355–366.

Zhiyan, T., & Singer, J. L. (1996). Daydreaming styles, emotionality, and the big five personality dimensions. *Imagination, Cognition, and Personality, 16,* 399–414.

Zhou, J., & Shalley, C. (2007). *Handbook of organizational creativity.* New York: Psychology Press.

Zuckerman, M. (1994). *Behavioral expressions and biosocial bases of sensation seeking.* New York: Cambridge University Press.

Index